REFORMING EDUCATORS

REFORMING EDUCATORS

Teachers, Experts, and Advocates

SAMUEL MITCHELL

PRAEGER

Westport, Connecticut
London

Library of Congress Cataloging-in-Publication Data

Mitchell, Samuel, 1936–
   Reforming educators : teachers, experts, and advocates / Samuel
Mitchell.
     p.   cm.
   Includes bibliographical references (p.) and index.
   ISBN 0–275–96366–7 (alk. paper)
   1. Politics and education—United States. 2. School improvement
programs—United States. 3. Educational change—United States.
4. Community and school—United States. 5. Teacher participation in
administration—United States. 6. Politics and education—Canada.
7. School improvement programs—Canada. 8. Educational change—
Canada. 9. Community and school—Canada. 10. Teacher
participation in administration—Canada. I. Title.
LC89.M58   1998
379.73—dc21   98–23551

British Library Cataloguing in Publication Data is available.

Library of Congress Catalog Card Number: 98–23551
ISBN: 0–275–96366–7

First published in 1998

Praeger Publishers, 88 Post Road West, Westport, CT 06881
An imprint of Greenwood Publishing Group, Inc.

Printed in the United States of America

The paper used in this book complies with the
Permanent Paper Standard issued by the National
Information Standards Organization (Z39.48–1984).

10 9 8 7 6 5 4 3 2 1

Contents

Charts

Acknowledgements

Many people have contributed a great deal of effort to make this book better. Marie Farrell wrote a draft for what later became Chapter 2 and contributed a commentary on one book for Chapter 7. Cari Gulbrandsen prepared a draft for the section on mentoring in Chapter 8. James Robertson wanted to write the section on school-based management, but was unable to do so. Marie Farrell, James Robertson, Catherine Littlejohn and Katherine Goods each read many of the drafts that were involved and contributed many of their ideas about innovation. Ursula Steele read Chapter 4 and suggested a number of sources for additions; she also made available to me the unpublished article by herself and Pat Boyle, which I have used extensively in Chapter 9. Several colleagues have read areas relating their expertise: Rudy Schnell has read Chapter 5 for the interpretation of progressive education that is developed there and Yvonne Hebert criticized the section on French immersion in Chapter 6. My chief assistant who becomes more valuable with each year again prefers to remain anonymous. The generous and constructive efforts of Martha Loeman made a camera ready version of this book possible.

Chapter 1

Prospectus

Two and one-half years later teachers still recalled vivid early impressions of the developers. As one said, "Those guys came on like a couple of hotshot salesmen who had just discovered planning." Another said ". . . He was lolling around with a cup of coffee in front of our library as he talked to us. The room was filled with teachers, and I thought to myself, 'How's he going to make school more businesslike?' But another teacher said to me, 'Oh, he's real cool.' . . . (Wolcott, 1977, p. 35)

Innovation means different things to each party involved. Teachers reflect innovations as they come from higher authorities and they refract the changes on to students and parents. Increasingly, these new developments come from leaders of formal political organizations who present programs of changes that are based on new and changing ideas. People in families and communities often embody traditions and react to innovations as singular issues that affect the web of their lives. The conflict between modernizing promoters of innovations and traditional resisters of innovations is the dominant recurring theme in the story of educational change. Innovations start as the gleam in the authority's eye, but lead to the birth of a baby whose presence alters the lives of many people.

When the baby-boomers were in school, education experienced an enormous explosion of innovations; there were few worries about consequences of change and advocates for new programs were particularly welcomed. The golden age of innovations was the period from the challenge of Sputnik in 1959 to the introduction of legislation for the integration of the handicapped in 1973. During that time, experts, with the support of administrators, initiated new programs for schools largely by themselves. Indeed, school board members often were unaware of the innovations that school administrators were implementing (Fullan, 1982).

In this earlier period, the major conflict occurred between the experts and administrators who pushed innovations in the name of progress and teachers who often stood against the tide of what they perceived to be fads. For example, the teachers were concerned about their own ideas of controlling students and used the mainframe computers to keep students working together rather than letting them work at their own pace (Carlson, 1965). Teachers had their own perceptions of innovations that focused on their crucial role of facilitating student learning. The unexpected problems of changes frequently involved the teachers changing the meaning of innovations. Indeed, the innovators' original meanings were often lost in the pressure for time, training and resources that limited the often isolated reactions of classroom instructors (Elmore & McLaughlin, 1988).

Though the conflicts between innovators and teachers were not solved, additional problems were added when parents and an increasing variety of other groups became involved with policy changes during the 1970s. Some programs survived because they had supporters, particularly Title I programs for low-income people, but those whose aims were solely innovations did not (Elmore & McLaughlin, 1988). These complications meant there were more parties to the issue and, ultimately, administrators and experts had to act before many more varied audiences. As a consequence of legislation, administrators had to inform parents about procedures that affected their disabled children (Sarason, 1982). Head Start and most other early childhood programs required parent councils and visits by teachers to homes; parent volunteers in classes also were encouraged. Parents were consulted even if educators would turn around and ignore their advice or input. In requiring parent involvement or other directions for education, legislatures were increasingly involved as their acts became more prescriptive.

Governance was itself complicated by the increasing involvement of business with education, a dominant power notably absent during the 1960s. Business people alternatively became critics of the schools, competitors to public education, and partners with schools in joint programs (Mitchell, 1996). Simultaneously, an increasing variety of other professionals became involved; education, health, higher education, and the arts have all become interrelated.

The transformation of educational decision making has included the involvement of an increasing array of such professionals. In the past, experts usually worked with the administrators from the school system's bureaucracy (Lind, 1974). As the power of the local school bureaucracy waned, community activists played almost as important a role as local school boards and administrators. Indeed, the leaders of some advocacy organizations have been called "the school board in exile" (Mitchell, 1996). Independent school councils or advocacy organizations have even hired experts to testify against the school system.

However, some select experts play ever more important roles at the state, national, or international levels. These experts, through their roles in foundations, joint agencies, such as the National Governors Association, and new consortiums among universities, plan new innovations for local groups, such as school-based management. Plans to integrate many innovations—systemic reform—very clearly reveals the role of new experts and ever broader planning. Unlike the market in business, the superexperts cannot remain an unseen hand, but must decide how directive they will be.

At every level, people must make decisions about innovations. Legislators decide on the relative support for an innovation among constituents. Administrators decide on the political feasibility of one innovation in terms of the resources they have available (Mitchell, 1992). Teachers must decide on an innovation in terms of its effect on their students in the local school and where they will find time to prepare for the change (Elmore & McLaughlin, 1988). Students and parents must decide if any one innovation is important to them as issues or for their futures. Businesses actually calculate the advantages of school partnerships with a formal, written approach; the Conference Board of Canada has such a procedure (Mitchell, 1996).

Though other partners in education may want to guarantee their interests, self-interest is often combined with broader concerns. Artists, for example, with a fixed roster of professionals to work with the schools and a stipulated honorarium for such work, are clearly protecting their interests (Remer, 1990); indeed, many of these programs were originally developed as employment opportunities for artists who lacked work (Dubin, 1987). However, artists in schools can increase student interest in schools in many ways. Basic literacy can be improved through art, academic achievements in other subjects increase, and attendance by both teachers and students improves.

Any group can see itself as acting on a broader or moral basis, while others are said by them to pursue a narrow self-interest. School boards are currently being attacked by both international and local experts as barriers to reform in finances and education; the Calgary Board of Education is currently under review by the province for these and other reasons (Mitchell, 1995). In the total reform of education in Kentucky, the major opponents of reform are said to be the school boards and their association (Mitchell, 1996). Today, experts see school boards as the most important problem for governance changes in schools (Mitchell, 1995). At an earlier time, similar commentators reported that teachers were the principal barrier to curriculum reforms (Sarason, 1982).

Supporters of innovations themselves represent diverse interests and contradictory ideas. The innovations are at least double-pronged because local interests are encouraged along with state or national policies by government leaders. Charter schools, for example, represent the aims of parents in local situations and voucher plans would, if adopted on a larger scale, make schools even more diverse. Diversity is, however, limited by the creation of national goals or indicators. National professional groups, businesses, or governmental reports and large-scale reform advocacy organizations usually have supported such goal statements as a part of systemic reform, while also encouraging decision making at the local school level (Elmore, 1993).

Though legislatures have set the national or provincial goals and administrators have established the system priorities, it is left to teachers and local administrators to implement the wish lists composed by them. The local groups, increasingly through school councils that include parents and sometimes students, are supposed to make the crucial practical decisions for which they will be held accountable by the external groups. The governance of the school is changed by local decision making, the technology of the schools is changed by the computer revolution, and the curriculum is changed by increasingly exact specifications.

DEFINING THE PROBLEM

Innovators usually agree that the school is the unit of implementation (Elmore & McLaughlin, 1988). Even though individual teachers create more variety within schools than exists among schools, the school is to be made the unit where achievements are measured and rewarded. Parents have more effect than any formal group on the learning of students, but parents themselves are not rewarded and punished—perhaps they should prove themselves with one child before being allowed to have others. Accountability, the current buzzword, can have many consequences.

Like the family, which is overburdened by the rising expectations of its constituents, schools are having problems with heightened hopes and unrealistic dreams. The emphasis on the individual school as the unit for reform has become a basis for standardizing results rather than individualizing programs. By the use of this alchemy, schools are expected to work towards external standards or indicators with sets of programs developed by experts, while increasing the satisfaction ratings held by students, parents, and employers (Alberta Education, 1995). While trying to drive out the school boards, reformers are replacing them with equally demanding gods. Separate subjects and isolated programs may yield to integrated activities, knowing a few things better, or teachers becoming coaches rather than lecturers, but schools remain artificial organizations that try to plan innovations while ignoring the existing sources of variation and change.

Definitions of change also involve a variety of viewpoints that the different players and institutions can bring with them as they introduce innovations. In contrast, an early influential view sees change as "the (1) acceptance, (2) over time, (3) of some specific item—an idea or practice, (4) by individuals, groups or other adopting units linked to, (5) specific channels of communication, (6) to a given system of values or culture" (Katz, et al., 1963, p. 252). This definition does not include the way people feel about the innovation or whether their perception of change is a key to there being a change. Nor are the people who are involved in accepting the change the ones who are initiating those ideas or practices.

Creative individuals can be the heart of the process and such individuals would try and include the perspective of the other players. Diversity is important in understanding the act of altering the status quo. Change is a creative process with struggle and conflict. The first year of innovations involves more problems one teacher has said, but it affects students more in that year than any other (Smith, et al., 1986). As noted by an economist, change can be a way of constantly renewing education, a perception of new uses for existing resources (Schumpeter, 1942).

Like the first definition of change, stage theorists have seen that there is an external entity to adopt. However, the development of individual attitudes, skills, and understanding is an equally important result of innovation (Fullan, 1982). For most people, the initial stress with the adoption of the innovation leads to an adaptation to local conditions. Finally, a stage of institutionalization means that the innovation is a part of the system (Berman & McLaughlin, 1978; Louis, et al., 1981). However, very different meanings of innovation are possible (Huberman & Miles, 1982). People can learn how to carry on future innovations, they can become more cosmopolitan about change, and they can jump over a stage and even develop their own ideas.

FROM EXPERTS TO SUPEREXPERTS

The reason why change is a problem is developed in the next chapter. The public may want the familiar goals of basic education, good discipline, and equality of opportunity from schools. Experts offer a very different menu that includes new subjects, school reorganization, and technological solutions. Chapter 2 critically, even cynically, views the disasters that have accompanied innovation, presents detailed accounts of classic studies, and raises many questions about the entire process.

Experts tend to neglect the context in which education occurs, while local people may be too adapted to traditional ways of teaching. Teachers are caught in between, playing the expert in their classes and resisting the plans of experts for educational policy. Even students, particularly those in gifted education, may play at being experts who develop one theme. Administrators are most closely allied with external experts, while parents may respond to them in times of crisis or when a particular controversy arises.

While other people think of particular situations and schools, the focus of true experts is on new subjects and new ways of thinking. Experts have developed new ways of thinking about change itself, thus we have innovation experts. Chapter 2 explores the meaning of change, focusing on experts who have attempted to develop a theory of change based on fixed stages. Particular situations, such as Individual Guided Education, reveal more diverse responses than stages that represent reactions to one common innovation.

Particularly as applied to different racial, gender, and social class strata, the innovation may differ substantially. Because the innovators often ignore these realities, the innovation may operate very differently from the intention of its inventors. For example, Individual Guided Education was used in working areas to control students and provide busy work, hardly the new meaning that the experts had wanted students to find. The distance between teachers and experts can be reduced by basing the change upon the interests and concerns of teachers, while teachers and administrators build the reform into the schedule, budget, and curriculum of the school. However, students and their families are not intertwined with the same movement.

The experts do not reflect the variety that students and their families represent. Such varieties could be the basis for innovations, rather than having plans superimposed on them. However, innovations from the grass roots require a new and changed basis of communication among the many players involved with education. The scientific community, which is the source for the applications that many professions offer to clients, provides one model of how such new links can operate. Changing our conception of this community to make it more representative of the divisions among people is a fairly direct basis for making experts more responsive to those they claim to serve.

Involving more people in the professional community and establishing links between them and the broader community are useful aims based upon past problems in transforming schools. However, increasing numbers of superexperts have appeared who work at the top level of institutions and organizations, and may cause even greater polarization in education between those more expert and those less so. Superexperts, who evolved from the research centers discussed in Chapter 2, are the source of many new ideas for involving teachers and parents in school governance and developing creativity among students, but they still make everyone more dependent on them since they have relinquished few powers themselves.

The evolution towards new, more limited policies is traced out from Chapter 3 to Chapter 6. Unlike the holistic account in Chapter 2, Chapter 3 offers a series of separate stories about the different ways teachers have responded to changes. As part of increased attempts to give recognition to teachers, a center in North Carolina has rewarded them with a beautiful setting in which they can create while being equals to any experts and while continuing to develop as teachers for that state.

This center, like ten others, marks the evolution of settings in which teachers have attempted to control their own education, a significant change in the hierarchical world where experts and administrators normally control teachers. Teacher centers came to North America from England and, for a time, were widely accepted as a basis for experienced teachers to prepare themselves for mandated changes and where beginning teachers could be inducted into the profession. When the centers became a political football, they were largely eliminated as an alternative. Teacher networks have emerged as a major new opportunity. Unlike the centers, the networks work with experts and exist through advanced technology.

Unexpectedly in the complex field of teacher evaluation, at times, teachers have become independent in reacting against the experts' position rather than in pursuing their own changes directly. After developing a basis for a common understanding with the establishment, teachers can become very articulate and expressive when confronting the authorities. In addition, three forms of evaluation are directly supportive of teachers: peer evaluation, self-study, and the approach of a critical friend.

Unlike the options within evaluation, the singular focus of systematic reform leaves little room for teacher independence, though it claims to advance teacher professionalism.   These limits are apparent in the program for advanced certification. Indeed, some of the reforms are so complicated that, even though they provide for teacher leaders and development centers, they may well spend several generations realizing these aims. One of the earlier approaches to legislated learning, integration of special education students, has shown that teacher resiliency can be encouraged with programs such as a team approach to mastery. There are many options for teachers as they demand their rights and attempt to achieve them.

Professional education, evaluation, and large-scale reform have been the sphere of experts and administrators. For teachers to be a part of these changes is an enormous advance, but one that would have to be repeated in many other places and for other constituents for a democratic vision to guide reforms. Systematic reform is overwhelming for teachers, while, in contrast, an innovation that four or five teachers can coordinate, such as schools within schools, is one they can control.

POWER AND VISIONS

Chapter 4 tries to reverse everyone's thinking while considering innovations most closely related to social and organizational power. From a personal sense of power affecting kindergarten students, the discussion moves to the most impersonal forms of business and governmental powers. The chapter develops through pursuing a number of themes including student part-time jobs, the relation between employment opportunities and discipline problems in high schools, the effect of business partnerships on those involved, the emergence of school-based management, and the politics of decision making.

Superexperts have developed plans for teacher and parent involvement, such as school-based decision making and peer evaluations. Teachers, in particular, have developed their own networks as they continue to react against innovations developed by higher experts. In Chapter 4, in order for alternative approaches to be developed, the possibilities of role reversals are explored as a way of overcoming status and caste differences. Imperial influences often mean that experts talk only to the higher experts; in contrast, opportunities are needed to develop more local meetings rather than so many summits. Social influences, which have always seemed to teachers to be so separate from schools, are increasingly impinging on them.

One such influence, the business world, has established an enormous number of links with schools in a very short time. Business is now an important partner with education in helping at-risk students, but a common community cannot be assumed between the interests of the two institutions. Superexperts from business have been almost godlike in proclaiming the virtues of many innovations, particularly school-based decision making and computers.

An alternative position seems to be demanded by the current crises in schools, which have threatened teachers with the loss of security. This impossible innovation, reconstitution, seems like a way to overcome persistent resistance by teachers; it replaces human improvement with formal evaluations. Formal procedures in bureaucratic systems, with power as its only true vision, is probably the most important reason for the appearance of purely symbolic changes. In a democratic community, everyone can be both friends and critics while teachers can be the first among equals in one unified community (Strike, 1993). This alternative may be more important than the current divisions among those preoccupied with current crises in education. These crises have led to distinct types of innovations, which are responses to separate financial, educational, and governing crises.

In Chapter 5, current values and beliefs that also are used to manipulate people are reviewed, yet these ideologies help to make sense of the present and to plan for the future. One of these programs, the concerns model of change, could be a means of bringing experts and their constituents together, instead of merely finding ways to make reforms more acceptable. Concerns as a basis for develop-ing innovations is one example of the process approach to innovations. Construct-ing one's own meaning of an innovation is a further development of this approach (Viadero, 1996c). Developing the capacity of people for many innovations is an even more enduring view of the progressive approach to change.

The contrasting position focuses on subject matter and student achievement, traditional or discipline-based ideology. This traditional position is product focused and usually derives from the disciplines, such as mathematicians developing the new mathematics in the 1960s (Sarason, 1982). Particularly when enhanced by national crises, discipline-based innovations, including back-to-basics, have been a source of new controls over teachers and students. These controls include exams, evaluation, and the manipulation of symbols. The symbols for these controls are currently the campaigns for standards and indicators. The return to tradition includes many changes; indeed, the word reform is often associated with more conservative values and controls (Mitchell, 1992).

People who usually are not at all ideological are often affected by innovations. Myths about creativity suggest how independence rather than ill-defined expectations of progress can be the focus of serious transformations. From seeing the power of myths, symbolic changes can be developed beyond the ridiculous ones suggested in Chapter 2. A group of teachers is shown to become active and theoretical towards education; its members acquired an alternative voice from the experts. Still other teachers and administrators are involved in education purely from the standpoint of power rather than ideology or theory.

In contrast to the varied themes in Chapter 4, Chapter 5 follows a small number of individuals to see, as concretely as possible, how they differ in their ideologies. However, many broader issues are the background against which the work of these individual actors can be interpreted. The chapter contrasts personal stories with research studies of differences between progressive and traditional education, on the one hand, and power differences, on the other. Unexpectedly, the study of power and ideology reaches the same conclusion that Chapter 2 did; the results of innovations can be personally meaningful, purely mechanical actions, or merely symbolic changes.

EXEMPLARY PROGRAMS: GUIDES FOR ACTION

Chapters 6 and 7 demonstrate, through concrete cases, how our best general understanding of change can be discovered and further developed. From among the leading innovations, French immersion demonstrates how effective an expert-inspired program can be, while the National Writing Program shows how exceptional teachers can be in organizing. Both of these programs are professional answers to perceived crises in education; respectively, the separatist challenge to Canadian unity and the decline of writing ability among American students.

Just as the writing program is concerned with all school subjects and French immersion teaches across the curriculum, two other innovations have attempted to influence the entire school. School-based management has tried to involve teachers or, alternatively, teachers, parents, and students in the management of task forces for the entire school, while the arts have been integrated with all other school subjects. Unlike the first two exemplary programs, these two more recent projects have remained connected with changes in the wider society. School decision making is related to similar developments in companies and also to political demands for democratic control over schools, while arts integration involves partnerships with visiting artists and alliances with more general reformers of education.

These four programs have been widely praised as successes but the positive achievements are contingent upon specific conditions. Each of the programs combines progressive aims with traditional directions; a degree of autonomy for teachers and the school, and promotion by advocates. Advocates and their organizations make claims for their programs and generate support for them. Currently, all of the programs show that program goals, which are often progressive, are being confined by evaluation procedures so that such accountability makes education more traditional.

Chapter 7 shows how any innovation can be developed for autonomous groups. Focusing research on common school problems, such as attendance, can lead to new programs whereby traditional understandings between teachers and students can be renewed as explicit contracts. Themes can be a basis on which daily classes are reorganized or a basis of orientation for the entire school. Themes or specialities also can be a basis for schools-within-schools. Teachers, as well as other groups, can organize so that their traditional isolation is overcome, while the unreformed rulers of education—individual universities—can be changed through confederations of higher institutions as well as partnerships with public schools.

Successful innovations often involve a combination of opposites, such as strong demands followed by understanding and support. Administrators often combine these opposites, as indicated by their attendance at planning sessions together with a recognition of teacher independence. Initially, administrators may need to shelter an innovation and, later, build it into the regular budget and accepted program so that it could not be eliminated during a budget cut. Similarly, teacher leaders and community spokespeople can both support changes and integrate them into the curriculum.

To accelerate the successful implementation of innovation, realistic time schedules for innovations are needed as well as a focus on service to students. Schools and all role players within them can be dramatically transformed. In a variety of ways, learning centered schools can be seen to contrast with traditional ones. Learning centered schools focus on shared aims that are important to everyone, whereas traditional schools show separate cliques where teachers, for example, share war stories about their problems with students. The staff and students both continue to grow and focus on their problems in alternative schools, while more stable schools often lead to the withdrawal of teachers from learning. Teachers who are learning and developing move from classroom alternatives to professional attitudes; this progress can be extended to community involvement. The stages of development from classroom routine to community involvement become a basis for evaluating the exemplary programs discussed in Chapter 6.

VOLUNTEERS AND ADVOCATES

Support for innovations can be mobilized either by involving more and different people or acquiring more resources through organizations. Volunteers who develop a sense of personal purpose and political direction may alter the opportunities, especially for at-risk students. In contrast, advocacy organizations view their people as constituents rather than just participants in the educational process, but they can build support through successful campaigns. These two seemingly opposite approaches can develop the basis for participation in a broadened community for professionals and a greater sense of commitment. The volunteers and advocates can widen the organized opposition to experts, as discussed earlier. Local advocacy organizations with special interests are the opposing power to total or systemic reform that attempts to introduce many innovations simultaneously, while volunteers and their commitment are the basis for a vision that evolves from people.

Power over others driven by singular motives can yield to power with people arising from varied goals. Such varied goals make possible more problem solving, while singular ones can produce, at best, compromise (Follett, 1924). Power with people can mean that each one influences others, while power over people can cause impotency for everyone in a school situation (Mitchell, 1995). Chapter 8 discusses these questions as a new contributor, the volunteer, becomes involved in education and educators become involved in the community.

Students have increasingly been expected, if not required, to perform community service; such service has been widely advanced by national programs and presidential summits in the United States. Within schools, students have helped other students through peer tutoring, support, and leadership in activities. Administrators have often removed the school's boundaries so that community leaders, experts, and ordinary volunteers could come to assist the school. Parents have been the usual source of volunteers for schools, but, in some instances, they have been joined by retirees and college students.

Volunteer programs have emerged as a result of the support by various foundations. Two organizations have frequently attempted to change the family while combining the efforts of its members with schools, the National Parent Teacher Association and the Junior League. More recently, organizations, such as Communities in Schools, have attempted both to overcome the limitations of the family and to supply volunteers to schools for the many social needs that students are seen to have. Perhaps the most important activity performed by volunteers is mentoring, which provides support for students, just as teacher mentoring was previously shown to help teachers. Teachers, parents, and volunteers need to have similar aims in confronting a variety of social changes and innovations within education.

The development of advocacy for change has become more than an expression of volunteer or parent support. Professional community organizers have developed the political awareness of those involved in reform, which many previous attempts have lacked. Though geared to conflict, the local advocacy organizations have shown signs of being coopted by the educational establishment. Even the most militant advocacy groups are still not yet organized into national organizations with political influence. Local community advocates usually have not been paired with educational promoters, even when such promoters were working with at-risk students on the same street with the poor people that the local advocates were organizing. The major programs for at-risk students are: Success for All, Reading Recovery, the Accelerated School Program, and the Comer schools. Success for All involves structured reading combined with tutoring, Reading Recovery is exclusively an individual tutoring project, and Accelerated schools attempt to enrich schools for poor students as much as has been done for gifted pupils in the past. The Comer schools attempt to involve poor people as paid aids as well as involving them in governing these schools. Most of these programs, particularly the Comer schools, also attempt to provide integrated services and operate through school-based management. Each of these programs has become part of an increasingly national effort to promote change that is financed by foundations; these programs have either been combined with others or have been expanded throughout the curriculum.

Two programs in different countries have attempted to involve government in spreading its message; the American Coalition of Essential Schools for general curriculum reform and the Canadian Parents for French on behalf of immersion education. Both efforts have been guided by exceptional experts, Ted Sizer and David Stern. The Coalition has had its schools sponsored by the government in at least ten states, while, in Canada, both provincial and national organizations of parents have been supported by the federal government as a means of achieving its bilingual goal. The American effort appears to carry more political costs than the Canadian one, but there is a huge difference between the scope of their goals.

Neither the national advocacy group nor the more local one seems to focus upon the varied forms of inequality that continue to exist. A local program of gender equity, surprisingly, was advanced by advocates within a school system, while promotional efforts outside remain rather fragmentary. General reform efforts, particularly the active one in Chicago, seem to hide from the gender issue. Various forms of inequality need advocates to develop awareness of their existence, but neither the local nor national advocates should encourage dependency on the part of those associated with them.

POLICY DEVELOPMENTS

Various recommendations and editorial comments have been made throughout the book, and Chapter 10 attempts to bring these together along with a reformulation of the experts' position, a general picture of the most significant parties to reform, and an account of the options that are available to individuals and organizations for future innovations. In each of these areas there are major contradictions to be resolved.

There are many known ways of overcoming the limits of experts at the local school level. For teacher-initiated innovations, experts can act as judges and work through local advisers; there also are a number of ways to reverse the usual status order while developing a common position between experts and laypeople. However, there are no such limits for superexperts who seldom confront teachers directly in schools. Rather, superexperts work through national institutions to promote computers, school-based management, teacher professionalism, and standards for student achievements. Local schools can best resist these centralizing tendencies by forming their own alliances with advocates who will help them resist the superexperts.

The increasing importance of promotional organizations, foundations, business, and government makes the actions of teachers, parents, students, and community leaders that much more critical. Passive resistance by any of these groups can wipe out the apparent victory of any of the increasingly superior forces. Furthermore, any victory without commitment will be an empty one because the battle is over minds and education, which is something that cannot be forced no matter how much the authorities would like to do so.

Alternative visions are as important as organizations. The visions must stress a broader sense of community rather than a specialized one. Teachers can see themselves as first among equals in a democracy. The major problems, whether the issue is evaluations or specific programs, are trust and power. Alternative visions that relate to other social movements, which are gender, racial, or social-class based, can establish meaningful alternatives for the local decision makers. The sense of calling can develop across these divisions as well as those between expert and volunteer. Experts themselves can become leaders of the people, rather than manipulators of the educational agenda.

A new consensus on the practices of education has ceased to exist. Different players may see the same change quite differently. The variation of meanings limits the players who will be present to negotiate or advise governments. Newer and more impersonal influences, such as foundations and the news media, including a specialized reform press, are influencing the path of innovations, as described in Chapter 10. Business and governments remain the dominant players in an increasingly political contest. Conservative governments, which also represent business interests, may assemble acceptable players for discussions such as the roundtables and forums that are increasingly organized to discuss new educational policies. There is a fear of special interests whose multiple paths may confuse the existing establishment.

In contrast, new alternatives require contributions by those who have not been involved with educational policy in the past: teachers, students, and community volunteers. To anchor new ideas with concrete experiences will yield a different but meaningful consensus. Such an alternative position can allow for meaningful criticism of the dominant position and its proposals; for the first time in education, there can be an articulate opposition towards new fads. The adoption process now relies on our best judgment and research-based plans, which can be discussed in terms of values. Rediscovering the best of the past in education can supplement trials of new approaches to deal with present problems, which also can be debated from the perspective of renewed meaning for people.

Chapter 10 returns to the division between experts and laypeople and attempts to show how these laypeople can develop their talents. Both groups can develop their understanding and sensitivity toward people and situations. The resolution of ideological and value conflict requires more than compromise. Each position must find, through problem solving, a way to arrive at a concrete solution without relinquishing its long-term goals. The parties can bring politics and education together, with a minimum of corruption and a maximum of new thinking.

Though ranging over many educational concerns from experts to volunteers, or from teacher centers to community advocacy organizations, our final concern is the effect of innovation and policy changes on students and the development of a new sense of community. Monopolistic professions and erratic experts can be replaced by more responsible change communities, change communities that can involve experts who have to live with the results of their plans and constituents who must come to see the consequences of their immediate choices.

By opening change to more participants with more ground rules and understanding of responsibilities, the roles of those in education can allow for the advantages of evolutionary variation in the process of planning changes. Many different meanings of change need to be considered. Change also must allow for the possible radical reform of the system and not just tinkering with classrooms. The crisis confrontations and less severe altercations are both important sources of innovations. The unplanned boomerang effects of plans and interactions of institutions must be considered as a part of change. Ideas, people, and power must all be included in our understanding of innovation.

Visions of democracy must contend with the scale of innovations, since distance between planners and practitioners has increased enormously. The complicated process means that different reforms and various ideologies are forever appearing.

Proposals and their opposites are constantly interacting. Attempts to develop alternatives to reliance on experts have gone hand in hand with changes in the role of experts. The invidious conflicts between those with more and those with less expertise have been compounded by the involvement of parents, and, occasionally, an active role for students has been preached or practiced. Parents, students, and community members represent social concerns that differ from the task preoccupations of professionals and the legislative demands of politicians.

However, these constituents also can be respected and expected to contribute to changes in education. Such changes can include altering the experts' plans or even initiating their own educational changes. By such actions, these groups clearly show that they have become the experts' equals. Attempts to overcome isolation and limited perspectives can empower these groups just as has happened for teachers. Parents have developed Internet sites in some areas and have become political forces in others. There also are some emerging signs of students becoming organized. All of these groups must be better organized if new meetinghouses for reform, which are neither purely local nor international, are to be developed in communities.

The inability of ideologues to develop a continuing and historically rooted reform institution and the refusal of many individuals of either persuasion to communicate across the divide, makes a power position more attractive than it might seem. Teachers often require shock by administrators before they even see an innovation as different from their current practices. All existing ideologies provide limited perspectives that need to be related to power realities. Indeed, educators, businesspeople, and professionals, as well as many others, together can help form a larger democratic community. Integrated medical and social services within schools require such an enhanced and widened view of service to the community to be more than a paternalistic attempt to improve the lot of at-risk students and their families.

Successful innovations involve combining affective ideologies and strategic use of power. Where there is a dominant stress upon technology and control, experts ignore people. When there is an opposite emphasis upon attitudes and interaction between groups, such as with the integration of special education students, results and discipline are needed. Innovations also must overcome resistance and the alienation of the people involved.

The problem of defining innovations is linked with major political and ideological changes in education and our society. Writers on education and the community should no longer be rounded up to discuss what should be done for other people. Practices, perceptions, and power will all have to change for innovation to be a new reality. It is necessary to include all the components; there are no simple solutions for changing education. Informed liberal and conservative interpreters of change can avoid accepting absolute positions. Greater democracy can be both the means for achieving innovations in education and the goal of those innovations.

A valuable new perception of the community is developed, together with a new sense of what innovations can be. Each chapter represents differences in the formulation of the problem, resources, and contributors who are drawn upon, and the method of presentation. This initial chapter is the only one to assert the argument for a variety of approaches, brief citations of a few illustrations and an attempt to convey a sense of new policy positions. Alternatives may widen the scope of planning, while having only one set of innovations may close off opportunities.

In a sense we can see the classroom system as a standardized invention that essentially drives out more idiosyncratic and individualized forms of schooling. (Goodson, 1983, p. 31)

Chapter 2

Sages and Sorcerers

Overall, the public seems to have a more traditional view of what should be happening in the classroom. They want to see students learning some of the same things—in the same ways—that they learned in school. (Johnson & Immerwahr, 1994, p. 17)

It is 9:30 A.M., classtime for 60 certified elementary teachers . . . . This is where they will learn to categorize children, put their classes into frequency polygons and histograms, measure their teaching by the off-whack leanings of the bell shape curve . . . . A rich baritone voice from a row of laughing teachers at the very back: "Might not that multi modal result just mean you have a rotten test?"

"I don't like that personal inference," says the lecturer, completely serious. . . . He repeats, slowly recitative: "The mode is useful when a quick, approximate measure of concentration is needed." Sixty pens tilt dutifully to paper, there is a quiet, studied feeling, a sense of relief at lecture sustained. (Lind, 1974, pp. 23-25)

Parents often represent the traditional views of education while experts usually symbolize the epitome of new planning for education. Experts initiate changes for practicing teachers as well as student teachers. Teachers usually are the connection in providing explanations of the changes to both parents and students. If the explanation by teachers is not adequate, the school's clients react against all those associated with change and resist the innovations.

Teachers are a crucial link in the process of change, but they also are a conceptual intermediary between expert and client or professional and layperson. Because they are between these extreme positions, teachers sometimes play the role of the sage on stage who provides advice and knowledge about innovation. In the classroom, students react in amazement when teachers observe, listen, and take notes; they are used to teachers talking at them. At other times, teachers parody, satirize, or passively accept the higher experts. In one example, teachers took bets on how long an expert on integrating special needs students would talk (Cusick, 1983). If the tests are elaborate, the research procedures difficult to understand, or the presence of the expert is overwhelming, the teachers may defer to the sorcerers whom they do not understand. Intermediate agents may, of course, change sides in this drama.

To examine the role of the experts and related professionals in the field of educational change is to enter a complex and perplexing area of debate. As a concept, nothing is so potentially loaded with implications, assumptions, and interpretations as that of educational change. With its labels of innovation and reform, educational change is a vast enterprise and begins to take on a life of its own. In this field, various actors play their different parts and therein lies the problem. The roles, which the actors play, vary in scope and power, and encompass groups within which there are hierarchies of position as well as social and academic legitimacy. The script of educational change itself can generate competing notions of authority, both professional and pedagogical. While it may be extraordinarily difficult to define or properly explain, educational change has become a regular part of life in schools.

The nature of educational change is the basis upon which any discussion of reform and innovation must rest. Problems with change include taking the definition of the idea for granted, hedging the propositions with prescriptive ideologies, and frequently misinterpreting the extent to which the change is actually practiced. In theory, the purpose of educational change is "to help schools accomplish their goals more effectively by replacing some programs or practices with better ones" (Fullan, 1982, p. 11). In practice, educational change is a complex process complicated by the interactions of the many stakeholders involved in current educational practices in the schools.

HOW PLANS BOOMERANG

Change, in this context educational change, is an experience "characterized by ambivalence and uncertainty" (Fullan & Stiegelbauer, 1991, p. 32) and, most particularly, by conflict. It is the conflict, which permeates the process of educational change, that is the central action in this play. If any paradigm can be used to describe the area of educational change, it is that of conflict. The entire field is rife with conflict among the various players. However, the essential problem is the tendency of all players to polarize along the continuum between lay and expert positions while inventing new programs. The paradigm of conflict encompasses the gap between the ideals and the realities of educational reform. In this context, there are gaps between the abstract theorizing of the experts and the concrete experiences of practitioners; the proposed innovation and practice of the innovation often differ enormously.

The aims and objectives of reformers and the perspective of those who use the program show the difference between activities for reform and the resilience of institutional life. Between conservation and adoption there is the contrast of professional groups and laypersons, between educators and parents. In effect, the whole area reveals potential conflicts and divergent opinions. Much of the conflict stems from the fact that each player in the drama of reform is in a particular position relative to the other players. The teacher, for instance, is an expert in the classroom context, but is not one outside it. He or she can dominate the discourse and activities in the classroom, a "sage on stage" as they describe their lecturing to students, but outside of schools they have limited recognition as either experts or actors. In the view of progressive educators, teacher talk that dominates classrooms is often an impediment to reforms that require greater activity by students (Sarason, 1982).

In the context of educational change, proposed reforms are rarely presented to individual teachers for their consideration and, as a result, the teachers lag behind in the reform process (National Governors' Association, 1994). Teachers believe that they are more targets of reform than partners in the process, and they do not perceive themselves as having any control regarding proposed changes to education (Sykes, 1996). For reformers, in contrast, educational changes are the symbols of the expected conversion of ancient school practices to modern ideas. However, the prophets of future changes do not always relate their broad ideas to the narrower halls and classrooms of teachers and students. Other groups of skilled professionals jump into the gap: school administrators and consultants try to link the ideas of the innovators to the world of practitioners. Teachers are a primary constituency for building support for educational change; they are presently included in reform planning to a greater extent now than they have been in the past (National Governors' Association, 1994). However, it is hardly surprising that teachers are often skeptical about innovations and proposed reforms in what is, after all, their everyday world of work.

There is a panoply of vested interests, expertise, and professions promoting educational reform. Unfortunately, these other agents of change are outsiders themselves from the practical world of teaching and classrooms, leading to a continuing conflict between established schools and new ideas until the change agents become a part of the school world. Against this array of players who want changes are the rituals, requirements, and rules that surround teaching, learning, and schooling in modern society. Therefore, institutional life is as significant as educational reform and innovation for effective change.

In this context, the planners and designers of educational change have often failed to consider the resiliency of patterns of institutional life. While the appearance contains a rhetoric of reform and program change, the reality that remains is the "conservation of existing arrangements and have little theory . . . to explain the stability amidst the fervour of change" (Popkewitz, 1983, p. 8). Why does this happen? Where do ordinary people, laypersons, stand in this conflict? Are they relegated to the sidelines, included in the debate—if only with lip service—or are they ignored altogether? Can individuals overcome the conflict inherent in their respective positions, to develop their own expertise, knowledge and conclusions, or will they retreat to the safer and more comfortable ground of unexamined assumptions? How can change happen within the paradigm pursued here, in order to resolve, to some degree, the conflict between the opposites?

In exploring these issues, one possible avenue would be to look critically at the discourse of schooling itself. Educational innovation and reform involve a range of proposals to change and restructure the various elements of schooling, from teacher education and curriculum, to organizational and administrative reform, yet within these efforts, the concept of schooling is rarely questioned. It is made to seem "natural and inevitable," (Popkewitz, 1987, p. 2) but it has been "socially constructed." Only when school hours, the place where education occurs, or the rhythms of education are altered will the experience of going to school be changed for students and teachers (Sarason, 1990).

Besides the stage and setting, the plot of education also must change. Talk within schools, particularly talk that teachers do about their subjects, often seems fixed and determined by the curriculum (Cusick, 1973). The discourse, while ostensibly conveying the impression of schooling as a neutral endeavour, hides the socially constructed nature of education and schooling. Changes over time sometimes reveal what we now take for granted. For example, in the nineteenth century, drawing was a required subject for all students, but in the twentieth century, art became a frill or an option for only the talented (Darras, 1996). The basics of education are a social construction whose existence is assumed; the current work of cognitive and constructivist psychologists has tried to show that there are different ways of knowing and different kinds of truths to learn (Viadero. 1996d).

A few mental experiments also can help reveal how many other beliefs about schooling are now assumed. Current assumptions about education can be examined by considering how schools would be if we did not have some actors or parts of the usual script (Sarason, 1982). For example, if one did not have physical education, teachers are prone to say that students would not have a place to let off steam; since they also admit that students come back from these classes more active than before, the possibility exists that it is teachers that relax or let off steam. Other subjects, such as mathematics, or roles, like the principal, can be analyzed for alternatives once they are no longer seen as inevitable.

As change is critically considered, subjects and school requirements can come to be seen as part of a changing and contested terrain. The curriculum content itself represents the intersection of social, cultural, political, and economic interests. Business, government, and other professionals are increasingly involved with school innovations (Mitchell, 1996). While the focus of the interests involved in the contests may change over time, the school remains a site for competing interests in society. For example, since Sputnik, science education has been an almost continuous conflict between scientists, educators, politicians, businesspeople and, occasionally, the people in classrooms (Sarason, 1982).

Past curriculum patterns never entirely disappear and always remain the background to which those in the foreground are reacting (Mitchell, 1995). There also is the impact of past patterns on the present understanding of what constitutes schooling and a "good education." All ideologies are affected by belief systems that come before and will influence those that develop afterwards, even if their meanings are opposite (Mitchell, 1995). Ideologies are, of course, influenced by the parties who are interested in educational change or offer resistance to reforms. All of the above also generate conflict between their surface and their underlying meanings, between the explicit values inherent in late twentieth-century schooling and education, and the implicit values and meanings conveyed at the same time. There is a tension and conflict between the medium and the message, between curriculum objectives and the hidden curriculum (Meighen, 1986).

EXPERTS AND THE PROFESSIONS

Experts and their organized body, the professions, often bring in innovations that laypeople resist and resent. Policy studies suggest that the division between experts and other people becomes as much a problem as the failings, which the innovations are designed to overcome. The selection of innovations must be done very carefully. Cases considered in later chapters show the difference between innovations that overwhelm subordinates and those that allow for their development. The cases in this chapter suggest that the very definition of innovation should show that an innovation is not dependent upon the status or power position of its proponents and adherents. Whether it is acknowledged or not, the expert-lay relationship, in terms of educational change, is a status relationship, which brings its own tensions and conflicts to bear on the reform process.

The conflict arises from the nature of professional expertise, its history and culture. Anthropologists believe that the shaman or medicine man is the origin of the expert role for most societies (Moore, 1970). In Western Europe, the priest was the basis for the current structure of independent professionals (Znaniecki, 1940). In underdeveloped countries, expertise of trained cadres is a part of government because there are no other sources for financing the professions. In developed countries, experts try to avoid government controls and seek status and self-regulation, such as that associated with the medical model of expertise.

Educational experts have emulated the medical model, particularly in areas such as special education, where a hierarchy of experts with medical-like approaches, has developed (Tomkins, 1986). However, those approaches increasingly have been under attack (Meighan, 1986). Nevertheless, professionalism as a social category has instrumentally defined the hierarchy of institutional life and, as a result, of schooling. Like being on an elevator in a department store, what problem you have depends on which experts greet you when you get off on different floors. The professions, with their history of expansion and credential ism, occupy a special position of power when it comes to defining pedagogical practices.

The special occupational groups, which serve as experts in the field of education, can label social groups, create categories of students, and dominate the language and discourse of schooling and education. The power to do this then serves to further increase the legitimacy of the professions, which have used the ideology of their "disinterested" approach to exert social control (Popkewitz, 1987). Furthermore, people's faith in claims to scientific expertise and knowledge serves to widen the gap between the layperson and the expert. The expanding role of the universities in defining society's "sacred knowledge" (Popkewitz, 1987, p. 13) and the role played by philanthropy in North American professional education both contributed to legitimating the knowledge generated by the universities and the status and power of its holders. The ensuing professionalization of knowledge and the degree to which credentials are important in American society only served to increase the social and cultural authority of the expert. Academics and other consultants became the experts consulted by policy makers when intent on change.

Knowledge itself became a commodity in the organization of work and in the ongoing formation of structured communities of experts. The professions, indeed, have their own hierarchy, in which "hard" categories of knowledge are more highly valued than "soft" categories. Hard areas are more abstract and more removed from everyday experience. The public sees scientists and engineers as specially gifted elites because they occupy a separate sphere (Immerwahr, Johnson, & Kerman-Schloss, 1991). In contrast, the place of education research would fall at the lower end of the spectrum, reflecting its lack of status in terms of pure scientific research. When attacked, educators are likely to retreat into the methodology of their approach rather than its substance; this is probably a way of finding a more scientific path of least resistance (Mitchell, 1992).

At present, despite the continuing perception of expert status, there tends to be more questioning of all expert authority. Today, the public seems to be more skeptical about experts, leaders, and professional institutions than previously (Johnson & Immerwahr, 1994), a fact that may be linked to the communication gap existing among these groups. The very success of the professionalization project may make its continuation that much more difficult.

A CLASSIC CASE: CRESTWOOD HEIGHTS

The influence of experts is intimately related to educational change in this affluent Canadian suburb, called Crestwood Heights (Seeley, et al., 1956). The community, whose real name is Forrest Hill, was, at the time, an independent suburb of Toronto. Because of its wealth and the availability of experts, the community demonstrated the lengths to which experts could carry on the innovation process. However, the changes and innovations led to increasing differences among the various actors taking part in the reform process. The experts, the practitioners, and the public (in this case, the parents) became more stratified and alienated from each other as the innovations progressed.

Crestwood Heights, despite the largely progressive innovations, such as counseling classes, a mental health clinic, and reading programs, reinforced a hierarchy of expertise that has continued. If anything, the recent innovations have been drawn from experts higher in the pyramid who emphasize administrative controls and technology (Wolcott, 1977). The hierarchy starts with the international experts at the top and ends with the parents at the bottom. The international expert who deals with hard areas of knowledge or who can help control organizations would have greater status than these social science experts. In fact, the experts in this case tried to avoid the expert title by claiming incompetency, but the status was still thrust on them.

The international experts could only avoid their status by avoiding their clients and, in that event, their clients would turn to more local or amateur experts. Both groups of wizards were the sources of advice and often gave speeches to a waiting audience. The audience was from a community that had abandoned tradition, the usual basis for child rearing and education. In addition, the community members were so caught up in the game of social climbing that they were not likely to be creators of their own solutions to problems of child care and education. If the experts had not been present, they would have had to be invented. The expert role tied into the bureaucracies as well as the family so that stability was insured in spite of the many changes. Within schools, the superintendent for curriculum assumed the mantle of expertise; in the Ontario case, this was known as the Director of Education. Any top level supervisor is concerned with the innovation as a plan or program. The principal must establish the activity in the school. Currently, this plan would include a vision statement.

The international and amateur experts are close to the source of broad, new ideas, while the director of education, principal, and specialists are the administrative experts whose role it is to carry out more specific changes. The principal supports the change by overseeing it and indicating interest in its success. Specialists in the school, such as a counselor or reading consultant, can give more definite specifications to the idealized version of the innovation.

THE MORE THINGS CHANGE, THE MORE THEY REMAIN THE SAME

The actual practice of the change is carried out by classroom teachers. In the sociological classic, *Crestwood Heights*, young female teachers with the lowest status, formally or informally defined, were most likely to adopt the progressive innovations. The innovations also appealed to the women in the community while the men in the schools or families were either unconcerned or were more likely to see traditional education as more important. Teachers and parents are in the lowest positions, while students are left off the list entirely. Though the position of women has improved within society, schools have not acted to improve their position independently from the rest of society. These hierarchical differences within education are not necessary. Fullan (1982) comments that those who introduce change, such as policy makers and administrators, treat teachers in "precisely the same way as they criticize teachers for treating the students" (p. 119).

The introduction of innovations occurs in a way that ignores what teachers think about different proposals since often only the expectations and aims of the change are set out for them. In general, teachers are on the "receiving end of new policy and program directions, either from governments, the local district, or the school" (Fullan,, 1982, p. 123). They rarely initiate change. As Fullan (1982), to be fair, points out, "the culture of the school, the demands of the classroom, and the usual way in which change is introduced do not . . . facilitate teacher involvement" (p. 20). The potential of teacher involvement in the process of educational change could be considered and their role as partners in the implementation of reform programs would be neither ignored nor underestimated.

Why are the teachers not given greater consideration? Fullan (1982) would suggest that it may be because the experts do not conceive of the teachers' position, or their own, as adult learners in the reform process (p. 119). Thus, the principles and wisdom from experts in the field of adult education are entirely overlooked. The experts' own position is not seen as an object of change because they do not adopt a relative conception of change for themselves, just the rest of the universe. Schooling is not the neutral endeavour, which many often assume, and as Popkewitz (1983) reminds us, it can have the result of actually conserving the very relationships that reformers and reform-minded people intended to change. Experts treat teachers as children; neither experts, teachers, nor anyone else expects students to change the mold.

STUDENTS AT THE CROSSROADS

The writers who describe the community of *Crestwood Heights* tellingly did not even include students in their hierarchy of status. Students, who might have something to contribute to the debate, were not then participants in the reform process. An even earlier account provides an example of how student subordination of students can be created for purposes of control by experts (Waller, 1967). A difficult boy was stripped and examined by a doctor in the presence of a female nurse. As his previous tough identity was eliminated, the boy would, according to the doctors, become very cooperative.

The situation of students has not changed dramatically today, but plans for students are increasingly made in the statement of innovation objectives (Joyce & Calhoun, 1996). Students view innovations pragmatically in terms of the effect upon their lives, unlike the ideal beliefs of experts. Even when students are involved with changes, it usually is because of a personal identification with a teacher, not a generalized commitment.

In the ensuing conflict of Crestwood Heights, the "students often get thoroughly lost in the shuffle" (Seeley, et al., 1956, p. 147). They are relegated to the bottom of the heap, where their power, either to conform or to resist, is limited. It can be effective, however, as shown in a study of working-class youth resistance in a British high school (Willis, 1978). There the "lads" bypassed the formal goals and objectives of the school and the curriculum; they found the middle-class values of their educational environment irrelevant and oppressive. Students from the British working class represent the polarization of students from the establishment of experts, but this is just an extreme version of the situations in more favorable schools, including Crestwood Heights.

The development of gifted programs in education usually reveals a pattern that accentuates the difference between students following the experts' ideals and those reacting against them. Gifted programs often assume that they are working with junior experts who will pursue research interests, follow themes across the curriculum, and offer positive contributions to their teachers. Unfortunately, neither the students nor their parents see the research scientist as the model that such programs are following as do the specialist coordinators (Ferrell & Compton, 1986). Neither teachers nor students believe they have a coordinated program that provides intellectual complexity (Ferrell & Compton, 1986, pp. 184-185). As a separate program, gifted teachers and students feel the tension with regular peers; it is only as an elite headed for college that students participate in class discussions and suggested educational changes (Fullan, 1982).

Students who are not trying for college are alienated from education and "impatiently waiting for the day they could leave the school and get out and make money" (Fullan, 1982, p. 150). Students in lower ability streams prefer to do regular work that is beyond them rather than try an innovative curriculum that exposes them to an approach that they think is childish or not a true school subject (Metz, 1979; Spradbery, 1976). Even students who are preparing to be experts are noted as lacking the motivation of true experts (Sussman, 1977). Students in the higher professions learn to be students first and professionals later in practice (Becker, et al., 1961; Bucher & Stelling, 1977).

Perhaps, any student is too marginal to the adult culture to achieve the central importance of expert status (Woods, 1983). As future professionals, students do not experience any significant involvement in curriculum change. As a result, the student role, which is passive and marginal, reinforces the status quo in education. Students expect education in the future to be what they have experienced in the past.

A REVEALING DISASTER: IGE

These concerns were largely absent from the development of the reform Individually Guided Education (IGE) in the late 1960s. A research and development center at the University of Wisconsin created the program, using a systems analysis approach, in an effort to make school programs more individually appropriate and responsive to individual needs. That it was designed and developed at a time of perceived crisis in American education has no small bearing on its aims and the methods it advocated. At a time when America's social problems seemed overwhelming, "educational reform became a potent symbol for responding to the nation's social predicaments" (Popkewitz, et al., 1982, p. 3).

It also was developed at a time of strong belief in scientific management, which would, it was hoped, provide a "rational and efficient scheme for manipulating the school environment to achieve desired outcomes" (Popkewitz, 1983, p. 54).

Studies of school management, including zero based budgeting, exposed similar polarized groups that resulted from another example of rationality carried to extreme limits. Such changes are always expected to have universal applications, but they seldom spread very far (Wolcott, 1977). In contrast, IGE eventually was implemented in approximately three thousand elementary schools during the 1970s and was to be the centerpiece of school reform efforts. It was the object of a four-year study by Popkewitz, Tabachnick, and Wehlage, whose results were published in 1982. Their findings were fascinating because they revealed that, in most cases, there was merely an appearance of change, while the school structures and practices remained fundamentally unaltered. The IGE program was important because it tapped into attitudes that have become prevalent in American educational thought, primarily a strong belief in individualism and an equally strong belief in the power of scientific expertise to address educational problems (Popkewitz, et al., 1982, p. 33). Its particular appeal lay in its combination of "systems management, behavioral objectives, and criterion-referenced measures," which seemed to be supported by psychological research. Its Instructional Programming Model, composed of individual teaching/learning units, was to provide for students who learn at different rates, and was "a systematic attempt to reform schools" (Ibid, p. 35). It also was to encompass both external agencies and internal school structures. Its aim was to create a single delivery system that was "effective in any community or social context" (Ibid, p. 161).

In the pursuit of this aim, the focus of IGE was on the transmission of skills and information, which could be pre-specified, and evidence regarding the approach was to be cumulative and hierarchical in nature. This approach depended on the belief that teachers should respond to individual needs and learning styles with a variety of technologies and methods such as the use of curricular materials, equipment, and pacing. In the opinion of Popewitz and his colleagues, the main thrust underlying the reform was that it would make schooling a meritocratic process. Merit theories generally assume that those best qualified for the expert role will rise to the top (Hurn, 1993). In effect, IGE ignored the social conditions that affect children's development and instead demonstrated the belief that a "universal method of reform could be devised for all schooling" (Popkewitz, et al., 1982, p. 172).

This was apparent in the model of change advocated by the developers of the IGE program. It was believed that the program could be centrally developed and then disseminated to the schools. If properly implemented, IGE would result in improved efficiency and improved learning. As the writers point out, the flaw in this model is that the impact of social structure and its significance for schooling and upon individual development is not considered. Just as gender is not seen as a variable in Crestwood Heights, other forms of social stratification were ignored in IGE.

Popewitz and his colleagues (1982) believe that the reform effort of IGE merely conserved "existing pedagogical relations rather than changing them" and that none of the schools they studied used the technologies as the "Research and Development planners had envisioned them" (p. 173). The approaches were used selectively to further the purposes and practices of individual schools. In most schools using IGE, the reforms only reinforced entrenched patterns and attitudes regarding teaching and learning. In effect, "traditional practices were given new credibility through the adoption of the IGE reform" (Goodman, 1995, p. 3).

As can be seen in the study of six IGE schools, the reform was adapted differently in the three "types" of schools identified by Popkewitz and his group in the orginal study (1982). They labelled these, based on their relative school practices, technical, constructive, and illusory. In the technical schools, techniques became an end in themselves and the focus on skill acquisition. Here, constant evaluation filtered out opportunities for analytic and creative thought. Record keeping became paramount, and test results, charts, and lists were prominently displayed. Of course, to the communities involved, this record keeping showed that the school was accountable, another slogan of the reform and one that is again in the forefront.

In the technical schools, knowledge was standardized and a "deficiency" model of learning was adopted, contrary to the intent of the developers. This model was evident in the procedural language that came to dominate the school, along with its talk of "diagnosis and remediation," language that was not used by the developers. In the process, knowledge was fragmented and teachers and students lost control of their work. Professional autonomy was sacrificed at the supposed altar of educational expertise as embodied in the technical schools "take" on the IGE program. What had been envisioned as components of a larger whole became not tools, but ends in themselves.

In some cases, teachers "resisted the routine produced by the testing programs" (Popkewitz, et al., 1982, p. 67), and relied on their own judgment when assigning children to groups. On another occasion, tests were thrown into the wastebasket when the children had left the room, an incident that serves to illustrate the frustration felt by an individual teacher trying to cope with the system. There are many similar cases of testing and procedures becoming an impediment for reform, including the total system change in Kentucky that will be discussed later. When it was not the intention of the programs, why does this happen?

The researchers argue that the emphasis on functional skill in the technical schools was supported by the surrounding communities. The professionals in the schools held assumptions and expectations regarding their students, which were shaped by "concepts of social and cultural class" (Ibid, p. 91). Any debate about the underlying social and cultural values inherent in these views was suppressed by the emphasis on efficiency and accountability and individual needs. The IGE implementation guides had managed to separate "purpose from procedure" (p. 92), and this only helped sustain the patterns of schooling already in place. Technical language and rituals drew attention away from any critical scrutiny of "institutional beliefs, priorities, or practices" (p. 93). People were so caught up in maintaining the system, that there was no opportunity to reflect and critique the program they were so busy implementing. Later literature supports this description as a typical response of traditional schools to innovations (Mitchell, 1992).

In contrast, there were very different, more progressive assumptions regarding education in what was labelled a constructive school. In this setting, children were viewed as capable of building knowledge through their experiences. The ways in which knowledge is created and integrated formed the underlying pedagogical principle, a position that was reinforced by the school being situated in a university town. The technologies of IGE were modified to reflect this pedagogical belief and were used to support what was perceived to be the particular requirements of the school. The unit and team teaching structure of the IGE program merely provided the framework used by the teachers to carry out their programs. Record keeping was kept to a minimum, and it generally was used to prove that the skill development aspect of the program was being implemented.

However, the priorities of the staff were centered on the belief that education involved problem solving and the development of aesthetic forms of knowledge. Children were presented with opportunities to integrate various forms of knowledge and were encouraged to become self-motivated and responsible. In this context, the language of objectives, charts, and systems was not considered appropriate to describe the educational environment and beliefs of the school. As a result, evaluation became a subsidiary element of the program. Most notably, the teachers in the school viewed themselves as professionals who had the right to make expert decisions regarding their teaching both within and outside the classroom.

Not unexpectedly, in the context of the constructive school, teachers valued their professional autonomy and were at pains to protect it. They perceived that this was being threatened by central administration and its demands for district-wide consistency. The idea of specifying curriculum objectives was thought to be the thin end of a wedge that would undermine their professional control and expertise. This conflict between the district administration and the ideologically motivated teachers meant that burnout became a problem since the teachers were so involved and committed. In all of these respects, this pattern is very typical of progressive schools that will be discussed in Chapters 5 and 7. Though other, more independent progressive schools have been caught up in their own conflicts and divisions, the schools in the IGE system were more slowly extinguished. Trying to maintain the founding principles of the school, while also trying to "get around" district requirements, proved to be a difficult task. In this context, the IGE program was modified and adapted to suit local conditions and became a mere symbol of change.

Finally, as IGE was used in a third category, that of illusory schools, it came to represent a totally different set of beliefs about the nature of education and the practices of schooling. In contrast to either the technical or the constructive school, the model of schooling was one of "social pathology—a belief in the cultural inadequacy of the children who attend these schools" (Popkewitz, 1982, p. 127). Students were deemed to come from unstable homes and backgrounds and the schools in this category were situated in low-income areas. In this context, the structures and technologies of IGE provided a framework for maintaining order and discipline in the schools.

However, while teachers and students went through the motions of teaching and learning, very little was actually taught. Education was an illusion; the tasks set by the teachers were known to be inconsistent with the level of students' ability. The focus of the program was directed to making the children look and feel busy. The emphasis was on organizational control of the children's school lives and on rules to be obeyed. The routines were ceremonial in nature and lacked content; they created an image of schooling that served to convince the staff that they were providing some form of order and structure in the children's lives. They believed that this was a valuable contribution, even if the children actually learned very little. The approach could be rationalized because of the overwhelmingly chaotic social conditions outside the school that magnified what happened within the classrooms. The form of schooling became an end in itself and the ceremonial rituals employed validated the pedagogical principles espoused by the school. The preoccupation of school systems with reorganization and power makes this a frequent, if unfortunate result of other innovations.

The innovation of the IGE program was accepted in the different schools because it was adapted to suit the individual needs of the communities involved. Teachers were not always conscious of the ways in which they adapted the structures and technologies of the program to suit their individual school philosophies. The analysis indicates that the reform program "responded to the institutional imperatives of stability and legitimacy" (Popkewitz, 1982, p. 169) despite the professed intentions of its users. "Reform" as a concept became a slogan that legitimated the various practices of the schools that adopted the IGE program. For the rituals and ceremonies of the reform program it is said:

team teaching or computerized record keeping, can be used to justify . . . a variety of institutional practices, and to provide symbols of credibility by suggesting that the institution is meeting its social mandate." (Ibid)

RESEARCH TEMPLES

The institutions where experts were educated and are employed vary as much as the schools in the IGE study. But the experts always assume they can steer the schools toward rational improvement plans. As suggested by the study of *Crestwood Heights*, plans and ideas rather than social practices are paramount. The major national effort in the United States, the National Institute of Education, was premised on the inferiority of those in educational research compared to other disciplines. The initial attempt was to find better people to conduct research (Sproull, et al., 1978). The quality of individual teachers has similarly been seen as the cause of school problems (Sarason, 1982).

The social organization of both schools and research institutes needs to be considered. In the case of research centers, in addition to individualism, the separation of the centers from school practice is a major problem. The largest Canadian center, the Ontario Institute for Studies of Education (OISE) particularly reveals the contradictions that are caused by this separation. In 1960, an original broad and voluntary organization for curriculum development led to a Joint Committee of the University of Toronto and the Toronto Board of Education (Tomkins, 1986,). In spite of an initial equal balance, patterns of deference rapidly developed within the Joint Committee. Secondary teachers looked to university professors to speak and elementary teachers simply deferred to most others as more expert than themselves.

The Ontario program also accepted the expert hierarchy when it came to developing a curriculum policy. OISE became an imperial subsidiary of American research. The ideas of Bruner were followed with respect to procedure as well as a basis for inductive learning. This institute also provided opportunities for American researchers (Tomkins, 1986). To provide more academic and specialized work, the Joint Committee was replaced by OISE in 1966; the focus sharply shifted away from practical matters.

In sacrificing cooperation with teachers for research work and graduate studies, OISE appears to have built in the problem of relating theory to practice. This conflict became acute as declining funds made all research institutes more subject to political pressures. Research institutes in Alberta and the Atlantic provinces have faltered for similar reasons. In the United States, regional laboratories as supplements to the National Institute of Education and educational programs as a part of national scientific institutes were responses to political demands.

The Ontario center has revived as it has provided opportunities for teachers to study and change schools in a Canadian context (Tomkins, 1986, p. 312). Field programs and very elaborate programs of partnerships with school boards have been developed (Erskine-Cullen, 1992). Like other research centers, this program has started to overcome its preoccupation with academic research in favor of more practical concerns, but an emphasis on cooperation among researchers and between the university and schools has only slightly reduced the admiration for outstanding work by individuals. The sorcery of science, and the status recognition associated with it, continues to lure experts to dangerous areas.

THE EXPERTS REFUSE TO LEAVE

Conscious criticism by those in their temples of research is still no more apparent there than in schools. The experts can change their own ideas and structures in ways that the accountability movement can never reach. These experts can make contributions to practical solutions, rather than critical analysis, but they must first change their role conception. The acceptance they have enjoyed from the community also must change. Ironically, the community must provide the experts with the support that will decrease their insecurity and allow them to change themselves.

In the Crestwood Heights study, there existed a market for new ideas that was due to the considerable wealth of the parents and their desire for the "best" education for their children. When the supply of experts met the demand of parents and teachers, the market for educational expertise operated. Psychologists, social scientists, and various educational experts came on the scene to plan the reform enterprise, bringing their particular brand of expertise with them. In effect, they imported innovations and the parent community accepted them rather than barring their entrance. Recent research has shown that external experts have such a gift of influence that they can have a positive effect on the acceptance of innovations.

A variety of connections between teachers and experts can be developed. The external experts need only direct their communications to internal experts who can connect with the world of teachers better than the experts can themselves. Similarly, links between top level administrators and teachers can be developed by intermediate roles, such as consultants (Daft & Becker, 1978), rather than higher level administrators (Bauchner, et al., 1982). When teachers develop more cohesive groups they are able to resist the power of experts (Sussman, 1977). These alternative relationships, together with partnerships with teachers, are all realignments of part of the educational profession.

It is the relationship between the experts and the public that is in most need of change. The experts are particularly likely to be crosspressured; they have neither the security of the upper class nor the passivity of a subordinated people (Seeley, et al, 1956). This insecurity of the experts derives from their marginal position (Levin, 1986). They are said to appear like shooting stars and one expert takes a position exactly the opposite of the previous experts. The experts change their own position and might be even criticizing themselves if they were able to admit it.

The experts try to control their situations by dominating communications. Not until they receive more financial and social support are they likely to diminish the war of words. Teachers who are more insecure than other experts are particularly likely to dominate classes, and recitation constantly has been shown to be their most typical expectation for student contributions (Cusick, 1973). Alternatives to the experts require that others help them to change.

The double pressure on experts is particularly revealed by the pattern of gender differences. In *Crestwood Heights*, even when the experts were female, they emulated the men in their profession. A large number of mid-level experts are now women, but they are insecure and don't usually reveal different options from men. The experts in *Crestwood Heights* used their influence to persuade the female parents in particular of the validity of their ideas, but it was the practical men that they would have rather have convinced, not the women admirers who were their "harem." It is conflicts between expertise and gender that are most revealing.

In a variety of other ways, the expert-lay difference exposes the conflict in status and authority that can exist in the relationship between players in the drama of educational change. In terms of superior and subordinate relationships, moreover, the higher experts who talk the most, appear to do the least work (Mitchell, 1981). The experts' role in promoting, and even inflating, innovations, reflects a preoccupation with rhetoric rather than with practice.

This situation is common within almost all professions, just as is the pattern of external experts receiving the most respect. It is the consultant or specialist, rather than the general practitioner, who gets the rewards in medicine for developments. The power of the professions in the educational hierarchy, as shown in the Crestwood Heights study, is considerable. The revolts of the clients and demands for accountability by governments have signaled the limitations of experts' powers as usually practiced.

More than controls on experts are needed; their considerable powers must be unleashed. The experts are a good resource because they are one of the least expensive alternatives for change that can be found; external assistance remains an important resource even after project and local organizational characteristics are taken into account (Louis, et al., 1981). The mythical qualities associated with the expert position may be just what is needed to engender commitment to innovations. The experts also are more useful in working with established innovations rather than ambiguous and new ones; they also are better as judges of innovations started by teachers than they are as original planners (Mitchell, 1992). For each of the known problems with experts, a specific answer is needed. The arrogance of experts can exacerbate the problems with top-down innovations (Lind, 1974). Experts can learn to work together with others; abstract knowledge can be combined with social sensitivity.

Forms of stratification including gender, social class, and race have been shown to be involved with both the experts and innovations (Baldridge, 1975). The gender results are particularly shocking; sex subordination clearly is reinforced by the reform process as revealed in *Crestwood Heights*. Gender stratification and beliefs about women affected the parent community more than the experts. Since the women were usually the parents involved with educational innovation, the authors of this classic study described parents as "passive females." Both writers and experts should clearly be more supportive of women. Women can become experts who are very different from men. They can remake the wizard role by seeking sociability, variety, and their own ideals (Mitchell, 1971; Peterson, 1985). However, women reveal these aspects of expertise only when operating in uncharted roles or are no longer having to constantly fight for recognition.

There is one critical concern about discussing experts and stratification. The experts do not possess power as much as they are associated with the powerful people. In societies and organizations, experts want to see their abstractions realized and implemented; they seek the government leaders and top administrators who can carry out their projects. For experts to express and articulate the ideas of the powerless in society is a revolutionary change for them and society.

REFORM: ADOPTION OR ADAPTATION?

In the more usual sequence, the experts' innovations engender resistance as they filter downwards. This, of course, poses problems for the promoters of innovation, who tend towards imposing the adoption of their particular program. This model of educational change has been predominant; it does not deal with the complexities of institutional life. It divides the players involved in the changes into groups of reformers and users and can generate further conflict in terms of the process of educational change. The various barriers to innovation, such as the impact of social class and gender, the historical separation of categories of thinkers and doers, and the problem of defining innovation itself, then come into play. The pulls exerted by the relationships in the educational hierarchy also pose their own problems regarding implementation, as do local conditions and the wider sociopolitical agenda.

All of these barriers have the effect that "change is not a fully predictable process" (Fullan, 1982, p. 93) and that it has many dimensions, all of which complicate the total picture of reform implementation. Researchers and theorists have tried to deal with these problems by positing a theory of graduated adoption. Three stages have been generally distinguished. Stage one would be the stress of the initial decision to adopt the innovation. Stage two would involve the first two or three years of use, which would see the adaptation of the innovation to local conditions. Finally, stage three would be the developments leading to the institutionalization of the innovation, whereby it integrates into the original system (Berman & McLaughlin, 1978; Louis, et al., 1981; Fullan, 1982). Stage theory still stresses that there is an external entity to adopt, but this approach has led to increasingly varied views of implementation. The basis for the stages, such as power, local situations, or abstract ideas, will affect the various views espoused by the theorists (House, 1979).

Innovations cannot exist solely in abstract thinking. They must be looked at in the light of the uses to which they are put. This approach has been incorporated into the Concerns-Based Adoption Model (CBAM) proposed by researchers at the University of Texas. This model and the research accompanying it emphasizes "an understanding of the change process as it is experienced by individuals who are implementing innovations within an organizational context" (Heck, et al., 1981, p. 1). Although the authors primarily are concerned with the measurement and evaluation of innovations, some of their observations about the process of change are worth mentioning.

As they have noted, an innovation is "dependent on the human element" (Ibid, p. 5) and the process of adoption is extremely complex. It involves blending many different perspectives to implement the innovation. On the one hand, developers "can often be too close to an innovation to see things from a teacher's perspective" (p. 24). On the other hand, the teacher who is isolated in the classroom may not be familiar with, or interested in, the big picture. This can mean that an innovation is subject to different uses by different individuals, or that parts of an innovation can be used in different ways.

CBAM attempts to measure the innovation from the standpoint of its expert developer. The components of the innovation are set down and ways of measuring the extent to which they had been adopted are developed. For example, a program for science at the elementary level could have twelve components including time devoted to science, use of the environment, materials available, inservice arrangements, and instruction sequenced for inquiry learning. One dimension could be the extent to which each component was ignored, had begun to be used, or was mostly employed. Consideration also would be given to whether current practice represented the best use of the component (p. 119). The more diverse the dimensions included, the more complicated the adoption of the innovation was revealed to be.

Though CBAM clarifies the meaning of the innovation from the standpoint of experts and many of them found the approach of the innovation configuration helpful, it did not help understand the innovation as a part of institutional life. It shows how, from the standpoint of the expert, purely symbolic cases of change could be avoided; it does not show why administrators or others would want a mere show in implementing innovations.

The question remains: How does institutional life, such as that of schooling, affect the implementation of innovations? As Popkewitz, Tabachnick, and Wehlage (1982) suggest, innovations are first incorporated into existing patterns of behaviour and belief. The initiating process, critical decisions to implement, and continuing survival strategies are shown from the large-scale study in Chart 2.1 (Huberman & Miles, 1982).

In the initial stage, the administrators must often protect the baby and support it. It is necessary to go beyond the initial support and include the program in the regular budget and in other ways make it the norm rather than an experiment. Further teaching and the diffusion of the innovation requires that it survive budget cuts and personnel changes. These extensive system reforms only begin to provide support for norms among teacher colleagues that are favorable to reform.

The implementation of reform at the classroom requires much more. To avoid superficial change, school routines and assumptions must be changed. The innovations can legitimize ongoing patterns of educational conduct as in slogans for reform (Huberman & Miles, 1982). Elliot Eisner (1995) characterizes such approaches to reform as "replays of past efforts" that fail to deal with what it is that "makes school practices so robust and resistant to change" (p. 759). Various government ministries and organizations invoke the language of standards, accountability, measurement, and excellence as the raison d'être of reform efforts, but in Eisner's view, these are merely slogans that obscure the "deeper . . . problems that beset our schools" (Ibid, p. 764). Slogans of reform such as these distract from the real problems, such as socioeconomic ones, that make a difference in people's experience of schooling. This limited view distracts from those multiple perspectives and interactions that take place in the educational field among "teachers, curriculum, evaluation, school organization, and the . . . pressures from universities" (Ibid, p. 764). What is needed, in Eisner's view, is a conversation about reform that will deepen our understanding of the educational process, its culture, and its possibilities, one that will encompass vision and ignore "the glitter of bandwagons" (Ibid).

Chart 2.1
Institutionalization

Supporting Conditions

Core versus peripheral application
Operate on regular, daily basis
Provide benefits and payoffs to users
Eliminate competing practices
Receive support from:
    Administrators
    Users/staff
    Clients (kids, parents)
Other: external money, laws, etc.

Passage Completion

Goes from soft to hard money
Job description becomes standard
Required skills are included in formal training program
Organizational status is in regulations
Routines for supply and maintenance followed

Cycle Survival

Comes through annual budget cycles
Continues after departure or introduction of new personnel
Skills are taught for successive cycles
Widespread use is achieved throughout the organization
Survives equipment turnover or loss (including materials)

ALIENATION: THE OTHER PROBLEM

Merely to look at the slogans and indicators of reform adoption is to ignore the various relationships at work in schools. Schooling itself is a complex "social, moral and political enterprise" (Popkewitz, et al., 1982, p. 178). Any study of reform and innovation that does not address this aspect is a superficial one because the "biases of social organization rest unexamined" (Ibid).

The organization has to support the powerless, provide security for experts, and provide for a better education. This is a difficult set of expectations but not an impossible one. The trick is to overcome the polar positions in policies and practices that divide the educational profession and its public. Chart 2.2 summarizes the opposition that can occur among the players.

Institutionalization is the problem from the perspective of trying to integrate the experts and administration within classrooms. However, from the perspective of the more subordinated teachers and students, the problem is alienation from ideas, schools, and themselves. Those at the top of the hierarchy are likely to see general, conceptual changes as more important than specific, instrumental variations (Rich, 1981). Symbolic change is a likely turn for the administrative mind while single issues, which are separated from any context, can become the concern of parents. For example, the practice of teaching classical myths in a Waldorf type of public school recently has led to charges of teaching witchcraft by a group of parents because of their misunderstanding of the teaching (Sanchez, E., 1997).

Though best documented in terms of teachers and administrators, conflicts can develop into polar divisions that are like the tribal divisions, moieties, in which differences periodically are settled by a tug of war (Wolcott, 1977). System makers would rebuild the entire house for a new refrigerator while individual changers would choose a new appliance which is slightly better than the previous one (House, 1974). Similarly, the evaluation of innovations can be split between those interested in long-range effects and increased scientific decision making and those who are concerned with immediate results and specific applications of any knowledge (Caro, 1973). The first group, like the critics of IGE, is likely to see any problems with innovation in the assumptions that practioners make. The second division is more suspicious of innovation generally and more prone to attribute any problems to the lack of resources for the project.

Central to this continuing conflict is the tendency of experts to be absorbed with abstract ideas while the other camp denies that there are any problems that require experimentation. Though important to consultants, a session on the philosophy of the new social studies was poorly attended; a meeting on methods of teaching the same subject drew hundreds of teachers (Serediuk, 1977). Teachers and administrators may be caught up in this process as was the case of the IGE constructivist school; there is a strong link between professionalism in education and a progressive education position that will be discussed in Chapter 5. The conservatives want to cover up problems with the current system while relying on tradition and intuition for decision making. The functionalist school in the IGE study shows some of the ways that change can be interpreted in a more traditional setting.

For either traditional or progressive receivers of innovations, the source of changes are people in a very insecure environment who are likely to follow fads and who are personally very insecure (Britian, 1981). The experts have a hidden agenda in battling over changes which is particularly revealed by *Crestwood Heights*. However, the same insecurity for experts as well as their opposition also is strikingly shown in a study of a governmental agency doing environmental research (Britian, 1981). Scientific hypothesis testing to improve the environment received little support and the experts retreated to a position that emphasized methodology. Such withdrawals have been common for educational research centres, particularly when their innovations are not successful (Sproull, et al., 1978). When successful, more scientific claims by researchers and increased attempts at large-scale implementation of ideas are made. Concentrated power

Chart 2.2
From Experts to Practitioners

Role	Perspective	Criteria
The Expert	Philosophy	Long-range concepts are explicitly research based but implicitly reflect changes within the profession and personal anxieties.
Administrator	Program or system	
Principal	School plan or vision statement	
Teachers	Methods or teaching aids	
Parents	Help for their own child	
Students	Practical requirements to get through the system and comparative requirements made of others	
		Short-term views are based upon personal experience and school traditions; innovations are supported if they are publicized in the mass media.

can apparently diminish the doubts of the experts and overcome the obvious signs of opposition from subordinates. However, in this situation like many others, less drastic alternatives are needed to improve the capacity of subordinates before larger, more fundamental changes can be tried.

LINKING THE SCIENTIFIC COMMUNITY TO PEOPLE

The greater involvement of subordinates, with greater recognition for them, can occur through a number of models. Social movements have been a pattern that educational reform has followed in several places and which involves many activist groups. Religion with true believers was the nineteenth century pattern for educational reform that is still like the conversion experiences that many advocates recall today. However, the one model that is closest to the professions and which the related experts should understand is the scientific community.

If all the constituents of reform could be included, then the excesses of reformers and a possibility of progress for educational research as a part of an enlarged community would be enhanced. Though the scientific model has emphasized the independent observer separate from the observed phenomena, it has always insisted that the determination of what would be studied and what evidence will be accepted is dependent upon the scientific community. As soon as the scientific community is shown to be dependent upon its constituents, which feminists have persuasively argued it is, there is no longer a separation of experts from people with other types of knowledge and it is possible for a common understanding to develop with them (Code, 1991).

The welfare mother has a knowledge of how to survive that is every bit as important as theoretical knowledge for the future development of the community and its members. Games that have been invented to understand the perspective of welfare mothers have only helped to sustain their subordination as they are judged insufficient by the standards of the experts. The aim of reforming welfare mothers is to make them into the image of the experts (Code, 1991). But all groups must recognize their interdependence on each other and, in turn, to the environment. The ecological interdependence in our planet also is the basis for overcoming the limitations of abstractions and studying the dependence of abstractions on the interaction of nature, society, and our concrete experiences.

In aiming to change the scientific community so that it is inclusive, it is important to recognize the variety of people's experiences that can be as validly used for innovations in education as the abstractions of experts. For example, six women in British Columbia, Canada, who were on welfare, designed the poverty game; the game enables others to understand the isolation of women who must survive on few resources and who must deal with an exhausting variety of welfare workers and other officials. The women who designed the game now have new options:

They receive an announcement of an innovative community program that provides free transportation and child care, and their new welfare worker is accessible and forthcoming. Out of the two developments—knowledge and solidarity—the six women are empowered to the extent that they can embark on the project of devising the game. Its success allows them, slowly, to overcome their inertia and—as they say in their recorded narratives—to draw on the strengths of commonality in taking charge of their lives. (Ibid, p. 285)

It is crucial that the game inventors recognize that they continue to have ties with other welfare moms, and the experts must see how much both groups have to teach them. The labeling and isolation of people as deficient must be seen as dehumanizing to all.

In the following account, LaJoe, her children, Lafeyette and Pharoah, and her husband, Paul, are a poor family. One organization, social services, denies family assistance when Paul is found to be in the home and becomes a possible source of income; the human drama continues:

Confused and upset, LaJoe walked silently out of the room, slamming the door behind her. She would later apologize to her inquisitors for her impoliteness, but she wouldn't offer much defense against the department's charges. She didn't deny that Paul occasionally stayed over. She didn't ask whether she was entitled to legal counsel. She didn't ask for a caseworker to come out and look at their home. Now, as she made her way through the labyrinth of desks, she wondered how to break the news to the kids.

Lafeyette knew his mother had gone for a hearing and that the department was considering cutting her benefits, so when she came home that afternoon he was by the door to greet her. As she walked into the apartment, his eyes locked with hers. His long fingers cupped her face.

"What'd they say?" he asked.

"Off," LaJoe replied in a voice that barely approached a whisper. Lafeyette's shoulders sank. LaJoe hugged him.

She chose not to tell Pharoah, at least not yet; she was protective of him. Because he had lately responded to nearly every instance of violence and family trouble with the same refrain—"I'm too little to understand"—she feared that the problems, when he was at last ready to confront them, would be too deeply buried for him. (Kotlowitz, 1991, p. 97)

Aside from completely changing the model for educational reform, there are opportunities for creative participation by teachers and others in a variety of reforms that are described in Chapter 3. The ways that experts can perhaps work themselves out of a job are discussed as they develop the abilities of others, much like physicians supporting self-help groups among patients. However, Chapter 4 shows the problem has become worse in the United States where the experts have become a more concentrated group with greater power. The increase in federal programs and planning to integrate innovations has created a small group of superexperts. As a result, the conflict between these experts and laypeople seems greater; in later chapters the dream of a completely changed community for science and humanity will reoccur in opposition to the professional dominance in more specific forms.

Chapter 3

Contrary Colleagues

I am always being told to suggest something feasible. What in effect is being said to me is that I should propound the ordinary methods or at least combine something good with the existing evil—Jean Jacques Rousseau. (Boyd, 1956, p.6)

We have a governor's school for gifted students. Why not something similar for teachers . . . to study some of the great books: Plato, Homer, Virgil, Shakespeare, and others? Include the opportunity to visit an art gallery, see live performances of Shakespeare's plays . . . . If that kind of learning experience doesn't turn on teachers of the humanities, I don't know what will. That excitement will be communicated to students—Jean Powell. (Rud & Oldendorf, 1992)

Few have tried to do the opposite of what usually is done as proposed by the philosopher Rousseau in 1761. The experts who were discussed in the previous chapter have not been placed at the bottom of the hierarchy. Instead, various attempts have been made to strengthen some of the constituents of reform. Jean Powell, North Carolina Teacher of the Year in 1983-1984, proposed a different kind of teacher training that would reverse the usual order in staff development. Teachers would broaden their horizons and meet with the experts as intellectual equals. Furthermore, the very instrumental and controlling experience of in-service education (Lind, 1974) could be replaced by an expressive and liberating encounter that recognized the excellence of teachers.

Ms. Powell's dream became a reality when a teacher center was established that nourished the mind, body, and spirit of those in the profession (Diegmueller, 1996b). This one example of traumatic change should be seen against an increasing trend to recognize teachers and provide places for them to meet, and develop standards to judge their performance. Parents, community volunteers, and students have been involved in education more erratically. However, as the players develop their own networks and plans independently from the experts, a new order develops where different ideas and experiences compete with the ideas of experts.

The multiple views among these players can add many separate contributions to an understanding of innovations; these different perspectives are a sharp contrast to expecting a single correct answer from experts or letting them unilaterally set the agenda for change. The more varied conception frequently is referred to as postmodernism, while the experts led the world into modernism (Efland, 1995). Postmodernism recognizes groups and cultural differences, which means theories and practices will be related because there is no one polarity between the two. Similarly, there can be a mutual recognition and acceptance of the difference between experts and laypeople.

Innovation programs have often gone in opposite directions and affected constituents differently. The integration of handicapped students has raised the ire of teachers who are against all reforms (Alberta Teachers' Association, 1993). However, it was the development of such programs that first led to the involvement of parents and made them a key group for integration. Programs aimed at parents and community members like school councils and those oriented towards teachers and administrators, such as the Coalition of Essential schools, have led to students being touched by the reform movement (Mitchell, 1996).

Other innovations tend to involve all of the actors without even realizing it. Teacher evaluations are an interesting example. The primary conflict over evaluations is between teacher control and administrative dominance, but influences by parents and students also have been part of the story. Furthermore, divisions among teachers suggest that none of these groups is monolithic. Peer evaluation and teacher evaluation of their own work are proving to be, perhaps, the most revealing sources of accountability.

For any of the groups considered, a primary question is whether the reform is overwhelming or does it contribute to the development of the individuals involved? Teacher centers and new activities have become entangled in political conflicts, but they have aided new teachers to come to grips with the realities of teaching and older teachers to renew themselves. Mainstreaming was the first major attempt at legislated learning on a large scale, which has generally been overwhelming for those most affected. The politicians appear to be having second thoughts about mainstreaming or inclusion because of the costs it involves rather than the educational effects on students and teachers (Zernike, 1997).

Finally, teacher evaluation reveals almost constant tugs between conservative speakers who want to achieve accountability and liberal advocates whose aim is to empower individuals. Accountability can lead to the complete change of staff and the loss of tenure by its members (Poe, 1997b). Support for teachers has come to include assessment from a critical friend in addition to peer and personal evaluation (Costa & Kallick, 1993). The contrast between soft and hard views of evaluation, summative versus formative ones, has never been greater. The problem of choice for those from each perspective in education has become tremendously difficult.

CHANGING THE GUARD

In the 1970s, the problem was to provide resources for teachers as they became more involved in the process of changing schools. Today, many groups are organizing themselves, particularly through the use of technology. Impact II is a network of creative, professional teachers who appear to have more supporters than any of the speciality groups, such as the mathematics teachers' computer network (Meyers & McIssac, 1994). Other more local groups of teachers are publishing newspapers and taking over the teachers' union, as in Milwaukee (Peterson & Tenorio, 1994). However, many teachers' unions have been very conservative and often a prime example of only symbolic support for reform (Toch, 1991).

Parents, students, and community volunteers have not had previous forms of organization to overcome; they have been scratching out new possibilities. Parents are now active in school councils and confederations of the councils (Mitchell, 1996). In a number of communities, parents have set up their own web site. In Evanston, Illinois, parents established such a site during a teacher strike and have continued it (Trotter, 1997b). Student leaders are active through large-scale newspapers and with plans for use of community television to have direct access to the student bodies (Mitchell, 1996). Such actions by parents and students may begin to scare the current captains of schools.

There has been an increasing involvement with education of many groups other than students and teachers. Seniors have become active volunteers with many schools. Former President Jimmy Carter has become an exemplary leader of efforts to involve volunteers in education (Mitchell, 1996). Uncles at large and similar organizations have increasingly involved community members as volunteers (Levine & Levine, 1996, p. 151). Extensive media exposure probably has led to a wider involvement in schools by many people, including businesspeople.

Our knowledge of these and other developments is often dependent upon the reporting and publicity of the mass media though the internet has represented a source of increasingly diverse information. However, the new technology became organized when a few sites, including *Education Week*, made available a large number of other sites; the dominance of media experts reappeared. The organ of American reform, *Education Week*, has become a large marketing and reporting organization, not just the newspaper that reports on educational changes. The polarity of experts and laypeople has always been greater in the established media than in education (Elliot, 1972). Media experts and those who relate to them have dominated the news, while the laypeople were limited and could, at best, be articulate enough to be quoted in the media. As they become more successful and better known, media stars become generalists with very pervasive influence (Elliot, 1972, p. 94).

PUBLICITY AND SOCIAL CONTACTS FOR TEACHERS

As initially suggested, the North Carolina Center for the Advancement of Teaching (NCCAT) has attempted to recognize and encourage exceptional teachers in an unconventional way. In other places, teachers have been given recognition as "teachers of the year," though other teachers have resented such recognition. In Kentucky, exceptional teachers are being recognized as distinguished educators who, for twice their usual salary, are expected to turn a low performing school around (Mitchell, 1996); some companies, such as Ashland Oil, have made and distributed a large number of videotapes of teacher talks on educational reform. Because of the increased publicity, teachers are no longer as isolated or anonymous as they once were (Lortie, 1975).

In 1986, NCCAT emerged as a showplace for teacher development (Diegmueller, 1996b). Teacher development was once so unappreciated that money spent on it was hidden in school board budgets (Fullan, 1982). Teacher centers, imported from England, made their in-service education highly visible and, when these became "political footballs," the centers were strongly criticized (Mitchell, 1992). In the last decade, teacher professional development has become a corollary of change efforts (Rud & Oldendorf, 1992).

In the context of a series of reforms that stressed education for economic growth, Jean Powell, who was recognized as the teacher of the year in North Carolina, was able to secure a grant from the state legislature to recognize other teachers and to provide for their renewal (Diegmueller, 1996b). She won support from three powerful forces to secure a budget request: a governor who was very interested in education, the resourceful speaker of the House, and the respected president of the University of North Carolina. Everyone expected the initial request to be reduced or the idea eliminated entirely from the package; none of this happened and the governor's request for an initial grant for $2.5 million was passed in 1985 (Rud & Oldendorf, 1992, p. 32).

In a number of different ways NCCAT was related to the arts. The program was modeled after the Aspen Institute in Colorado, which has a similar liberal focus. When the initial proposal appeared, the North Carolina Humanities Committee provided support. The program was also supported by those in the arts and provided a model for art and other intellectual subjects for teachers. When the actual program developed, a number of the scheduled seminars involved art, myth, dance, and architecture. One such program was called "The Design of Earthly Gardens" and involved a comparison between the magnificent gardens in nearby Asheville, planned in the nineteenth century with current ideas of landscaping. The teachers participated as equals with an expert landscape architect. Since the program was residential, art objects were a crucial part of the experience as were the gracious living arrangements.

Other programs involved politics and ethics. Only in rare exceptions was a teaching interest, such as teaching psychology in high schools, included in the curriculum. More typical for the center, time was left for teachers to pursue their own interests. In the center's second year, a teacher scholar program was established to free teachers to do creative work. They submitted individual plans; one teacher created fifty-one works of sculpture in three weeks, another began a biography of her son, and another needed a week to read the poetry of Wallace Stevens.

Still, regardless of the subject, the arts seem crucial for this summer experience, high in the mountains. Many teachers have described the residential week and its follow-up activities as a peak experience in their lives. The planners clearly saw aesthetic practice rather than remediation as a crucial part of teacher renewal. In interpreting the experience, the colleague-like directors stressed how they wanted teachers to see the world as it might be, rather than as it was.

The teacher-students formed study circles among themselves, which also included their expert-teachers. These circles were concerned with ideas, and they have developed alumni reunions to the mountain peak residence where art and hospitality are united. One former teacher-student wrote a moving poem to express the experience to others. The teacher networks sought corporate support and made their own contributions to programs in other parts of the world including Canada, England, Mexico, and Costa Rica.

The alumni have become a significant source for nominating new applicants for the experience designed for excellent teachers. Originally, superintendents and principals made recommendations and teachers prepared an elaborate form that included examples of their writing. Now, the alumni have replaced the superintendents while principals still endorse and support the applicants.

Some connection has been made between teachers for NCCAT and the San Francisco Center for the Advancement and Renewal of Educators. In the past, lecturers for seminars came from the Highlander Research and Education Center, which trained the civil rights protesters and works with similar advocates today. However, few links between the students in the North Carolina program and other state-supported programs have been developed because the program has never been replicated as originally planned. In recent years, some ten different centers have been established over the United States, but all of them are structurally different (J. Franson, interview, July 18, 1997).

NCCAT is an inspiration for the future in the way that New College at Columbia University was in the past. New College was a progressive education program for teachers during the 1930s. The creative experience of New College recently has been rediscovered (Smith, et al., 1986). Together with classes, New College students traveled to Europe, worked in rural areas, and experienced continuous intellectual stimulation. Unfortunately, the graduates of New College went on to become education leaders rather than teachers.

Unlike New College, NCCAT has tried to keep teachers in the classroom. A specific aim of this program was to provide recognition so the best teachers would not leave North Carolina. NCCAT seems to be achieving that goal since past participants at NCCAT have returned to teaching in overwhelming numbers. However, there is a self-selection process related to race and gender that appears to keep many teachers from coming to the center. White teachers are far more likely than Black teachers to apply, while women in the profession are far more likely than men to come. Possibly, Black Americans, who live more in the lowlands of North Carolina, do not seek the mountains, which has been the home of mainly Whites, as a place for their peak experiences. Perhaps the aesthetic purpose of curriculum and the residence have made the program more appealing to women. One commentator believes the Center mirrors the way "women think, work, and create and support relationships" (Rud & Oldendorf, 1992, p. 139). However, more direct reasons for the underrepresentation of these two groups need to be found.

The only apparent bias in the planning of the center is toward the usual expert way of thinking. The planners have accepted the perhaps male, instrumental ways of thinking about stages; women might consider an affective process as a guide. The actual planners thought of the center as moving from interim activities to instutionization of the approach as discussed in Chapter 2. For an artistic conception of change, there is no final product or organization, only continual recreation of the context for new experiences (Mitchell, 1997). It is, of course, possible that if the center was more consistent with an artistic conception, it would be less appealing to some teacher groups.

THE CONTINUING CHALLENGE OF TEACHER CENTERS

Both NCCAT and New College broke with the restrictive tradition of viewing the education of teachers as a means of overcoming moral, psychological, or technical deficiencies (Rud & Oldendorf, 1992,). The North Carolina experience is an extension of the more open and creative teacher center movement that came to the United States from England in the 1970s. That movement did not include aesthetics as a part of its purpose, but it did try to work with teachers rather than dictate to them.

One of the founders of an American center, David Hawkins, argued for a Stone Age conception of knowledge. Like the Stone Age man, teachers should pick up ideas and accidentally adapt them to some other end. They would creatively use these ideas for some new purpose. In a similar handicraft fashion, another movement leader spoke of "weaving relationships among participants who give as well as take" (Thompson, 1982, p. 136).

With a world view that stressed voluntary, personal efforts, the early leaders of teacher centers were unable to deal with the effects of institutionalization as their program was adopted throughout the United States, England, and parts of Canada. Their efforts emerged from teachers who wanted help and who sought change. Little consideration was given to reluctant teachers who were unwilling to improve or who were preoccupied with their own survival. The omission of power and the avoidance of more structured approaches was behind the early leaders' opposition to systematic research. It was feared that experiments, surveys, or quantified case studies would all lack an understanding of the movement's unique aims. NCCAT has stressed that their questionnaires originated from the verbatim testimonials of participants in the program and the survey items derive from these qualitative statements. Power with people rather than power over them is stressed both by the original teacher centers and NCCAT.

Like the North Carolina center, the teacher networks developed as a reaction to external reforms. Both of these teacher efforts have tried to develop teachers' understanding rather than be "rule governed" by the demands of their masters (Rud & Oldendorf, 1992, p. 4). Originally, teacher networks arose from the need to implement the new science programs of the 1960s. The leaders of teacher centers tried to avoid the problem of innovation developed by their predecessors, such as the inventors of Educational Resource Information Center (ERIC) who thought that the library system would immediately make the latest research available to teachers. They did not want any technological changes that must later be explained, if not sold, to teachers. In moving for acceptability to teachers, there has been no concern for stretching teachers' ability to contribute.

The concern for all teachers with the assumed motivation to change was only slightly modified. The centers attempted changes that the authorities had ignored in the past. In both England and the United States, teacher centers focused upon the demands of teaching students from the working class (Thompson, 1982). These centers offered small rewards to help teachers with innovations (Hering, 1983). Such awards allowed teachers to hire a teacher consultant, buy materials, or visit another teacher's program.

The awards program was followed by government programs that offered minigrants, which proved to be one of the most successful government programs (McDonnell, 1985). The teacher centers were adopted by the federal government and became a "political football" when President Carter had legislation enacted to support them (Thompson, 1982). The legislation required school boards, rather than existing teacher centers, to apply for federal grants. The school boards and, even more, the teachers' unions with which the boards dealt, treated the teacher center movement as an elite group from whom they would not accept direction. Federal support was terminated by President Reagan's administration, which claimed teacher centers were only "union hiring halls" (Mitchell, 1992, p. 24). Though neither side realized it, the ideal of local determination of individual teacher needs and strengths had been lost.

The original teacher centers failed to use the opportunity provided by the federal legislation to promote either themselves or their ideals. As the political wars ended, all remaining centers were thrown back to individual states for financial support. The leaders of the original centers claimed that education was political, but they refused to act like politicians. Instead, they reacted with the resentment of generations of teachers who believed they had not been appreciated. One activist said:

The Feds think only of their 89 teachers' centers. They don't remember there are all these *wonderful* centers from which their ideas sprang plus England. . . . I'm ignored or dismissed when I mention them. (Thompson, 1982, p. 146)

The original center movement went into a form of moral retreat that prevented it from developing more extensive contacts with teachers who had not been involved with them. Though those in the initial group continued to claim a leadership role for all centers, they did not admit that they had been outmaneuvered. These leaders even backed off from active collaboration with the federal centers because of the "risk of destroying the center's status as a place where it is safe for teachers to admit inadequacy and to experiment without fear of being evaluated" (Thompson, 1982, p. 138).

The leaders of the original movement appeared to have withdrawn from an active political position because of the limitations of the human relations or counseling approach that they adopted, which saw its future as the development of interpersonal relationships rather than power brokerages or new ideas. They promoted small retreats or working meetings where teachers could compare experiences, share ideas, and solve problems. Bulletins on selected topics were among their most indirect approaches.

THE NEW IMPACT OF TEACHER NETWORKS

Though some teacher centers survived the loss of federal support, it has, ironically, been teacher groups that used technology and contacts with authorities that have been more recently active in promoting teacher innovations. In the interim, experts were shown to be effective judges for innovations, which teachers initiated (McIntyre & Entwistle, 1983). Teacher networks increasingly used the internet since for them technology was not the controlling force that the early center leaders had feared.

These networks provide an opportunity for teachers and administrators who are very much a part of the formal system to bring people together so that they have a personal investment in the meetings of the network. The new new networks have also wanted to garner wide support and have worried about calling progressive educators since this label would not be appealing to foundations. Even specialized networks, such as mathematics teachers, are thought to be a problem if they permanently divide teachers.

Though the newer networks existed before they started using the electronic bulletin board, they have consistently sought new ways, including the internet, to reach innovative teachers. Unlike the original teacher centers, the newer networks have sought legitimacy and guidance from research studies and experts. One of the most general groupings, intriguingly called Impact II, was based on pilot programs, which began in the public schools of New York City and Houston between 1979 and 1981 (Meyers & McIssac, 1994).

After the pilot programs, they sought formal evaluations with the assistance of experts. The initial assessment by Columbia University showed their teachers were more likely to use new ideas, presentation methods, and classroom management techniques. In 1987, a four-year study by the National Diffusion Network led to further recognition of Impact II as an effective approach. The evaluations or their continuing search for "indicators" does not show the concern for aesthetic experience that NCCAT demonstrates for teachers (Meyers & McIssac, 1994, p. 44).

Impact II primarily acts as a bridge between the world of the wizards and the workplace of teachers. New journals and studies are stressed, but it is the "recipes" that teachers can exchange that are at the heart of the approach. A "Blue Plate Special" of ideas for the classroom is advertised. The exchanges between teachers reflect progressive education ideas, such as a student citizenship project or schools within schools, but they constantly attempt to find new forms for communication with teachers. Impact II is particularly concerned that teachers become more than implementers, by designing and developing new programs.

Teachers involved with Impact II are always linked with the ideas of outsiders, such as the work of Howard Gardiner on multiple intelligence or the ideas of Linda Darling-Hammond on teacher leaders as a form of renewed emphasis on professionalism. Teachers who also are writers, such as Nancy Atwell, are particularly important because they are models of what other thinkers can do while remaining in the classroom. It is a mentor relationship among teachers that is most frequently demonstrated in their materials; peer tutoring among teachers is the parallel of peer tutoring among students. Impact II makes small grants to mentors who develop and write about their ideas and to those who adopt them (Chicago Foundation for Education, 1992-1993).

Ironically, the program appears to appeal to teachers for whom traditional logical thinking rather than the visual arts is more dominant. Much of the material published by Impact II reflects this orientation whether it is the handbooks for teachers, videos, or the interactive television program of the menu on the internet [http://www.teachnet.org]. Their conferences appear to be designed for idea-centered teachers as does their recent publication *Teachers Guide to Cyberspace*.

A concern for ideas also seems to be more important than policy changes. Some of the policy plans that Impact II has made do not appear to have been realized. The Teachers Voice Initiative was supposed to provide a "teacher's voice to the national dialogue on school reform" (Meyers & McIssac, 1994, p. 4). Neither this program nor similar ones appear in their current listings on the web; their menu claims to provide forums on educational policy making, but these could not be located.

The results of Impact II are more limited than their agenda suggests. The Institute for the Future of Education attracted 50 teachers from across the country and appears to have considerable impact on them as well as their students. Local programs to promote educational leadership currently are underway at Santa Barbara County in California and Dade County (Miami) in Florida as well as New York City and Chicago. The lists of mentors show that they are concentrated in large urban areas.

The editors of the Impact II study speak of surveys that show that most teachers feel they are "targets" of educational reform (Meyers & McIssac, 1994, p. 5). As an alternative, professional communities are stressed as a powerful means of achieving reform. However, most teachers are not members of such communities and confine their outside reading to popular magazines (Clifton & Roberts, 1993). Joyce and Showers (1980) have found that many teachers require a demonstration of a new approach in their own school; other researchers have shown that most teachers have difficulty with the technology that these advocates assume for their message to be received. The development of mentor relationships probably requires a much larger cadre of teacher leaders than appears to be available.

THE EVALUATION MANIA

Despite the problem being the number of mentors of technology, Impact II has not managed to reach the reluctant or isolated teachers any more effectively than did teacher centers. Evaluation efforts appear to have shocked some of these teachers into a new awareness. Confronted with demands for accountability, some teachers have actually felt that they benefited from these programs. Such teachers have often felt they were ignored and that remediation by administrators meant that the leaders were paying attention to the followers for a change (McLaughlin & Pfeifer, 1986).

The new evaluation efforts have gone beyond the simple check lists used in the past. The dominant impact of Madeline Hunter has been to focus on a detailed record of lessons as they were actually taught. A discussion of these actual experiences with a common framework usually follows the observation sessions, and corrective behavior is suggested for the teacher. Limited as this approach is to direct overt teaching, it has been sufficient to promote professional development for teachers as well as counseling for those who want to be promoted or to leave teaching (Wise, et al., 1985).

Teacher acceptance of the new evaluation procedure is conditioned by their traditional desire for authoritarian control in the unpredictable world of teaching. Rigorous measurement, documentation, and review procedures led teachers to see principals and administrators as closer to the omniscient observer they want their leaders to be (Lieberman & Miller, 1984). Teachers have been shown to prefer bureaucratic procedures over arbitrary management (Moeller & Charters, 1970). The most admired teachers often have been the ones who were thought to have eyes in the back of their head (Smith & Geoffrey, 1968,) and new principals frequently have treated teachers as they previously related to students (Waller, 1967). Teachers usually have wanted more systematic and comprehensive evaluations (Wise, et al., 1985).

Traditional evaluations have been characterized in a parody of Socrates. The great teacher received a very low score for external behavior, such as not using visual aids or appearing not to know his subject since he asked students questions. Truth is often more shocking than fiction. At the elementary level, a principal reprimanded a teacher because she told the students there was no Santa Claus (Wolcott, 1973). At the secondary level, teachers were disciplined for failing to have students participate in a tricycle race (Wasserman, 1970). Teachers who were facing dismissal often had charges dropped because of minor technical mistakes (House & Lapan, 1978).

In contrast to the past practices, teachers may not always like the new evaluation approaches, but even the sharpest critics become much more focused in their views about both the approaches and teaching. In a tense situation aggravated by charges of discrimination against older teachers and resentment about the use of student surveys, a teacher says, "I'd have to pitch a perfect inning just to get rated satisfactory, whereas other teachers just coast along" (McLaughlin & Pfeifer, 1986, p. 182).

A requirement for verbatim transcripts is seen by teachers as a usual first step in removing subjective and arbitrary procedures when evaluations are made. A common educational program for both teachers and administrators is seen as a further advance. Legitimacy was given to the entire process when, after their training, teachers and administrators were certified as evaluators by the state.

The use of the procedure to improve teaching was the final and most important step. A system of observation, feedback, and coaching, called Effective Instruction and Support, was used to remediate teachers in a very traditional school system, which was located in Santa Clara, California (McLaughlin & Pfeifer, 1986). The principals in this system had a very stable relationship with teachers, which they did not want to disturb by acting against them. The principals actually did not place any of the teachers on remediation until the superintendent placed four of them on this program. The following year, ten teachers were placed on remediation by principals and the program had become more than a symbolic change.

The reality was clear when the first teacher required to have remediation resigned from the system. One teacher stated her perception of the general situation in this school system:

The principal now comes in and can focus on specific things that I'm doing and speak in language that he and I can understand. . . . I think I know what I'm doing is good, but it's important that an outside observer comes in and basically puts that rubber stamp and says "Yes you're on the right track." (McLaughlin & Pfeifer, 1986, p. 158)

Even when an evaluation program is developed in situations with far more conflict than Santa Clara, there is still a perception of social support that represents improvement in the teaching process. In Moraga, a Californian community with a long history of conflicts among parents, administrators, and teachers, teachers developed a strong sense of shared purpose. This common aim occurred after a new superintendent introduced a program of joint training and evaluation. One teacher with a particularly positive experience said, "The principal has made evaluation an ongoing process this year. Now there is no territoriality: I don't see my room as mine alone" (Ibid, 1986, p. 207).

Almost all teachers in this school talked about instruction informally, far more than before the program. Their bulletin boards showed many more new ideas. When asked explicitly about the training, the teachers stressed collegiality and shared experiences between themselves and administrators. One administrator said he had developed a "common way of looking at teaching" (Ibid, 1986, p. 207).

Even the most cynical of the teachers became more supportive when they saw moves towards implementing the training program and the evaluation procedures. Though the past history of conflicts could not be eradicated by the new superintendent, the teachers had become increasingly articulate and more able to address problems that remained between administrators and themselves. One teacher had a striking vision:

Schools are like a dark room with a large globe in the center. All the actors—teachers, administrators, board members and parents—stand around the globe with flashlights. If we all use our flashlights and shine them on the globe, we light the place up and we all can see. But if only one or two flashlights are on we grope in the dark. (McLaughlin & Pfeifer, 1986, p. 214).

Significantly, the superintendent set a strong example of modeling the behavior she expected. She observed teachers at least two days a month, which led other administrators to do so as well. She communicated with her staff and developed a goal-setting process whereby principals became teachers of teachers. Teachers became more articulate because their principals became clearer in their own communications. The power of all the staff to talk increased; many now said: "Some things make sense" (p. 199).

The ability to speak for oneself is important in all change (Pondry, et al., 1983). The verbal abilities of teachers have been shown to be related to successful innovations as well as effective teaching (McLaughlin & March, 1979). In another new evaluation program, which did not have a common education program and focus, teachers were less able to articulate their concerns (McLaughlin & Pfeifer, 1986. In this third California case, Mountain View-Los Altos, teachers who said they were positive about their own evaluations believed other teachers in the district were dissatisfied with their results. Similarly, administrators were not attacked over the use of student evaluations nearly as much as students were considered inadequate for the task.

The tendency of teachers to talk around a problem when personnel conflicts are involved means that conflict did not become creative in Mountain View-Los Altos. Traditional teachers in isolated schools are particularly likely to be indirect and inarticulate because they are so separated from others in the school system or society (McPherson, 1972). At Mountain View-Los Altos, the divisions between teachers and administrators were initially sharpened by training administrators separately in the evaluation procedure. Twice as many negative evaluations occurred in this third case than in Santa Clara. The evaluation process became very legalistic and lawyers acted as consultants.

The conflict was far greater in Moraga, but teachers were also becoming more independent. Resignations because of the evaluation procedure occurred three times more often in Moraga than in Santa Clara. In Moraga, teachers are not as dependent on their administrators. They could see them "warts and all"; one teacher says of the superintendent: "She plays no favorites. But she is like the tundra in the summer time—go down a foot and she is as hard as a rock"

(McLaughlin & Pfeifer, 1986, p. 194).

In contrast, in the situation with some conflict but less focus, a teacher in Mountain View-Los Altos states her acceptance of administrative actions: "We need people to come in and check on us like anybody else. As long as it is done in a positive and constructive manner, all it can do is benefit education" (Ibid, p. 180).

This need for administrators to provide guidance and structure has been reported in many traditional settings, particularly among elementary teachers (Lortie, 1975; McPherson, 1972). However, many teachers may have been simply overwhelmed by the elaborate procedure and the difficulties with appeals.

In a fourth situation there were even more elaborate programs for both experienced teachers and new ones. In Charlotte, North Carolina, there were not the independent and articulate speakers as in Moraga. With a state-wide program and administrators devoting over 30 percent of their time to evaluations, teachers could still sound like Uriah Heap: "My chairperson has contributed so much. I feel badly using those people free of charge. . . . Yesterday morning we had a meeting at 6:45" (McLaughlin & Pfeifer, 1986, p. 231). The superintendent at Charlotte has recently gone to work for a real estate company that plans schools as a part of its package; perhaps he can help program teachers to fit into corporate plans.

Creative conflict can lead teachers away from dependency on the judgment of administrators. Because of the ambiguity of teaching, teachers want guidance from administrators (Lieberman & Miller, 1984). Administrators have often covered themselves and evaluation procedures in trivia (Sarason, 1971). A large-scale set of surveys found elementary teachers often wanted their principal to act like a superego who would check on their human failings (Lortie, 1975). One detailed case study found elementary teachers would imagine that their principal was checking up on them even when he was quietly eating his lunch (McPherson, 1972). To achieve independence from administrators while openly discussing evaluations is like coming out of the closet for those who have wanted to hide their failings (Lieberman & Miller, 1984).

CAN TEACHERS TRUST EVALUATIONS?

Though evaluations have not tried to develop teachers and respect them consistently, there have been some further experiments that could contribute to these goals. The superintendent in Moraga was respected by teachers because she maintained the evaluation program in spite of severe budget restraints and because she wanted to extend it to peer tutoring. Peer evaluations, self evaluations, and a critical friend are all ways in which teachers have been challenged to improve. (Rooney, 1993; Haertel, 1993; Costa & Kallick, 1993). A particularly brave principal has taught in front of teachers in order for them to criticize his teaching, which, in turn, was a way of improving their own teaching (Turnbull, 1985). Equally brave teachers have increasingly sought the views of students (Gorham,

1987).

Each of these evaluation approaches develops the social relationships of teachers and eliminates secrecy about the craft. Teachers are increasingly involved in thirty-two reported cases of school system evaluations (Wise, et al., 1985, pp. 72, 85). However, the support that teachers need is perhaps best revealed by the critical friend approach. The critical friend builds trust by listening well, respecting the person's integrity, understanding the work, becoming an advocate for the success of the project, and offering value judgments or evaluations only when asked by the learner (Costa & Kallick, 1993). The approach can be used by anyone—administrators, students, or, presumably, parents—because it builds on mutual understanding, which, in turn, allows higher order thinking to develop within individuals.

The critical friend approach has been developed as a program by the Annenberg Institute for Social Reform at Brown University through its National School Reform Faculty (Olson, 1998b). Since 1995, this program has reached 5,000 teachers and administrators in 200 schools. Critical Friends Groups, as they are called, observe one another at least monthly, select a coach to advise a group of them, and the Annenberg Institute conducts external evaluations. Many other major reform efforts that are discussed in Chapter 9 cooperate with this formal approach to improving teachers through critical friends.

However, the critical friends initiative can be informally spread by osmosis to an unknown number of groups since it involves a very simple approach. A critical friend is a way of bringing a different perspective so that teachers can better see themselves. They can have the views of critics, which people in the performing arts have. Over time, those in the various arts internalize criticism so that they "become more sharply self-evaluative" (Costa & Kallick, 1993, p. 51). Internalized criticism may overcome the limitations of self-assessments as a source of information for teacher reflection and a way of making teacher reflection more closely related to a change in teacher actions (Haertel, 1993). Self-reflection usually is advocated because it overcomes the trivial basis of administrative evaluations and teachers who continue to distance themselves from the actions of others. However, self-evaluation can be confined to a checklist as much as traditional evaluations carried out by principals, and nothing ensures that videotapes or portfolios will be creative as teachers view their own work.

Without greater support from their peers, teachers may not trust their own evaluations. A teacher stating her reaction to team teaching said: "Maybe they would find out how bad I am" (Mitchell, 1968, p. 27). Reports on peer evaluation often focus on tasks, new techniques, and the variety of people who can be involved, including university faculty (Askins, et al., 1994). There also is a preoccupation with the effect of this or other forms of evaluation on student achievement (Olivero & Heck, 1993). Social support to develop trust among teachers and within teachers still is not seen as the critical issue.

It is the lack of trust in educators by the public that has led to a proliferation of evaluation and demands for greater accountability (Johnson, 1978). Administrators and teachers have contributed to the cycle whereby greater distrust leads to more evaluation and more evaluation leads to still higher levels of suspicion. No source of evaluation evidence is greeted with distrust and arouses more suspicion than student surveys (McLaughlin & Pfeifer, 1986, p. 185). However, the learning of students is the aim of teachers and the objective of all forms of evaluation.

Students themselves have some interesting views on how trust and communication could be better developed in classrooms. One student leader has proposed that students should become more active (Belton, 1996, p. 68). Volunteer students would visit classes, speak with students, and form discussion groups with teachers. Student evaluations would be far more than students sitting passively in the classes where with paper and pencil they anonymously evaluate the teachers who instruct them. Active communication could be built upon the basis that students generally use to evaluate teachers: direct instructional effectiveness, classroom management, and responsive personalities (Gorham, 1987). It is possible that with direct communication about evaluation, students could overcome the known limitations of such feedback. Students have been shown to be inaccurate in judging pedagogy in terms of questioning techniques and visual aids (Cohen & Manion, 1981); the reasons for these limitations would probably emerge in terms of typical teacher practices, such as recitation, or the frequent attempts to fill time with films.

Finally, the issue of social relationships should be used to consider reactions to the advanced teacher certification as it is being developed in the United States (Bradley, 1996a). This program, National Board for Professional Teaching Standards, is dear to the hearts of most expert reformers and claims to have the involvement and support of classroom teachers. Like teacher of the year awards, teachers resent those who have achieved advanced recognition in the profession; at least one teacher who who was recognized in the new program was fired. For the people who undergo the program it is demanding and appears to be more personally challenging than financially rewarding. Teachers involved with NCCAT should find it appealing. Like both reform emphasis on standards and teacher centered innnovations as discussed throughout this chapter, advanced certification does not, in any way, ensure that those who most need to achieve its goals will do so.

SPLINTERING THE RANKS THROUGH LEGISLATED LEARNING

Legislatures have increased the distance between reform agendas and classroom experiences by adopting detailed programs and sponsoring model schools. These activities frequently have reinforced the difference between groups, particularly teachers. They have not developed a greater consensus based on the political realities of specific situations. For example, in Kentucky the entire educational system was systematically changed and, as part of the change, student portfolios were required (Mitchell, 1996). Portfolios are extremely demanding for teachers; the requirement that portfolios in both mathematics and language arts be done in the same year was only changed after the teachers were exhausted.

Most professional organizations do not try to operate with tightly specified requirements from a distance; they allow for the adjustments that professionals will make in the situation (Thompson, 1967). The classic case of specifying a great deal and ignoring what may matter the most is inclusion of the handicapped. Canadian teachers in at least one province have complained so much about the requirements for mainstreaming that they have sought to have all innovations treated as experiments with controls (Alberta Teachers' Association, 1993). American teachers have apparently resisted the spread of mainstreaming so that the practice may now be decreasing (Mitchell, 1992, p. 37). In both countries the difference in the education and beliefs of special education and regular teachers is ignored in either the legislation or administration of the program.

Nothing usually is done in the training of teachers to prepare special education and regular teachers to work together. One general course in special education is often only for regular teachers; teachers training for special education receive many specialized courses, but there is seldom common training for both groups so that they can work more effectively with special students. At the university there appears to be two types of psychology: one for normal people and another for those with special needs (Sarason, 1982). Special education students learn an array of classifications that provides them with a special language (Tomkins, 1986; Berlak & Berlak, 1981). Within special education, gifted students also become a separate arena though that status is often marginal to those who are seen as having more difficult problems (House, 1974; Sapon-Shevin, 1994). In none of these situations do regular and special education teachers learn to work together.

The three cultures of teachers develop from educational perspectives. Regular teachers see the small student-teacher ratios and think special education personnel have the ideal world, whereas special education teachers see regular teachers as passing on all of their problems to them so regular classes are more uniform if not smaller (Sarason, 1982). Furthermore, regular teachers are relieved that they do not have to meet the needs of the gifted, and they think it is time to spend money on the gifted since too much had been spent on students with disabilities (Sapon-Shevin, 1994).

These differences are not reduced by mainstreaming, and the inclusion of others—parents and students—often accentuates the differences. Separate organizations among teachers are paralleled by parent groups: the regular Parent Teacher Organization, Parents for the Handicapped, and Parents for the Gifted. Even among those with handicapped students, some parents are opposed to integration of the handicapped. Particularly at the high school level, opposition among teachers to inclusion is sometimes intense. In a suburban high school, teachers regularly organized a betting pool during inservice education classes, gambling on how long experts would talk, while a school board psychologist who advocated integration was openly ridiculed (Cusick, 1983, p. 117). Governmental leaders have become increasingly critical of mainstreaming since the costs have escalated (Zernike, 1997). Ironically, divisions among teachers and other groups are diminished when separate positions for different kinds of teachers are eliminated during budget cuts.

However, there are some innovations that have systematically attacked many of the divisions that are involved with inclusion. The Team Approach to Mastery (TAM) combines preservice education, inservice programs, and a single framework for all educators, teachers, consultants, and district staff, to participate together (Johnson, et al., 1994/1995). TAM teachers build upon previous efforts of special education teachers in jointly developing individualized programs and then team teaching these programs (Mitchell, 1992). TAM teachers teach in teams, diagnose individual needs and learning styles, strengthen self-confidence, provide direct instruction, offer reinforcements regularly, and get feedback from peer dialogues (Johnson, et al., 1994/1995, pp. 46-47). Even broader programs have been proposed by tying all students on the margins—special education, English as Second Language, and poor students—together since the categories overlap (Wang, et al., 1994/1995). Support for this proposal is found in the increasing practice of employing teachers across the programs.

Integrating approaches to special education is a way of tying these programs to more general reform efforts in education. The model schools, particularly those of the New American Schools Development Corporation (NASDC) have been the clearest example of the current emphasis in educational planning, innovating through a number of different programs, rather than a single innovation at a time. In 1991, systematic reform was given a major boost when then President Bush persuaded a number of American business executives to develop model schools that would break the mold of current education. Though a non-profit corporation, NASDC represents the power of elite groups, which can be very separate from individual communities and schools.

For people in Bensenville, a village governmental area of 17,000 people outside of Chicago, NASDC became a power attempting to decide the fate of this community and legislating the structure of education. Initially, one governmental agency, the Bensenville Intergovernmental Group, two separate elementary school boards for the communities of Wood Dale and Bensenville, and one high school board for both communities appeared to be supporting a proposal to create a "lifelong learning community" (Mirel, 1994). Later, to parents and teachers in the wealthier community, Wood Dale, as well as others who saw their children's lives disrupted, if not threatened, the New American Schools became "the New American Fools" (Ibid, p. 483).

The proposal that won a planning grant of $1.25 million dollars for the Bensenville area was based on a number of progressive education ideas that had not considered many of the area's political and cultural realities. By citing John Dewey and many of his ideas on linking school and home, individual differences, and persistent life situations, the county expert, along with representatives of the key groups involved, were able to win the grant, one of eleven winners out of 686 proposals submitted. However, soon after the state and federal politicians had gone home, it began to be realized that the award might mean amalgamation of the two elementary districts, loss of contract rights and possibly tenure for the teachers, a likelihood of higher taxes because of salary differences in the two elementary districts, uncertainty about the arrival and departure times of young students, and even fear of abuse by community mentors who might seek contact with young people for sex. The essential interests of the constituencies and the protections they might need were never considered.

Each of the constituencies was to have been a part of lifelong learning with the community as educator. All of the groups had been a part of town meetings that helped to develop the proposal along with a representative committee (New American Schools Development Corporation, n.d.). The proposal included many areas that other winners hardly mentioned such as fine arts in schools and developing a new teacher education program. After the richer community and teachers had withdrawn and NASDC refused to provide further funds, the teachers in the poorer area continued many of the innovative ideas on their own. An interdisciplinary program combined technology, history, geography, computer simulation, integration of work in fine and commercial art, joint enrollment by parents and students in language classes, and an early childhood center (Mirel, 1994).

Later accounts of NASDC and subsequent research on their continuing seven programs have shown little awareness of the political issues raised by the Bensenville fiasco (New American Schools Development Corporation, 1995/1996; Sommerfeld, 1996a). No explanation for dropping Bensenville was ever given; a lack of time for fine-tuning the ideas was the only apparent way the plan was related to political events (Mirel, 1994). New research by the Rand Corporation stressed the comprehensiveness of the innovation. Core designs that focused upon a single area, such as tutoring for basic achievement, were more readily spread than programs that included integrated social service and governance with a core curriculum, such as the Authenic Teaching, Learning and Assessment of All Students (ATLAS) project (Sommerfeld, 1996a). The ATLAS project brought three titans of education together: Howard Gardiner with his theories of multiple intelligence, James Comer with his plans for community health through changes in the way schools are governed, and Ted Sizer with his emphasis on active learning in a common curriculum. The Atlas project is discussed in more detail in Chapter 9.

However, the Atlas project was less complex and easier to implement than the one even larger "systemic" project, the National Alliance for Restructuring Education. The National Alliance is trying to change the school systems of five states and four large cities with over five million students in over 9,000 schools (Olson, 1995a). Named after a report that stressed the choice between high skills or low wages, the Alliance has stressed a comprehensive school approach called America's Choice. The curriculum stresses higher order learning, school to work transitions, new standards and authentic assessments, integrated health care and social services, and total quality management and staff development (New American Schools Development Corporation, n. d.). The program is to be spread by a national seminar, teacher leaders, and, most of all, the Teacher Development Center. Teams of teachers visit centers to learn by practice; center coordinators check on the teachers over the next year to determine their progress (Olson, 1995a).

The National Alliance and NASDC as a whole were trying to spread their innovations to 30 percent of schools in eleven sites over the next five years. However, it functions like a business with very instrumental goals; there is no political program and little awareness of human ambitions for art and religion. Schools have often chosen programs with little idea of what is involved. In one school, teachers chose a program based on purposive learning because they thought they needed a purpose and another group thought the technology emphasis would give them free computers (Olson, 1995a). The Rand study stressed how unprepared teachers were for the New American School efforts, but the corporation seems to see other agenda items as more important than teacher receptivity. The same study found that after two years only half the 40 schools studied were implementing the core elements of the new designs (Hoff, 1998). NASDC President, John Anderson, and the National Alliance founder, Marc Tucker, have both stressed how important it is for individual schools to begin paying for assistance and that this pushed them into the "competitive market" and the current period will be "chaotic while things sort out" (Hoff, 1998).

As in Bensenville, the competitive market can mean divisions between teachers, communities, and programs over political and personal concerns. There is still no strategy for getting beyond the small number of educators who are interested in innovative ideas (Elmore, 1996). Though there are a large number of partners, including advocacy organizations, the National Alliance still does not have a platform. The organization's position is linked to the issue of national standards, which has gained momentum. Like integration of the handicapped, the national models may further divide teachers and parents.

OPTIONS FOR TEACHER INVOLVEMENT

First of all, most innovations have appealed to the small group of teachers who are attracted by interesting ideas (Elmore, 1996; Joyce & Showers, 1980). Close social relations, immediate demonstrations, and creative expression, such as those that art partnerships can bring to schools, can involve many more teachers. Finally, teachers who resent innovations can be minimized, in the long run, by innovations that make their ideas more creative and, in the short run, by remediation that removes them from the school where they have become too adjusted.

Second, innovations such as NASCD have tended to be extremely instrumental. Language from business and computers so dominates discussions that it is difficult to find any innovations that combine expression and action. Recently, the meaning of innovations and emotional intelligence have been stressed as a way of developing better student judgment (Hargreaves, 1997). The structuring of emotional expressions through the arts has long been recognized as a way of overcoming the emotional desert that classroom research has repeatedly found (Remer, 1990). Only the NCCAT program has focused on the arts.

Chart 3.1
Types of People and Reform Aims

Types of People	Reform Aims		
	Expressive	Instrumental	Comprehensive
Idea-centered	NCCAT	Teacher Centers	TAM
People-responsive	Moraga	Santa Clara	Charlotte
Resentful or power-centered	Bensenville	Mountain View-Los Altos	Separate cultures

NCCAT, North Carolina Center for the Advancement of Teaching; TAM, Team Approach to Mastery.

In the arts as in writing, teachers must be creative themselves before they enhance the students' work (Mitchell, 1997). Defining a comprehensive program to include more emotional expression by teachers and for students would be an important direction for innovation projects. Generally, the programs that have been reviewed, which are shown on Chart 3.1 as comprehensive, are simply more elaborated rather than more fully human and aesthetic.

The resentment against NASDC continues to be ignored though the "New American Fools" label should serve as a reminder candle. More calculating approaches do not see the need for sensitivity to political and individual needs. Moraga, because of the sustained joint education program and conflict, made the teachers far more articulate than in the more complicated evaluation programs in Charlotte. Some of the school model programs, such as Atlas, lead to an enormous amount of coming and going among staff; others in the NASDC set of designs apparently are too large for teacher change to cover. The re-sorting of teachers might lead to teacher learning as in Moraga.

Finally, some of the programs, such as the innovative program of inclusion, TAM, seem to overcome many of these limits. TAM and the original program at Bensenville tried to go to the heart of existing divisions among teachers by changing preservice education together with the field innovations. Separate cultures among teachers are developed at universities. Furthermore, the divisions between research and administration and teacher concerns are reinforced at universities (Clifford, 1988). All innovations must still give more attention to how and when they will overcome the division between experts and lay; when they play the sage on stage, teachers must consider the same change in their classroom behavior. Both administrators and teachers must establish new relationships with parents.

This division is the heart of an alternative conception of the change process. Staff training at NCCAT allows teachers to be recognized as creative generalists and to be accepted as equals by experts. Evaluations at Moraga could stimulate teachers to reflect and express their ideas and new experiences. Neither staff training nor evaluations usually play this stimulative role; a Canadian study of exceptional schools found only one such school focused upon evaluations for staff training and innovations (Gaskell, 1995). The resiliency of teachers to control is revealed by the few successful teacher responses to inclusion attempts and model schools; the resentment against these imposed dreams also is important. Teachers need to be expressive and forceful so that they can be more fully human than the experts.

The preferred politics of pedagogues is the politics of the priest-craft protected by its putative mastery of the mysteries of educational expertise, supported by the public's response to sacred values, and proceeding within the privileged sanctuary of its private preserves. (Iannacone, 1967, p. 14)

Chapter 4

Perceptions of Power

Kindergarten children used the social context of their activities to help them determine if they were working or playing. If the activity was one in which they were required to participate, the children labeled their activities work. . . . Only when the kindergartners perceived themselves to be free of adult supervision did they call their activities play. (King, 1983, p. 263)

At their first encounter with schooling, kindergarten students sense the controls that are exerted on them by an institution in which all adults have more power than they do and where individual teachers can change the meaning of play to work. Policy has been seen to change people's perception of the world rather than just exerting rewards and punishments on their behavior (McDonnell, 1994). In Chapter 3, the meaning of teacher education in several cases was shown to be very different from the more usual inservice education. Similarly, the meaning of evaluation and integration of the handicapped depends on the situation and the relation of this reform to other innovations and the priorities among these changes. In Chapter 5, specific ideologies will be shown to be related to the tide of innovations.

In this chapter, perceptions that lead to changing behavior are explained through role reversals that alter the way things are assumed to be. The normative changes can result from orchestrated campaigns by experts, as in the case of school-based management, or the perception of crises, as in the cases of youth unemployment and civil disorder in urban cities. The differences can occur unexpectedly, as in the case of accepted dominance by one country or group over another, or as a result of interaction between belief in innovations and another set of norms, such as teacher independence in the classroom. Differences in power perceptions cannot occur until common understandings between experts and people are developed and personal conflicts are reconciled.

THE WORLD TURNED UPSIDE DOWN

Temporary reversals of the status order, when students act as if they are authorities or when all the rules are suspended, can reveal the potentials of power sharing. As mentioned in Chapter 3, principals setting themselves up to be criticized in their teaching is an appealing basis for teachers to improve their teaching. When elementary teachers and university professors were involved in an experiment in which they reversed roles, the elementary teachers were noticeably wanting to do anything—cut, paste, or knit—so they could avoid the abstract discussion with university professors (Lanier, 1983).

Similar reversals can occur among subordinated students. An effective way for students with handicaps to improve their own educational performance is to tutor regular students (Top & Osguthorpe, 1987). Like the handicapped, other marginal groups often are expected to contribute to the educational system as controlled by the dominant group (Lind, 1974). Racial groups have been so subordinated by the social authorities that their relationships with the majority resemble colonialism.

Extremely subordinated groups react against the usual way of doing things (Mitchell, 1997). Similar to delinquents who would be clean and work hard if the norm was to be dirty and lazy, racial groups will react against their colonial-like subordination over many generations. Alternative music and art, such as the Sex Pistols, is full of these reversals that are particularly appealing to groups who have been made to feel inferior in so many other ways. In the past, Jews in the ghetto and, today, Aboriginals and Blacks from their slums have expressed such resistance to dominance (Mitchell, 1997).

Aboriginals became adept at delaying and manipulating their masters even in the extreme situations of residential education. Native students could delay and stay on the playground or copy others' work in the classroom even if it meant their own education was undone (King, 1967). Today, Native Americans are attempting to become masters of their own education though the system of band chiefs and councils that Whites imposed upon them has become a barrier and source of corruption for the Native elite (Mitchell, 1997).

A more effective opportunity for Natives occurred in a few places where Whites show respect and attempt to learn from them. In St. Benedict, a Calgary Separate school, a principal and some of the teachers developed a program where the school's 300 White students learned the Native language (O'Hara-Escaravage, n.d.). The remainder of the teachers did not realize how much the sixty Native students felt a sense of confidence in having their language accepted.

The supporters of the program developed a strong position: The group first met with parents both Native and non-Native to get their views on incorporating Sarcee culture into the curriculum. While many were very positive about this, they were afraid, being Catholic, that some of the old traditional religious ways may be taught to their children, and they didn't want this. The non-Native parents objected to Sarcee as a seocnd language, if it was going to replace French, which they felt was necessary for their children's further education. After much controversy and many meetings, the differences were resolved within a year. . . . Central to the program was the Sarcee language, which was offered as a second language in the curriculum. Native people were brought into the school as culture resource persons in a way that helped achieve another of the program's objectives: to develop a common base of experience for White and Indian children alike. In our class, for example, someone from the Reserve may teach the kids about Indian teepee designs or beadwork. Indian dances would be incorporated in the phys. ed. class. (O'Hara-Escaravage, n.d., p. 3)

The development of a voice in one's own language and a way of speaking speaking with the majority developed concretely as a necessary stop in learning to think and learn in the White people's system.

The *Calgary Magazine* gave the program an A+ rating and sharply contrasted it with all the educational programs that were generally reported as news. The magazine said:

[The program] is systematically trying to make adjustments for the dissimilar backgrounds of the two student groups. It is trying to do something about the dilemma that has always faced the Indian students in a white system, whereby he is expected to succeed on white terms. . . . Children mix in the playground and Indian kids are proud to speak up in class and contribute their reserve experience to the general discussion. (Ibid, pp. 4-5)

However, in less than a year this program was abandoned at St. Benedict and apparently was never expanded into any other part of the Calgary Separate system. The program was ended when the supporting principal left the school: neither the remaining teachers nor the new principal had the same ideals as the original principal. Other school principals found the program so absurd that they referred to it as "an Indianization of White kids" (Ibid, p. 5). In retrospect, it would require an incredibly strong leader or one who had a great deal of support to bring about this or any other role reversal that has been discussed.

TEACHER EFFICACY

Institutional reform efforts continue to create paradoxes, particularly for teachers. The conflict within the reform movement is that it wants more professional teachers and, at the same time, it wants to control them more than ever (DeYoung, 1986). In the first wave of school reforms, a preoccupation with student achievement and productivity was matched by teacher exams and career stages. Thus, the heavy hand of the Texas program for both teachers and students led to this program being called "the Texas chainsaw massacre" (Timar & Kirp, 1988, pp. 65-80). Evaluation of teachers' improvement in a Virginia program was based on very explicit expectations as follows:

Instructors are directed not to offer their own unique, in some cases highly idiosyncratic, views of effective teaching, however successful these views might be. Instead, they are encouraged to transmit sensitively a standardized curriculum that reflects public knowledge of the competencies. (McNergney, Medley & Caldwell, 1989, p. 70)

In the current less structured and more progressive second wave of school reform, the teachers are made more responsible and given more attention. The National Commission on Teaching has been established and teacher leaders have been widely discussed as an option (Bradley, 1997; Wasley, 1991). The biggest challenge to teachers has been school-based management, which gave teachers the opportunity to participate in decision making and held them, together with principals, accountable for results.

Though the National Commission provides long overdue recognition to classroom teachers, its ideas on work jurisdiction seem to reflect the views of its expert executive director, Darling-Hammond, rather than views of teachers. The commission was supported by the Carnegie and Rockefeller Foundations. Who else would support a blue ribbon panel making decisions for teachers? For example, the concern of the report, "What Matters Most: Teaching for America's Future," for teachers who teach without full qualifications is striking; there is no evidence that this is a major concern of classroom teachers (Bradley, 1997). What matters most for teachers is the opportunity to study and influence the decisions being made (Rosenholtz, 1989; Coleman & LaRocque, 1990). Similarly, accreditation, licensure, and advanced professional certification—the "three-legged stool" of teacher quality—do not come from teachers; they also represent a dubious comparison with the group mobility projects as practiced by other professions.

In another related issue, an educationist was hard pressed to find enough teacher leaders, another proposal from the Carnegie Foundation (Wasley, 1991, p. 23). Teacher leaders represent a repudiation of bureaucratic hierarchy and procedures; the concept does not seem to have been thought through. In addition, since team teaching has always encountered enormous resistance from the individualistic world of teaching, similar problems can be expected from making some teachers more equal than others.

The dreams of experts have been brought much closer to reality through a vigorous campaign to establish school-based management (Ogawa, 1994). Teachers become leaders as part of the numerous committees that tend to accompany this reform. Teachers increasingly report that they are involved in budget and personnel decisions; the majority of the members in the National Education Association said that their views were considered in these areas (Sanchez, R., 1997). However, the limits of teacher influence still seem to be confined primarily to their own classrooms (Anderson, 1994).

Established power differences in schools are difficult to overcome. No group of teachers is seriously influencing inservice education: urban public schools, private urban schools, or rural schools. Though teachers in private schools have more influence on school discipline policy and hiring of new staff, and teachers in rural areas, generally, have more access to school decisions, neither of these groups influenced inservice education in any way. Professional training remains the world of administrators and experts; as a result, the teachers' ability to generalize their competency in teaching is still limited. In an organized program of school improvement, staff training and innovations should be closely related.

Similarly, school-based management does not often provide training for teachers (Robertson, 1997). Principals are not any more efficacious than teachers; however, they may act as if they are knowledgeable and they definitely control more of the keys to schools that are to be administered jointly. Learning how to learn in an organization that makes repetition and consistency its actual goals, while attempting simultaneously to change as its proclaimed purpose, is the dilemma that teachers must challenge.

CHOICES FOR SCHOOLS

The movement to restructure local school decision making developed rapidly after 1990 (Ogawa, 1994, p. 525). The key event was the publication of *A Nation Prepared* by the Carnegie Forum on Education and the Economy (CFEE); the publication was important because it led to more conferences, videos, a speakers' bureau, and an outpouring of academic articles on the subject, particularly those geared for practitioners. The publication represented the longstanding influence of the Carnegie Foundation. This foundation has usually supported research and policy positions that have been conservative, such as the reinforcment of segregation in South Africa before World War II; it has helped finance and publicize school consolidation and progressive positions in the United States during the 1960s, but it has never supported a radical position, such as deschool ing (Berman, 1984).

In this instance of modest reforms, the Carnegie Foundation's point man in the case of CFEE was Marc Tucker, who was mentioned in Chapter 3 as the key executive for the National Alliance, the largest of the model school programs. The National Alliance evolved within CFEE together with programs that addressed the country's needs for skilled workers and national standards. For this effort, Tucker persuaded the Carnegie Foundation to create its own unit rather than finance an outside group since the relation between the economic demands for competitive- ness was so crucial for the foundation's interests. The business bias of a major foundation seemed to be recognized in 1985 when CFEE was created and Marc Tucker, an "entrepreneur," was named its executive director (Ogawa, 1994, p. 540).

Earlier, Tucker had emerged as an expert while he was with the think-tank National Institute of Education (NIE). Through NIE in 1970s, Tucker became an operative for many educational reforms, including science programs at teacher centers (Thompson, 1982). Though currently focusing on business, Tucker has learned to bring together a number of national organizations around issues, particularly school-based management. Tucker is representative of the type of person who articulates new ideas through joint organizational arrangements, hence the label "institutional entrepreneur." Aside from working for NIE, graduation from an elite university, particularly Harvard, was a useful background for these institutional experts whose organizational memberships were more important than any individual attributes.

Influence was determined by means of ratings by those in organizations as well as individuals (Ogawa, 1994). Similar entrepreneurs had worked at NIE in the 1970s and later became staff members with the National Governors' Association (NGA). The NGA published its own report, *Time for Results*, which was only half as influential as the report by CFEE. The report for CFEE was supported by a third group, the Educational Commission of the States. All three organizations worked together for the same reforms. The institutional leaders of the three groups coordinated their efforts with those in still other organizations, especially teacher unions, and a group of academics at Rutgers University, the Center for Policy Research.

In 1988, the Carnegie Foundation provided support for the NGA to bring together a number of accepted reform groups to support school decision making (Ogawa, 1994). Probably because of the involvement of a number of key governors, such as Bill Clinton, academics were not needed to legitimate the cause. Professors generally act as interpreters and promoters of the ideas for changing school governance. Academics attempt to rationalize more spontaneous movements so that, for example, a consortium of universities were said to have the "fix" in for reform in Chicago (Mitchell, 1996). For the orchestrated movement for school-based management, key academics were more independent, but they were not likely to reject the idea of involving those at the school level in decisions (Ogawa, 1994). Jane David and Dick Elmore were the academic entrepreneurs selected to do sponsored research or edit conference proceedings.

These institutional experts bring together a number of strands in the educational reform movement. They are the logical link with the earlier innovation of effective schools, which showed the importance of principals and teachers leading by example and setting common goals. Researchers divided effective schools into groups and increased the number of factors that were believed to be essential for these groups to improve school practice. Perhaps, in terms of how many decisions can be included in the agenda, school-based management is as ambiguous as the effective school research (Mitchell, 1992).

The varied and changing terms used to describe the movement make it possible to include the efforts of business to decentralize its management as a similar development. Coinciding with business becomes important as its rapprochement on school innovations grows (Gerstner, et al., 1994; Mitchell, 1996). In addition to the business merger, there are several significant political connections for this movement. Some states, such as Florida, had adopted legislation supporting something called school-based management in the 1970s. The Carnegie group gave impetus to these early efforts and at least one institutional entrepreneur advised each of the key governors, Clinton in Arkansas, Alexander in Tennessee, and Kean in New Jersey (Ogawa, 1994). However, because of the social distance between the superexperts and those they wish to ultimately influence, there is a need for each of the advisers to have a teacher or principal as a consultant.

SCHOOLS AND SOCIETY

The elaborate web that institutional experts have created is very different from the world of teachers within closed classrooms. These practitioners' immediate concern is with day-to-day school events, and they do not usually develop any sense of social continuity. Individuals in schools have a view of schools that separates them from those outside the system. For students, education appears to be the responsibility of individual teachers (Everhart, 1983). Teachers limit many of their views and actions in their own classrooms (Lortie, 1975). Administrators see themselves as evaluating the entire school system without usually thinking of how permeable the boundaries of the system are (House, 1974).

Few of the players in schools are aware of the more impersonal influences that affect their work and aims (Sarason, 1982). Crises, such as budget cuts in government grants or drug problems among students, bring about an awareness of the background against which these performers act (Johnson, 1983). However, once the crises disappear, schools go about their tasks in isolation from society unless a new pattern of interaction and mutual dependency develops. Such isolation appears to be the norm even in communist countries whose claims to a larger vision fade when revolutionary movements lose the vitality of their songs and slogans.

Schools do little to enhance either students' understanding of impersonal power or the staff's perception of how they are influenced by the unseen hand. The difficulty of individuals perceiving the relevance of economic phenomena is shown by a series of conflicts. Teachers in high schools within industrial areas seldom think of the high unemployment rate as affecting classroom discipline even if job shortages are shown to mean that students stay in school because of lack of opportunities and that their forced attendance produces considerable resistance (Mitchell, 1966). Farming cycles are better understood in rural areas in terms of such effects. Students who have well-paid labor jobs do not particularly see the relevancy of vocational education programs for job placement (Stinchcombe, 1964).

For students in urban areas, academic programs are a mirage in relation to their future careers. Similarly, teachers do not see their own performance as influenced by the salary increases they may receive (Lortie, 1975). Teachers do see themselves as being cheated when they look at the rewards that businesspeople receive. Though administrators have more developed relationships with businessmen than do many teachers, they have struggled to develop even simple sharing of meeting facilities as a form of barter with industry. Businesspeople who occasionally become teachers have undergone a culture shock as they deal with undisciplined students in vocational education (Ryan, et al., 1980).

Cooperation between businesspeople, teachers, and students has been shown to be difficult and the distance between these three roles is substantial. The relation is beyond impersonally providing for qualifications for the labor force. A life-style can be developed from the efforts of a grade one teacher and can have continuing effects on students' careers (Pederson, et al., 1978). Schooling can develop ways of living, as Europeans have long recognized. In the United States, cooperative education has revealed that industry and education find it difficult to work together because of the differences between the two institutions (Feldman, 1985). Programs from the excellence movement, which have developed in both education and business, are having very different effects in the two institutions. Educators have found it difficult to believe that economic effects should be primary; businesspeople believe that they are always primary.

Business executives, who have complained loudly about the low standards in education, have seldom had direct contact with local schools or even the experience of hiring many graduates of their local system (Hall & Carlton, 1977). North American businessmen have not had the experience of English or German employers of being actively involved in the business of training and certifying students (Vickers, 1991). In Canada and the United States, a number of links between business and education are being made that may alter the experience of schooling for unwilling scholars. For example, business has begun to examine the school records of students when hiring them; students can be expected to work harder when their academic record is going to count for employment (*Washington Post*, 1997). After over 100 years of coexistence, educators and businesspeople are beginning to perceive how they can be complementary to each other, though many of the efforts are still at the show-and-tell stage, such as one business sponsoring a school (Mitchell, 1996). Education and business need to realize their mutual dependence in a common community.

THE AMERICAN CONNECTION

It is through the instrumental ties created by a common economy that many links develop between very different educational systems, such as Canada and the United States. The histories of these educational systems are very different; Canada is more closely linked to the stability of European models, while the United States creates much of the booming, buzzing confusion of continuing innovations. Business in both countries has an unparalleled influence on schools, which no other institution in society can claim. American business combines the greater power of itself as an institution with an unequaled influence by individual companies on education.

In many parts of the world these joint forms of imperialism are very significant; the Canadian case needs to be seen against these large and widespread differences. The consequences of cultural imperialism are revealed by examples, such as Northern Ireland, the first British colony. Only government can begin to counter American business and its related allies, but North American states have loosened their controls as a means of focusing on measured results in schools. This removal of direct controls has opened the door for businesses to run schools on a profit basis as well as for non-profit, public schools to be similarly measured by their results (McDonnell, 1994, p. 404).

Business colonization of schools and state or provincial programs for education converged in the call for school-based management. The movement co-opted the most significant Canadian experiment that had developed in Edmonton. Edmonton's Superintendent, Michael Strembitsky, joined the National Alliance as high performance management director (Plattner, 1994). To share its experience, Edmonton cooperated with the Cross City Campaign for Urban School Reform of American cities.

Some other examples of U.S. colonization have been much more striking, such as the plagiarism of the *Nation at Risk* by bureaucrats for Saskatchewan's program (Stewart, 1987). In Chapter 2, the extent to which the Ontario Institute of Educational Studies emulated American ideas was discussed. French immersion has influenced similar American innovations, such as Spanish immersion for English speaking children, which is cited in Chapter 6. However, the dominant trend has often been for American ideas to come to Canada. Nevertheless, British ideas are sometimes drawn upon as a balance against American ones. Canadian innovations, like Canadian football, have encountered the dominance of a superior country, which, unlike the political or economic challenges from Russia or Japan, have not threatened them.

Until the twentieth century, Canada was heavily influenced by British or French imperial models (Poignant, 1969). There were no grades; there were forms and standards. The language used in education is, at times, still European. Streaming of students is discussed rather than mere tracking of the same pupils. Until recently, grade thirteen was a requirement in Ontario that was accepted by European universities as close to the equivalent of sixth form. Though there is the recent case of Calgary preferring the British practice of effective schools over the American work, almost all of the Canadian innovations now come from the United States (Mitchell, 1992). In fact, one teacher stated the point sharply when she said: "Any innovations the Americans have tried and found to fail we are sure to adopt" (Mitchell, 1995, p. 15).

Emulation of American innovations has been resisted whenever it touches the nerve of Canadian national character, as it does in other countries when a conscious awareness of cultural imperialism develops. Before World War II, American progressive education was adopted, particularly in Alberta. However, American terms such as "project," were resisted in favor of the British word, "enterprise." The practice of progressive education was always constrained in a formal structure that made controlled practice the norm (Tomkins, 1986). Ironically, after World War II, Canadians berated themselves for falling into the disorder and confusion of progressive education; Hilda Neatby's book *So Little For the Mind* was written for the wrong country, because Canada had never abandoned traditionalism in practice (Mitchell, 1992).

On other occasions, Canadians have assumed that criticisms of American failings apply to them, including the more recent excellence movement. Without any court actions challenging the inequality among school districts, Alberta took control of finances away from public school boards to provide greater equalization. The attack on school boards and a broader campaign to reinvent government are examples of very direct American influences (Mitchell, 1996).

The decade of innovations, the 1960s, began unleashing the flood of American innovations. Revealingly, in spite of provincial control over education, every urban school system in the country in 1968 began to build open area schools and they have not completely returned to separate classrooms (Martin & MacDonnell, 1982). Though the open areas were never used and in many cases were separated by dividers, even wealthy parents, who offered to pay to have the walls put back in, have been resisted by schools. Architects and planners developed open areas without concern for people, much like the experts who planned the new mathematics and science programs.

Abstract approaches encounter covert resistance. The problem was assumed to be the separation of theory and practice and that the ordinary teachers must remain passive. As one teacher said: "Make sure brain is engaged before putting mouth in gear" (Mitchell, 1992, p. 11). Whole programs may be similarly categorized. Drawing upon direct approval of their efforts by the original British researcher, Peter Mortimore, the Calgary effort at effective schools claimed its superiority to American efforts (Mitchell, 1992). The American effort is focused on the single goal of higher achievement scores, is directed at lower social-class areas, is dependent on expert identification of weaknesses, often ignores British research, and has a narrow concern for educational efficacy and accountability.

In contrast, the Calgary program includes a concern for pupil satisfaction as much as their productivity, is used as a tool by any school after the people in the situation determine their own needs, attempts to build upon strengths in order to make good schools better, relies on British research of effective programs together with broad studies such as those of Goodlad on schooling, and emphasizes the process of change as a part of whole school improvement. This elaborate rationalization keeps Americans at bay by combining a progressive education approach with British support to produce a program for Canadians.

However, neither rationalization nor social distance alone accounts for variations in American imperial influences on education in any country. Physical social distance also separates the reformers from any laggards. An evaluation of all programs for the gifted in one state shows how the road map can reveal this dominance (House, 1974). Large central cities on divided highways are the most likely place for innovations to be both developed and to spread from; the least likely location to design and assimilate innovations is a remote rural area. The development of innovations is dominated by large areas, such as New York City within the United States and Toronto within Canada. Cultural centers are everywhere the showplace for the empire. The ways that distance and innovations are related are shown in Chart 4.1.

Like geographical stratification, other forms of statification influence innovations. The dominant social class has been the first to accept innovations. French immersion was developed in upper middle-class communities and has not spread to the working class (Mitchell, 1992). Similarly, computers, particularly when they require fund-raising, have revealed enormous social class differences (Becker, 1985). Many innovations reveal stratification that encompasses a variety of

Chart 4.1
The Distribution of Innovations

Status and Innovations
Dense urban vs. Sparse rural areas
Central areas vs. Fringe provinces
Expert planners vs. Traditionalists
Higher classes vs. Working class
Dominant race vs. Subordinate race or ethnic enclaves

Economic Sources of Change
Competitive alternatives vs. Monopolies
Industrial societies vs. Traditional orders
Isolated nations vs. Competitive world

System Development—Imperialism
- Power position of home country
- Subsidiary colony
- Colonial elites identify with dominant elites
- Subordinates demand more equality
- International organizations coordinate or replace previously different groups

Relationship to Other Forms of Power
- Cultural forms, including science, can serve the interests of the dominant group, but knowledge determines perception of interests and opportunities for growth.
- Military leaders and politicians keep power via control of communications and transportation, but loyal opposition required for consideration of alternatives.
- Political controls influence exchange of ideas and consensus is basis for trade.
- Resources increasingly come to include education and cultural products but opposition develops against instrumental view of people.

Sources of Imperial Control Against Rivals
- Vertical integration of resources, products, and markets.
- Feudal interaction of elites with elites and no link between corresponding subordinates.
- Imperial capital functions as window to the world.
- Style differences become a part of product offerings with knowledge of style and products both initially limited to an elite

factors, particularly gender, race, and the ethnic allegiances as discussed in Chapter 2; the Native programs for White students are a striking exception. However, the likelihood of adoption is closely related to association with American ideas. Male business leaders or politicians have been most open to American ideas, such as charter schools that remove government controls on education (Mitchell, 1996). Even computer software programs reveal this regularity (Emil Vajda, personal communication, July 22, 1997).

The pattern of resistance offered by Canadians to American influences is revealing. Status differences have compounded resistance even when ties with the economy and power were not critical. For example, in the softer areas of social studies and English, Canadians have attempted their own home brew, though many of the American ingredients were present. For over ten years, the Canadian Studies Foundation produced materials in the softer curriculum areas. However, in the end, that foundation collapsed under the weight of provincial differences and "bureaucratic and institutional solutions to educational problems" (Tomkins, 1986, p. 334). Furthermore, under cover of the Canadian studies rubric, American approaches such as value clarification in social studies, came and went without any serious change in practice (Downey & Associates, 1975).

The major impact of American imperialism is to create a marginality between the Canadian practice of schools and American ideals for education that diminishes the possibilities of creative solutions being developed and accepted in Canada. Typically, for most Canadians, cultural developments must be endorsed by the elite in the United States because marginality produces insecurity and defensiveness. A standard interpretation of innovations by a Canadian was marred by a preoccupation with American literature and Freudian slips in its bibliography, such as the National Institute of Canada for the National Institute of Education (Mitchell, 1995). Such slips reveal the extent of emulation by a Canadian and a desire by him to be as powerful as an American.

The theory of imperialism developed by Galtung catches the sources of dependency, particularly with its focus upon elites talking with elites (House, 1974). In neither the superior nor the subordinate country, do ordinary parents, teachers, and students meet so that they can develop innovations. The ideas of ordinary folk on either side of the border were ignored when open area classrooms were developed. Rather, feudal liege patterns link experts between countries, high-level administrators to principals, and principals to teachers. Teacher involvement in innovations often means dependency on their superiors (Cusick, 1983).

Aside from feudal interaction, imperialism is claimed to develop from vertical integration of direct school services with suppliers of materials. Certainly texts, tests, and research studies have been heavily controlled by American sources. However, other than American universities and some private international schools, which increasingly offer their programs in Canada, there have been no direct service outlets controlled by the American suppliers. Until Chris Whittle enters the scene with his entire set of schools for profit, franchise operations have not completed the route to further the educational dependency of Canadian education.

Almost all the innovations involving business have radiated from the dominant power and reinforced it. Over ten years separates the development of corporate sponsorship in the United States and the same idea is being promoted in Western Canada. Canadians have also attempted to organize the influences into a hierarchy, even though hierarchies have been the major problem in developing alternatives to American ideas. For example, the Information Technology Association of Canada has proposed focusing efforts at adopting a school at the elementary level, career exploration at the secondary avenues, and joint research programs for higher education (Mitchell, 1996).

Rationalization combined with a status system does not greatly alter the actual experiences with innovations. An additional defense is the Canadian tendency not to join American associations, but to incorporate American ideas into their own schools and more limited associations. The belief that American problems with their urban decay, crime, and racial riots will not come to the safe middle-class world of Canada also tends to diminish an awareness of American influence. The problem is for Canada to recognize the influence of American examples and learn from them while teaching Americans that they must learn what any dominant power must know, that the poorer cousins can resist and teach their superiors some important lessons.

However, the larger significance of imperialism and resistance to it is that the analysis suggests the central limitations of concentrated power and control of innovations. The current fad of systemic innovation claims to coordinate innovation and to compound the effectiveness of separate reforms. However, the silver bullet of systemic changes also leads to a structure of decision making that is very similar to imperial rule. The more national reform organizations, such as the Getty Center in art education and the Coalition of Essential Schools, reveal an integration of training, materials, and teaching as well as displays in their capitals together with an emphasis on style to distinguish their products from others. Imperial efforts will be contrasted with more local and democratic ones in Chapter 8 and 9, but the bookmark from this section will be the criteria for criticizing concentrated power that any current Caesar may wish to wield.

SCHOOL-TO-WORK

No social or educational issue has more profoundly challenged confidence in any modern country more than the spiralling unemployment rates among all kinds of youth (Wotherspoon, 1991). Beginning in the 1970s and growing dramatically in the 1980s, the difficulties of youth in a great many countries in finding work has increased pressure on educational systems to provide solutions cooperatively with employers (Vickers, 1991). The school-to-work initiatives have followed the American practice of either attempting to keep at-risk students in public schools, or making educational programs meaningful for the large group, often said to be the majority, who did not go from high school to university. For the latter group, programs are sandwiched between high schools and community colleges are developed as career avenues. The concentrated power of business is seen as the solution if it can only be related to schooling and change the direction of youth.

The separation between business and schools should not lead anyone to ignore some obvious relationships that are developing between them. Students and employers are usually linked through part-time jobs. Such jobs are a source of immediate income to meet growing adolescent needs, but the jobs have little long-term significance (McNeil, 1984). The part-time jobs mean that students can work long hours, neglect their school work, and opt out of extracurricular activities. However, there is a large body of evidence that shows working in high schools has a very positive impact on career earnings (Stern, 1990). Though such work prevents or delays graduation, the impact on earnings is still positive (Lerman, 1996).

The problem is how to integrate the economic benefits of such work with a renewed appreciation of the significance of studying. At present, when students seek predigested courses and school social life disappears, the meaning of education can be transformed by these jobs. School, then, becomes "unpaid work" (Hall & Carlton, 1977, p. 69). In focus groups, parents have expressed their belief that combining vocational and academic programs would be beneficial even if the same parents ultimately want college for their students (Kallick & Jobs for the Future, 1990).

In a study of eight states and thirty-nine local partnerships, only 16 percent of seniors reported participating in a workplace activity (Olson, 1997c). In the same study, 88 percent of students who had jobs during high school found them on their own. Only two states, Oregon and Kentucky, had integrated work-to-school programs into their reform agendas. Most schools, in this study as well as others, ignore employment as a source of learning (Lerman, 1996). A significant clue to the puzzle is that there are striking benefits for at-risk students in combining education and work programs. A survey by Lerman (1996) reports:

Among at-risk youth, working between 15-29 hours per week as a sophomore in high school resulted in more than 25% higher earnings 8-11 years later as compared to those who had not worked while in high school. The impact was only a 10% earnings gain among all other sophomores.

However, a more negative syndrome often develops among at-risk students. This pattern can begin as early as entry into school, when some students disengage from schooling and neither identify nor participate in their education (Lerman, 1996). Later, students characteristically come to lose interest in school and confidence in themselves though they often blame teachers and other experts for their problems (Gaskell & Lazerson, 1980-1981). Students need to have their interests stimulated, their resources increased, and provision made for them to receive rewards where few have previously been found.

Early evidence from Career Magnet Schools in New York City shows gains in self-confidence among many at-risk students. Other studies report higher achievement in general subjects for those in this same group of students. When these same programs include job placement, the disadvantage of informal channels to jobs is reduced for poor students (Lerman, 1996). The programs can also provide adult peer groups that prevent the negative youth groups pulling students away from both work and education. Finally and most importantly, such programs can keep at-risk students out of trouble and ultimately out of prisons.

For the employers, participation in education to work programs changes their perceptions about the limits of young people. Employers have been shown to wait for young people to simply grow older as their only sure indication of greater reliability and ascertainable skills. School-to-work programs can drastically change this. Employers who participated in cooperative work programs with schools reported positive attitudes toward young workers. For example, 60 percent strongly agreed that such students were productive workers and 33 per cent somewhat agreed.

In contrast, a more general group of employers in focus groups reported great frustration with young people which echoes statements made by other dominants about other colonial's inferiorities; youth are said to lack "discipline as well as communication, numeracy, and literacy skills" (Lerman, 1996). Employers preferred older workers who had demonstrated their abilities in other jobs or through temporary help agencies. The main difference between the employers involved in the cooperative work program, and others, was that the schools were providing a reliable screening function. As a result, over half the cooperating employers wanted more students from the same schools.

An essential of school-to-work programs is the use of the computer, a skill sought by employers. A critical problem is the lack of home computers for at-risk students, which has been partially overcome by school or library computer loan programs, such as the one in Houston. At an even more basic level, at-risk students are often denied the use of school textbooks at home. The possibilities of using volunteers to help provide resources and support for such students is further explored in Chapters 8 and 9. The challenge is to develop career and education programs that will benefit those who are attracted by these ideas while raising the expectations of everyone with regard to the efforts that effective education can entail.

CORPORATE LEADERS AND EDUCATORS

The call for greater use of computers, a wider relationship to technology and science, and even greater awareness of cultural differences, has been part of the typical program that corporate groups, such as the Corporate and Higher Education Forum, have sponsored and published (Mitchell, 1996). These programs have received an enormous amount of publicity. Corporate power has increasingly been brought into both higher and basic education by joint programs with industry (Berman, 1986, p. 106). In the United States, programs such as the adopt-a-school program, the Boston Compact, and the Academy of Finance, focused on the problems of inner cities. In Canada, these programs developed later when financing for schools was more of a problem and such assistance has been their purpose. In neither country have such programs raised the academic performance of students, but they have improved the attitudes of students and made the school coordinators more involved (Mitchell, 1996). For both countries, the teachers involved with programs that had corporate sponsors were affected, as they were with programs for exchanging personnel between schools and businesses, known as the Ryerson Plan (Apple, 1982).

Cooperative programs involving industry and universities, have been more highly developed than those between industry and schools; joint research and technology efforts have been sought, particularly in Canada, by having businesspeople appointed to university chairs and by continuing grants to universities that can be monitored by business donors (Feldman, 1985; Mitchell, 1996). For example, the Xerox Corporation set up the Institute for Research on Learning, which it runs together with the University of California's Graduate School of Education. Industrial leaders like the president of Xerox, David Kearns, advise schools and universities on how they ought to be like "the smartest high tech companies" (Kearns, 1989, p. 7).

Industrial leaders have emerged as institutional entrepreneurs or experts, similar to those with CCFE and NGA. Louis Gerstner, formerly chairman and CEO at RJR Nabisco and now chairman and CEO at IBM, has become more influential than David Kearns was earlier. At RJR Nabisco he started a model school project, Next Century Schools, which preceded the New American Schools. Both the New American Schools and Nabisco have rewarded very progressive approaches.

Gerstner's most important experiment has been his use of the "bully pulpit" of his position with IBM to rally the reform troops. He became co-chair of a national summit of governors and businesspeople, which has attempted to create a permanent national organization, Achieve, to monitor the progress of reform (Lawton, 1997a). The educational summit brought together forty state governors, forty-nine business executives, and thirty-eight experts or "resource people" at IBM's conference center in Palisades, New York. Gerstner originally invited the governors to the IBM center to display the technological applications that were available to education, but the conference was enlarged to promote high standards and realistic assessments as well as computers (Diegmueller & Lawton, 1996).

The co-chair of the summit, Republican Governor Tommy Thompson of Wisconsin, helped broaden the summit. Thompson was head of the NGA as well as Chairman of the Education Commission of the States (another think-tank that will be discussed later). Thompson is typical of politicians with multiple roles just as Gerstner is among similar businesspeople. A careful mix of three Republican and three Democratic governors made the summit possible. One of the Democratic governors, James Hunt, headed up the National Commission on Teaching & America's Future; others became increasingly involved in a variety of educational roles.

For the organization to follow up on the summit, the politicians and businesspeople chose a typical institutional expert, Robert Schwartz, to head the Achieve organization. Mr. Schwartz had been educational advisor to former Governor Michael Dukakis of Massachusetts. Until six months before the new job, he had been head of educational programs for the Pew Charitable Trusts, the fourth largest foundation in the United States. In between leaving Pew and joining Achieve, he had joined the faculty of Harvard where he continues because the office of Achieve is conveniently located in Boston. Mr. Schwartz is described by a Washington insider, John Jennings, as someone who knows everyone and as a "pivotal person" for the whole standards movement (Lawton, 1997a).

The summit and its continuing organization have brought together many multitalented individuals. For example, the select group of resource people included Christopher Cross, now president of the Council for Basic Education. Mr. Cross was Assistant Secretary of Education under George Bush and education director for the Business Roundtable and is still head of the Maryland state policy board for education. The summit also rounded up the usual institutional experts, including Marc Tucker and Lauren Resnick, with the same Carnegie project (Harp, 1996).

However, all parent organizations and many grassroots groups were left out by the selection of summit participants. Such groups were invited merely to watch the summit and discuss the issues in the Chamber of Commerce's Washington television studio. Two tiers, which resulted from separate discussions, complement the hegemony that business, politicians, and dominant intellectuals have established, but the very existence of the two tiers is a nagging problem.

SELLING COMPUTERS, DIRECTING EDUCATION

A social concern for education and the implications of technology are not considered in the campaign for technology; only technological and economic benefits are stressed in the campaign. The slogan Gerstner has used over and over again to persuade politicians to spend more on computers and other technology is that public schools are "low-tech institutions in a high-tech society." His views are generally acknowledged to have given the impetus to states and provinces to direct their new expenditures for education almost entirely to technology (White, 1997). Certainly, in Alberta, the policy papers on technology have been dominated by technocratic considerations (the use people make of them is ignored); alternative views have not been considered.

Corporate power is augmented in society through involvement with government or policy commissions. The foundations or the nonprofit corporations give more support to those in business positions and suggest more of a consensus than any direct expression of self-interest by businesspeople would ever provide (Berman, 1984). Head Start programs, which were once so challenged, are now part of the consensus of efforts to promote excellence and to get the poor into the race for success (Kearns, 1989). However, the dependency of the poor is only enhanced through paternalistic programs. The chance of subordinate groups developing their own culture and education programs is diminished.

Intellectuals who help maintain the dominance of centralist programs are themselves caught in the corporate web. Communications, education, and more generally, culture, have long been recognized as varieties of imperialism that can include even the most selfless scientist (House, 1974). Moreover, the scholars who prepare background papers for business and government reports, from *A Nation at Risk* to the recent summit, are particularly subject to co-optation. What they tend to think and write is influenced by publicity and reward systems, which are governed by interests other than their own (Tomlinson & Walberg, 1986). Academic experts can provide a further cloak for the hegemonic consensus that corporate interests have so recently contrived in relation to schooling. Neither academic values nor the values of subordinate groups are promoted by their expedient practice.

Since joining IBM, Louis Gerstner has been particularly concerned with bringing together top minds in education to brainstorm and plan. Initially, the institutional experts were to think about the $100 million that IBM gave away each year. In addition, IBM began giving away $25 million to integrate technology with other reform efforts. All of these projects, called Reinventing Education, include site-based management and the math and science skills that are essential for the new, but not "radical" program (Trotter, 1997a).

However, many other programs developed by IBM try to provide critical information to teachers and administrators. In Armonk, New York, students who have specific learning disabilities can have resources located for them in advance by the use of the computer. IBM has devised specific teaching devices, such as computer programs with cartoon characters who read to students, correct their mistakes, and make a list of problem words. IBM also has announced an additional $10 million to refine these three areas, along with a portfolio assessment of a middle school science program that blends mathematical reasoning with computer simulated experiments (Trotter, 1997a). Someone should ask Mr. Gerstner about the things that computers cannot do and what experiments IBM has tried that have failed. Unlike the employers who were involved in cooperative work programs with high-risk youth, at the summit, there is very little sign of corporate or other leaders learning from subordinates.

WORK EXPERIENCE PROGRAMS

However, organized programs with businesses are not necessarily more effective. The computer addiction has been compared to candy that students enjoy, but that may rot their teeth and technology often ignores social relationships and the creativity of individuals. This adds to the contradiction between impersonal business approaches and the thinking of students, as revealed by work experience programs.

These programs often treat young people more like potential employees or future customers, than as maturing individuals. The possibility of making very young students more realistic and less creative at a very early stage should cause some hesitation, but those who write about school-work programs want others to worship these programs. Parents are skeptical that sixteen-year-old students can make a four-year commitment to the youth apprentice programs, whereas students are concerned that their peers and social life may be upset (Jobs for the Future, 1991). For the students, good work experiences that allowed them to learn about people, often have occurred outside youth apprenticeship programs.

The students want courses that will provide practical applications, even if they do not want to give up their other immediate concerns with people and events. Though programs for at-risk students more than justify a combination of work and education, there is a danger of education including only work as its focus. North

American students do not seem to believe they have ever had enough practical applications! Students always want more practical applications in their university programs (International Association of Students in Economics and Business, Carleton, 1993). Nursing students in Arkansas is the group most enthusiastic about youth apprenticeships, particularly in rural areas, because they see that such health programs could lead to preventive approaches.

Nursing has long been one of the professions with the most "hands-on" training and the least theoretical base (Mitchell, 1971); the enthusiasm of nursing students may be further grounds for suspecting that academic training and career education are not always being effectively combined in youth apprenticeship programs (Jobs for the Future, 1991). An earlier study reported opening the door for women as a learner expectation of a low-level vocational program (Lind, 1974). Extremely low-level expectations have led to student criticisms of special education (Mitchell, 1992).

However, it may be that the emphasis on limited practicality, like the use of testimonials, is a fumbling attempt to connect the world of students with business activities. The world of students is people-centered, and students' interactive knowledge is more affective than rational (Everhart, 1983). The very young students are in a stage of primary socialization where motivation is being developed, whereas adolescents are just entering the adult stage where power dominates (Brim & Wheeler, 1966). Only in supporting early childhood education does business begin to grasp how different education for children is from the education of managers. The development of students as individuals is ignored by the managerial approach toward student responses to school work. Consequently, those involved in youth programs often believe that they must be advocates for students who would otherwise be ignored (Dyckman, 1994); only in this way can superior imperialistic influences begin to be countered. Perhaps if American businesspeople started to see their occasional statements of interest in the arts as a basis for identifying with individuals, the chasm would be overcome.

THE CRISES PROGRAMS OF GOVERNMENTS

Radical changes in education have increasingly intimidated teachers, primarily because the testing programs that are often involved, control them. Kentucky has a history of centralized state planning, which led to the state's testing program (McDonnell, 1994). Kentucky's controversial testing program was a part of a total educational change that began when the state Supreme Court decided that the state was totally failing to provide a reasonable education as compared to neighbouring states. In Chicago, racial turmoil and a repeated series of teacher strikes led to a community and business attack on the educational bureaucracy, but the testing program preceded reform and has recently been given more emphasis. In Alberta, as in many other parts of North America, the selling of the fear of government deficits led to a drastic restructuring of education, health, and social services. Both Kentucky and Alberta share a long history of centralized testing, and they are now seeking to find effective indicators to measure government efforts in education.

Though California is often a center for curriculum changes together with major testing efforts, it is hard to see the same sense of recent crisis engendered there as in the total programs in the other situations (Mitchell, 1996). The crisis in Kentucky was educational, the intense conflict in Chicago was social and political, and the radical change in Alberta was economic. Though affected by racial and economic problems, California appears to have created a fashion center for educational innovations as a way of relating to growth industries in the state. Several of the art programs that are discussed in Chapter 6 originated in California.

For teachers, parents, and students, these three or four types of revolutions present many challenges and extensive opportunities; experts continue to cause problems for these more ordinary people. In Kentucky, an institutional leader, David Hornbeck, was suggested by the Educational Commission of the States as the guiding genius for its radical effort. A lawyer, Hornbeck had been chief executive officer for education in Maryland; he is now Superintendent for Philadelphia and also prepared the educational plan for the Business Roundtable. His complete overhaul has changed the curriculum and testing of the elementary program throughout the state and is beginning to change the secondary program, but his reward and punishment system, which is based on a state-wide testing program, has caused the greatest alarm (Mitchell, 1996). For example, authentic testing was initially required in both English and mathematics at the end of the unified primary set, grade 4. The demands of this testing were overwhelming for teachers so the tests were later modified by the legislature. In addition, teachers have not been able to lead parents and students into a complicated educational approach that they themselves did not fully understand or support.

Chicago, in contrast, has had an enormous involvement of parents and community groups in its program which is based on school councils. The Chicago program was initially supported by a variety of advocacy groups, especially Designs for Change. Don Moore, a Harvard Ph.D., had national interests, but decided to focus on Chicago in hopes of bringing about significant changes (Mitchell, 1996). He often works with local groups providing them with resources and letting them lead the opposition in filing a court case against the school board. Attempts were made to involve the teachers through a city-wide task force, a union-run innovation center, Quest, a minority set of positions for them on school councils, and school improvement plans where they were the creators. None of the efforts were very successful because they had been habituated to working within a bureaucracy with an industrial union representing their interests.

In western Canada, the reform efforts were engineered by a politician, Ralph Klein, and his cabinet (Ibid). Many school boards were eliminated, opportunities for conservative groups were provided, such as schools of choice within the public system, and teacher salaries were reduced by 5 percent; teachers reportedly seethe with resentment against the government . In Kentucky, salaries were substantially increased while Chicago reforms were fiscally neutral, other than one collective bargaining contract. The cuts in Alberta have been combined with pressure for results and continued expectations for rewards and punishments based on school exams. Alberta reveals how a basic threat, fiscal limits, can overshadow differences between elite and rank and file.

There are a great many common reforms among these extreme types of reform. School-based management, school councils, integration of health and social service with education, curriculum changes, and statistical controls for account-ability, have been a part of each reform. But each specific reform takes a different meaning in the separate contexts. For example, the process program of writing, the National Writing Program, has been developed in each case . In Chicago, this means that two competing groups have opportunities open up, because school councils, with their new autonomy, can hire them. Advocacy groups wanted competition of ideas and Chicago students' writing scores have been the first area to show improvement.

In contrast, Kentucky has made the same national program a part of the Kentucky Department of Education and it is not perceived by reformers as being an independent program. In Alberta, the same program has been ignored by the politicians and businesspeople who have focused entirely on more instrumental approaches to education; writing has not been seen to be a problem for the superior Canadian system of education. California has seen the writing program combined with business writing as well an attempt to forge a union of many diverse art and educational groups that are discussed in Chapters 6, 7, and 8.

DRIVING THE STAKE IN

None of the major alternatives has done a very effective job of developing evaluations or developing new policies together with these evaluations. Evaluation program findings of continuing problems with some schools, and the remedy of reconstitution, where the staffs of deficient schools are totally changed, have challenged the rank and file of education. The elite has indeed cooked up a strange stew when, on the one hand, autonomy is promised through school-based management, yet, on the other hand, if higher student achievements are not realized, staff will be removed and possibly even lose tenure entirely. In 1932, Waller wrote that there are two things that worried teachers: losing their jobs and not maintaining discipline in their classes (Waller, 1967). Though classroom discipline is not yet a focus of assessment and measurement, the current programs are enough for the staff to call out in terror.

Each of the radical types has reflected this emphasis on evaluation that is increasingly controlling people, but other areas also reflect the same trends. Kentucky, from the very start, has emphasised exams and rewards; the plan was influenced by the economist and former Secretary of Labor, Ray Marshall. It has also created a category of superteachers, Kentucky Educators, who are to come in and help turn a low performing school around. When such schools are placed on probation, parents have the option of transferring students, and teachers can be dismissed (Mitchell, 1996).

Initially, the advocacy organizations and their allies in Chicago tried to get more flexibility for schools in hiring teachers and eliminating teachers with super seniority; they were not concerned with putting schools on probation. More recently, with direct control of the schools passing to the mayor, Chicago has placed schools on probation, eliminated social promotion of students, and required summer school for students who might fail (Poe, 1997c). Kentucky provides Saturday classes or summer school for students who are deficient, but its main emphasis has been on improving the performance of schools over a long period. Alberta has not viewed itself as having a problem of deficient students or schools, but it has developed plans for student flexibility between schools, evaluation and rewards for schools, and greater centralization of the system in which autonomous schools operate (Alberta Education, 1995).

A number of American cities are developing plans for reconstituting school staffs, generally on the basis of standardized test scores. Houston has tried this approach (Olson, 1996) and Denver, with the agreement of the teachers' union, is in the process of doing so, whereas Philadelphia's plan to implement the overhaul of the staff at selected schools has been blocked by a court decision brought by the union (Jones, 1997). The state of New Jersey has used staff changes as a way of dealing with school systems, mainly Jersey City, that are corrupt and financially and academically bankrupt; however, they have had more success with altering the budget than in improving learning.

More than anywhere else, San Francisco has focused on educational aims in its plan for reconstituting schools. Since 1982, San Francisco has been under a court order to reconstitute the lowest performing school staffs in order to improve racial integration. San Francisco has had the most success in improving student achievement because of an education plan with high expectations that accompanied the reconstitution (Olson, 1996). However, because of teacher animosity and union opposition, the plan is now being abandoned, though a program for the individual transfer of teachers has been instituted (Reinhard, 1997).

Most of these approaches have encountered teacher resistance, parent disinterest or opposition, and an unanticipated set of problems. In Kentucy, right-wing political groups may have complained more than teachers, but teachers still have neither understood nor supported the approach. Four years after Kentucky started its radical approach, 60 percent of the community and 40 percent of parents did not understand it (Mitchell, 1996, p. 177). The teachers union in Chicago has apparently found the approach of politicians more helpful than that of the original reformers; but teachers are still not involved with the approach in any long-term sense (Poe, 1997b). Teachers in Alberta are already adjusting the curriculum and their teaching to the evaluation approach (Steele, 1996). Evaluation for control has almost everywhere led to a greater need for checking on exam cheating (Martinez, 1997). The complicated use of portfolio testing in Kentucky has led to rewards being obtained but having to be returned when cheating was finally discovered; more significantly, political demands are being made there for more and more checking on schools (Harp, 1997).

Testing to get the system under control and the practice of reconstitution have both failed to be a silver bullet for reform. Though politicians might be forgiven for wanting a quick fix, institutional experts, such as David Hornbeck in Philadelphia, have also tried to move in this direction without adequate preparation. Politicians and experts must learn the significance of institution building that includes testing but is not preoccupied with it.

Two of the largest studies of innovations ever undertaken, by the Rand Corporation and the Network, found consistent negative correlations between evaluation efforts and diffusion of innovations (Bauchner, et al., 1982). In the Network study, the more time experts spent planning and increasing the number of programs, the less time they spent on evaluation. The more time they spent on evaluation, the less time they spent in awareness raising sessions in local areas. Staff development and parent participation can also be related to evaluation in learning-centered schools (Rosenholtz, 1989). According to this last study, teacher evaluation is related to school decision-making and positive feedback to teachers as well as other innovative approaches for the school staff. Paralleling these general findings, a former administrator with a state department of education that has undergone massive changes, speaks of the war between the bureau responsible for evaluation and the agencies supporting innovations (Linda Hargan, interview, June 3, 1996).

WHERE WE NEED TO GO FROM HERE

Whether or not such evaluations improved teachers or students, these tests are conducted by high level experts. Their preoccupation is still with new and constantly changing forms of evaluations, which, even more than inservice education, is their turf. This development causes even more problems and requires more support for teachers, parents, and the community wherein the experts roam. The critical problem is to develop organic leaders from the people, who will bring broader visions to those in the trenches.

Among teachers, more cosmopolitan leaders have been found to aid the spread of innovations, such as the computer expert on staff (Daft & Becker, 1978). Some school superintendents, though currently embittered by their limited role in reforms, have long been shown to want change as a way of avoiding too much stability (Blumberg, 1985; Hendrie, 1997). Teams of community leaders from Latino and Black constituents are an even more obvious source of counters to the power of institutional leaders (Mitchell, 1996). In Chicago, one member of the leadership team would be a planner and the other would be a spokesperson who could articulate the feelings as well as ideas of the group, or one member would be the bridge to the ideas of experts and the other would be the politician who could mobilize people and resources. Such oppositional teams, similar to the loyal opposition in parliament, can act to reverse the status quo and create many more schools in which the opposite is tried. In Canada, alternative teams or leaders could be important sources to break the preoccupation with status and hierarchy.

Reversing many of the conditions shown in the theory of imperialism would probably create more support for organic leaders. Such support is crucial if these leaders are to bring about significant role reversals. Experts should not be caught putting words in the mouths of people, but the people should refuse to let institutional experts intimidate them. Especially important is contact among subordinates, teacher to teacher and student to student, not just everyone going to seek the oracle. Nor should one institution, such as business, be allowed to dominate others. The elite must know that they can be challenged and the subordinates must know that they can confront dominant leaders. Only then will a sense of community that crosses status and professional barriers be possible. A community can combine effective programs for at-risk students with efforts to raise the expectations of all students; unity can be built on more than a crisis scare.

In all these efforts, reformers must begin to test themselves, and the first question must be how they propose to overcome the chasm between superexperts and laypeople. The second issue is to show the limits of their proposals and to reveal that they are not infallible. The agenda must grow to include recognizing people as who they are, not who they are assumed to be. Students are not just future workers and consumers; people have educational options that can include their participation in democratic decisions, as in Chicago; and evaluations must be premised upon helping everyone to improve so they can become the sort of person they think they ought to be.

Efforts to evaluate support for reform and self-evaluation with critical friends are essential. Putting oneself in the position of teacher, parent, and student should be the test of all future leaders. The early reforms in Chicago reveal an ideal of community change that needs to be wedded to the theory of experts as teachers and of teachers as first among equals in a democratic community, rather than possessors of a monopoly on skill or knowledge (Strike, 1993). Building the community of interests for which such leaders can articulate the vision is the aim of the remainder of this book, whether the apparent issue is teachers, advocates, volunteers, sensitive individuals or successful programs. Aspects of each type of reform need to be combined just as all the constituents of the community need to contribute to schools. Finding the balanced weighting of all these elements is the challenge facing educational innovation and reform.

Fathers themselves, ought every few days to test their children, and not rest their hopes on the disposition of a hired teacher: for even those persons will devote more attention to the children if they know they must from time to time render an account.—Plutarch

Chapter 5

Visions

Two boys are drawing tanks and trucks, a girl is making paper pompoms, another apparently daydreaming in the midst of drawing a hand. Two boys are deeply engrossed in Lego construction—the like of which has not been seen in any classrooms we visited—a motorized cable station. A book on transportation lies open nearby as reference. Mr. Sprinter suggests that after they record them on paper they 'go outside to try them out.' Two girls who have been watching a snail for forty-five minutes ask him [Mr. Sprinter] a few questions as he walks by. He helps them record their observations. . . . . The greatest strength that kids have that we don't have any more really, that we have to recreate in ourselves as adults, is that way of looking. (Berlak & Berlak, 1981, pp. 98-99)

In Hamlet, Shakespeare writes, 'What a piece of work is a man!' Marva Collins, a recognized leader in education reform declares, 'What a piece of work is a child!' . . . Visitors to these [her private] schools are awed by first graders learning the metric system and geometry; second graders involved in astronomy; fourth graders reading flight schedules; fifth graders studying Latin; and sixth graders reading Nietzsche, Voltaire, Chaucer, Shakespeare, and Tolstoy. . . . [Marva Collins] 'I take the position that the more fetid a home environment might be, the harder a teacher must work to break that self-perpetuating cycle.' (O'Neal Mosley, 1993, p. 22)

Both Mr. Sprinter and Marva Collins are stirring up their local areas with practices that break the mold; they are challenging the experts to include their experience in theories about change! In Chapter 4, a number of approaches were suggested for joining theory and practice, such as viewing professionals as primarily members in a democratic community. Other approaches are developed in this chapter, particularly to combine the general approaches that are reflected in the difference between Marva Collins and Mr. Sprinter.

General approaches are often justifications for future actions, but they are very different from concrete experiences. Theory, or rather theories, constantly fragment actual experiences with educational reform whether in Chicago, Alberta, California, or Kentucky. Experts as leaders in the modernization process alternate theories rather like a parade of fashions (House, 1974).

The theories can attempt to seize upon changes of what might be, values. When values are formalized, even in school improvement plans, ideology and beliefs replace actual experiences. Plans for innovation, publicity about innovations, and research on innovations can all be affected by ideological positions (Editors of *Education Week*, 1993). Teachers, in contrast to experts, may, for example, want to bring progressive and traditional approaches of education together (Presseisen, 1985). Students, in turn, may want teachers to bring such combined approaches to the classroom. An integration of approaches will probably be difficult until images of each theory are seen to need supplements from other approaches to connect with experiences. Such an integration may require educators being brought together with innovations regardless of whether the innovations are a result of an individual creation or a social crisis (Pauly, 1991; Weiss, 1995).

Innovation is a multifaceted and complicated process. Experiencing innovation is an enhancement of individual experience. The individual, whether child or adult, must be given the opportunity to experiment. Opportunities can also be increased by competing organizations and conflicting professions. These differences also create tensions, which can challenge individuals or further subordinate them. As we saw in Chapter 4, power is a limiting condition for creativity. Combining alternatives as well as being encouraged by the awareness of them can establish the significance of organic leaders or institutional entrepreneurs at the local level or a national summit. The possibilities that the boomerangs or unanticipated results of innovations are the most significant result of innovations will be explored to enhance a realistic understanding of innovations as a part of day-to-day life in teaching.

A CREATION MYTH

Alternatives to existing approaches to innovation can arise from a different perspective. In the western world, innovation is closely related to progress, but the historical experience does not support this myth (Nisbet, 1980). Because of so many opportunities for mass destruction, there is growing awareness that human beings may not be making very much progress. In many simpler societies around the world, creation is related more to separation and independent growth rather than progress. Myths drawn from a different philosophical or theological conception are our first clue about how to think about innovation. The creation of human beings by God has usually been seen as the extension of an already existing form. Creation can, however, be thought about as an action of a dominant power that so contains itself as to allow the development of a new independent agent, say, the student.

This creation myth, which includes contraction and critical extension of power, has been used as a guide for developing the leadership of administrators (Simon, 1982). The original power must question and inspire the emerging power. The original source for this position is Isaac Luria, a mystical rabbi. The myth could be even more significant for teachers who need to develop independence among students since the human meaning that is suggested by myths is closer to the students' world than it is to that of the system makers. A myth about the iron cage of bureaucracy, where people are captured by their beliefs about what is required to be king or queen, would be more fitting as a "psychic prison" for administrators (Morgan, 1986).

Students' involvement and development through traditional roles or through more modern forms of power sharing are frequently mentioned in the literature written for administrators on how to relate with students (Rutter, 1983). However, these approaches to students are through extensions of the already existing professional structure. In the literature on administrative and organizational factors affecting students, more creative conceptions need to be added so that students will become more interested in learning, not just on becoming junior experts.

For example, concerning small and large classes, what options are available to students in small classes that are different from their alternatives in large classes? Very small classes have been shown to benefit very young and disabled students rather than the older and healthy ones who might be expected to work in a more independent manner (Rutter, 1983). In large classes, students may successfully avoid being smothered by teachers as they try to exercise their initiative, but they may not have received the grounding that they need. Teachers have been shown to be more interested in personalizing classes by relating to students than they are in individualizing instruction and curricula for them (Tyler, 1988). Do teachers use small classes to relate more to students and diagnose their weaknesses? Or do they teach in the same mechanical way as they have previously done in large classes?

Similar problems can relate to the current proposal for small school alternatives within existing large schools. Such schools can reduce alienation from the larger setting; teachers can know the names of their students while giving them alternative programs on which to focus. But do they question the students, direct them, or inspire more autonomous actions by them? Or do they create a temporary tent where students may be sheltered but not provided with the resources to construct further new alternatives for education themselves?

The school system can be thought about in a new way from the creativity myth. Consider the parallels between the findings on bureaucracy and community size. In both these areas curvilinear findings have been reported concerning organizational size and community numbers; order and size are both good up to a point but not beyond it (Tyler, 1988). We know that greater freedom is experienced under some structures governed by rules than under the arbitrary discretion of administrators (Moeller & Charters, 1970). However, the highly bureaucratic schools limit the likelihood of schools developing innovations. Student examination results in schools in communities of less than a million are higher than those in schools in either small towns or large cities (Tyler, 1988). No one has a clear idea of the reason for these results. Students may have both the order and freedom they need in structured schools in middle-sized communities.

The interesting findings concerning peer group balance might, perhaps, have the closest relevance to the creation myth. The findings show that the presence of large numbers of able students in a school raises the performance of individual students more than many things a school does directly (Rutter, 1983). Neither higher occupational background of students' families nor the students' racial origin is nearly as powerful as the context of intellectual ability in its effect on the work of individual students. Furthermore, the comparative ability context is unrelated to either school or teacher approaches, though more effective schools show that the peer effect is greater than with lower-rated schools (Rutter, et al., 1979). Because intelligence scores are generally known by students and incorporated into their own thinking, it is reasonable that the peer effect is part of the invidious comparisons that students themselves make (Werthman, 1963).

While a positive peer context for students in one school can mean that they avoid being alienated from one another and thus perform, students in schools with negative peer context could be in comparative disadvantage. In Chapter 4, the adult peer group was seen as providing a more positive focus in work transition programs. If students are to be a significant part of their own future, positive, more independent, and more responsible peer groups must be developed . The peer group could be both the beginning for poorer students and the continuation for higher-level thinking as part of a supporting and intellectual environment for all students.

As with teachers, students may be more motivated when they are more involved. One of the more detailed studies of innovation, the Network study, has pointed out that for both teachers and students the most striking effect of innovations is the sense of being "set apart" from other schools (Huberman & Miles, 1982). A sense of "a part together" can further lead students to identify with teachers who are particularly innovative. However, this social effect seems to separate schools and individual classes rather than expand them. Separate schools need to be a part of a broader movement.

Currently, the schools-within-schools approach has problems with the rest of the school. According to the myth, the whole school would have to recede and surrender many of its controls so that the school within could become more and more autonomous. Without support from outsiders, the internal conflicts engendered by schools within other schools may disappear. Another alternative would be to make the boundaries of school systems so permeable that many other plans besides schools-within-schools would constantly enter from the world of outsiders.

A TEACHER STORY

Teachers often lack the direction that is expected of students by the creation myth, but they can develop it and become more the peers of experts. The activity of a local teachers' group shows that teachers can handle theoretical matters and that they can do so when they challenge the powers that be (McDonald, 1987). As is true of most teacher groups, the group that evolved a theoretical position and sought power started with a purely social function. A meeting over pizza, which started with the teachers complaining about student aggravation, became, in this notable case, a discussion group because the teacher members wanted to be less "insular and self-absorbed" (McDonald, 1987, p. 27).

Though they initially were only a discussion group, the teachers increasingly became critics of educational reform. These criticisms began with a written review of one of the excellence reports that were current at the time. Next, the group took an increasingly political position by ignoring the advice of their school superintendent to take a more moderate stance. As a result of the teachers' publicized activities, an expert who was writing a new report came to talk with them before his new position paper was finished. He noted that "the teacher's voice can contribute to school policy essential knowledge that is available from no other source" (McDonald, 1987, p.31).

Aside from directly influencing the experts, this particular teacher group reached the power centers with their ideas. The teachers wanted the school district policymakers to listen to them for a change. The teachers' views were based on particular situations and could be stated, initially, as a story or parable. However, they later brought together anecdotes with theories so as to "use anecdotes to illuminate the insufficiency of anecdote just as the group was later to use theory to illuminate the insufficiency of theory" (McDonald, 1987, p. 34). Together with experts, they presented papers on policy matters to the public at large. From a discussion group, these high school teachers developed into and became a source of power; this is a much bolder stance than most of the teacher networks described in Chapter 3 would take.

PROGRESSIVE PROPHETS

As an attempt to realize new ideals within the existing power structure of education, educationists have made progressive education largely identical with reform. This is true only because a more drastic plan—vouchers or the deschooling movement—wants to replace or abolish the system, whereas more limited discipline-based plans only want to modify the existing curriculum (Whiteside, 1978). However, there is much more involved than a definition. There has been a constantly recurring circle of thinking that polarizes traditional and progressive education.

These polar positions are not always explicit. The differences can be hidden in the development of research studies, as in the study of educational change.

Neither elaborate analytical schemes nor longitudinal research has managed to escape the net of these polar positions (Mitchell, 1995). For some subjects, such as English or art, a progressive approach seems more effective; for others, such as mathematics or highly conceptual approaches, a more structured approach appears at basic levels to be superior. In general, progressive approaches involve more sociability and affective responses, whereas more traditional approaches include an apparent focus on character and school community (Mitchell, 1992). The more traditional Catholic schools and residential programs have been held out as models for public day schools.

The distinction between traditional and progressive education is almost religious in the ways it has engendered verbal symbols to which people are attached. The symbols can still be regarded as myths, but they are often more systematic than myths; as rational plans, they can be criticized from an outsider's point of view. These same symbols have limited the formulation of policy positions. Criticisms of the early reform movements in Kentucky and Chicago seem to have come from traditional educators, reinforced by extreme right-wing advocates. In other cases, more ideologically open advocates claim that only more progressive efforts have produced real improvements (Mitchell, 1996).

Sometimes the use of progressive and traditional positions becomes a center of major controversy, as in the work of an English scholar, Bennett (Strivens, 1980). Empowerment, as in the teacher story, is often interpreted from a progressive stance because both ideas are linked to progress or individual development rather than to the creation myth. More commonly, craftsmen versus bureaucratic teachers (Gracey, 1972) or transmission teachers versus interpretive teachers (Barnes & Shemilt, 1974) are in the mind of the writer just natural divisions, which they do not question in their study or argument. In unsuspecting places, like pupil deviancy from rules, one finds a distinction between coercion and incorporation, which is later characterized as "tradition, authoritarian coercion" versus "liberal, progressive incorporation" (Reynolds & Sullivan, 1979, p. 138).

Differences that are repeated are even more frequent in general theoretical positions or the writing about change. For example, even when the Progressive Education Association was going out of business, the theoretical sociologist, Talcott Parsons, made the difference between progressive and traditional education fundamental to his analysis of the school system (Mitchell, 1995). Though the terms continue to change, the literature on school change has advocates who insist that change is a process and that personally meaningful questions should be asked of students (Sarason, 1982). Research contrasts are developed between schools with an "overreaching" approach that includes alternatives and those with an "enforcing" scenario that focuses on information and organization (Huberman & Miles, 1982, p. 406).

In a general text on change, there is said to be a "tug of war of national proportions between intensification and restructuring advocates" (Fullan & Stiegelbauer, 1991, p.7). Intensification includes "increased definition . . . mandated . . . specification . . . and monitoring . . ." whereas restructuring means "many forms . . . enhanced roles . . . decision making . . . radical reorganization

Chart 5.1
Progressive Educators vs. More Traditional Educators

Progressive Syndrome

- Process emphasis and sociability practice.
- Reactive and polarized position from opponent.
- Less articulate about goals since react against the other.
- Individual and internalized concept of power.
- This power concept often reinforces moralism.
- Moralism is based on middle-class orgin and conservative policies.

Traditional Closure

- Product goals and frequent testing.
- Develops or rediscovers own original position.
- Within the defined discipline-based position, creativity is possible.
- Authority from society and organizations can guide individuals.
- Ideal of authority supports the status quo, but
- Options developed from aristocratic past, such as dialogue.

History

- Depression relates to tougher, more traditional position: 1890s, 1930s, and 1980s, but progressive stance, such as social constructionism in 1930s, can become more exteme.

- Economic expansion relates to broader and more expansive progressivism: periods before World I, after World War II, and the current period.

- Dominance of business and political challenge to the country support more traditional values: 1920s, Sputnik era, and present time.

- Status politics and style changes in society in general support modern, progressive position, but extreme right-wing positions become superconservatives, particularly when immigration increases.

Spheres of Influence
- Traditionalists are dominant in areas where accountability pressures are substantial: testing movement, basic education, and front-line administration that must relate to parents or politicians.

- Progressives are more involved in subjects and approaches where attitude or general change is emphasized, such as arts, special education, multicultural education or professional development. Portfolio testing has more support among progressives as does higher-level cognitive exams.

- Professional education, though dominated by progressivism, is complicated enough to confuse most outsiders and so influential that educators are isolated from even similar education for other professions. Very few mechanisms exist to relate professions to other groups, though this is changing.

Chart 5.1 (continued)

- The ideological differences relate to policy, but are less salient for those who are outside the inner circles of power and for the experts a particular position may be taken for granted unless a professional or political opponent attacks. During a different type of crisis, such as those involving race or drugs, this difference may be masked.

Limitations

- *Progressives* ignore power and often accept status difference within education, among students and within society. Teachers accept the general approach, but they need specific directions which include a consideration of power.

- *Traditionalists*, though directive, have been inconsistent in their interest in education, insensitive to school situations and willing to have dependency relationships develop with subordinates. The use of clearer components, concrete materials, and authoritative supports does not overcome the difficulty of seeing different meanings among individuals and at different levels of the system.

Interactions

- Some fields combine parts of both philosophies, such as experiential and structured approaches in French immersion or discovery learning even in the discipline-based approach of sciences. These could be a model for others.

- Approaches are usually alternating rather than institutionalized, which is what scientific and clinical medicine does. The advantage of counter power to correct or limit the excesses of the other needs to be realized. Debates can become a basis for considering innovations as part of a democratic process. Institutions, such as a loyal opposition or an independent judiciary, could be created for policy making and review.

- Change norms require more acceptance so that those most supporting innovations would be most accepted. Change itself must have more support than merely an act of faith. Ideological advocates need to be able to move away from the fringes. Advocates should be supported who combine ideological approaches as well as other polar positions, such as the insider and outsider perspectives.

- Advocates of either persuasion should broaden their position so that they are not so sectarian and professionally focused. Concern for students and social minorities could be expected together with a more direct political focus of a combined approach. However, political umbrellas may not make educational alternatives clear.

. . . new roles . . . and revamping and developing the shared mission" (Ibid). In the discussion of change, terms such as "reform," "renewal" or "monitoring" have long been used for more traditional approaches, whereas the slogans of "innovation," "change" or "process" have been reserved for a rather typical progressive position.

A more definitive position on this polar difference can come from an historical approach, which is tracked in Chart 5.2. The literature on evaluation and accountability is particularly suggestive:

> During periods when conservative ideas dominated, such as the 1920s, 1950s, and 1980s, efficiency and productivity were stressed. During periods when liberal values dominated, such as the 1900s, 1930s, and 1960s, access to educational opportunity was emphasized. (Steele, 1996, p. 12)

Educational opportunity was presumably stressed because the development of people could only be measured in the field by their inclusion in education. Progressive approaches are generally related to the expansion of education and optimism associated with periods of economic expansion, a reassertion of basic requirements, and structured approaches. Some issues, such as race, ethnic, and social class differences, have cut both ways. Greater diversity has led to demands for basic education, including demands in the United States for teaching or examining students only in English. However, racial differences were accepted by Dewey in *Schools of Tomorrow* (Dewey & Dewey, 1915), and English studies have shown progressive educators teaching the working class just as colonialists dominated the Natives in many places (Mitchell, 1995). Progressive educators' middle-class and dominant ethnic position has not usually led to them supporting a radical program; teachers who are educationally progressive have often been politically conservative.

The twin peaks of education are probably not influenced by any historical sense, and similar positions are maintained by similar reformers over different decades (Thompson, 1982; Sarason, 1971). For example, the problems of specific direction for general beliefs among progressives are repeated in the periods both before World War I and after 1968. Similarly, more discipline-based approaches showed little sensitivity to people and schools either after Sputnik or after the shrill report of *The Nation at Risk* in 1983 (Presseisen, 1985). The aim of finding approaches that were "teacher proof" was not made in the later period.

Neither researchers nor lay participants are consistent about their value positions. In fact, it seems that developing such consistency is itself a goal for education. Individuals can develop their ability to express experiences through language, symbols, and their own ideas. In situations that are very demanding, individuals develop a greater capacity to make decisions, including those about innovations. The teachers in Moraga have already illustrated this pattern. However, we need to know when and how individuals can integrate these two ideologies.

Adherents to the traditional position seem to give more attention to ideas than they do to people, power, or personality. Ideology is a reality for them that includes thinking as well as aims (Mitchell, 1996). Progressives frequently use analogies; Mr. Sprinter suggested that parents compare his diverse class to the order they would obtain in a party for a similar number of kids. Traditionalists often resort to parables to illustrate their ideas. Marva Collins compares the potential of Black males to the way Michelangelo saw a piece of marble, "an angel trying to get out" (O'Neal Mosley, 1993, p. 24). The two individuals differ on whether knowledge is relative or absolute. The extreme position to which one side or another goes may perhaps be reduced by greater contact with a variety of people. Mr. Sprinter was isolated as the only seriously progressive teacher in an English infant school of the 1970s, and Mrs. Collins endured isolation and suspicion for many years while teaching in the public schools.

As Marva Collins became more involved with organizations, she became less absolute. Aside from her four private schools, she became an contractor with the state of Oklahoma in a training program for teachers and a federal agency conducting a school in a housing project (Cohen, 1993). Now she talks about the ways that a teacher could be both progressive and traditional whereas, earlier she had attacked all progressive experts (O'Neal Mosley, 1993; Collins & Tamarkin, 1982). In the last two years she has been involved with planning the program for Chicago schools that have been placed on probation (Poe, 1997b). As a result of her involvement with a more conservative version of Chicago reform, perhaps her obsessive and self-centered nature has begun to mellow.

Though the career of Mr. Sprinter has not been reported, a similar progressive is Nancy Atwell who has been involved with teacher networks, writing projects, and her own private school. There has been an enormous evolution of Mrs. Atwell's thinking from a rebellious student who once said she wanted only to "marry my boyfriend, live in a trailer, and party" (Schultz, 1996, p. 219). An opportunity to attend college, and an English professor, Toby McLeod, who helped her to become an academic and whom she married, led to her being a creative English teacher. Her contacts remain with similar people and the model for classes is discussion at her home around the diningroom table with her family. However, when she opened the first of her private schools, she required teacher visitors to come in teams, sign a contract, write an essay, and get permission from their administrator in writing to make changes after their visits. If they were in more complicated settings, Nancy Atwell and Marva Collins might begin to talk; currently, they seem to have stopped reacting against stereotyped versions of the other's position.

In some subject areas there has always been overlap between the ideologies. Discovery learning in the sciences together with discipline knowledge has long been an overlap (Waring, 1979), but the use of the computer with the combination of analysis and surfing is another that has attracted the attention of historians, such as Larry Cuban who had doubted this possibility (Schmitt & Slonaker, 1996). In Chapter 6, we will follow the combinations developed by French immersion.

However, the curriculum is not as much a problem as is power. Either an "administrative progressive" or organizational man who would manipulate people and pretend to be meeting their needs is a more difficult problem (Tomkins, 1986). In fact, until the people doing the changing are doing as much learning as the students and teachers whom they propose to change, it will always be questionable whether any progress toward joint positions is being made. Research on undermanned settings suggests that under such difficult settings people think more of the task at hand, think about the contributions that others must make, and draw on their general skills to solve their horrendous problems (Sarason, 1982).

Though neither the acceptance of a lower level of admission and performance standards nor increased insecurity associated with undermanned settings is probably desirable, some use of both shock therapy and common demands for service seems to be necessary to overcome this philosophical feud.

The ideological separation does not seem to promote the modernization of education. Though the pursuit of the expert ideal has meant that education has often emulated medicine, it has not acquired the dynamic quality of this profession. In the nineteenth century, medicine combined scientific study with its older clinical tradition; the two types of medicine are still in opposition to each other (Jamous & Peloille, 1970). The conflict leads to new discoveries and organized procedures for the introduction of new approaches. In medicine, the norms of innovation have been so accepted that the earliest adopter of a change can often have the highest reputation and acceptance among his or her peers. Teachers do not show such acceptance of early adopters (McPherson, 1972). In fact, as far as innovations are concerned, the resentment of teachers is often only matched by the arrogance of experts (Wolcott, 1977).

STUDENTS AS OBJECTS

The experts and administrators keep control through manipulating and controlling other people. Unfortunately, this power orientation prevents them from learning to change. The same people who want to introduce changes "for the kids" want control primarily in schools (Mitchell, 1992, p. 47). Most reformers cannot decide whether they want to treat students as people; perhaps, similar to American slaves, students are only three-eighths human. The position of English progressives against working-class students has already been mentioned.

The strongest example of treating students as objects was found in a study of Chicago reformers, most of whom initially wanted progressive reforms (Diana Lauber, interview, November 11, 1993). Student members of the school council were reported to sit in the audience on occasion (Mitchell, 1996). A student leader, Philip Bleicher reported that his phone calls to the most important leader of an advocacy group were not returned. Bleicher believed that reformers were only interested in having students out as supporters in a meeting. Susan Herr, the editor of the student newspaper, *New Expression*, reported that reformers did not even believe in freedom of expression.

However, the most striking example of ignoring any relationship to students as people was revealed by a survey conducted by the consortium of universities and advocacy organizations in the Chicago area on students' reactions to reform (Mitchell, 1996). The thinking of students was not sought in the survey or as advisors on the survey. The reaction of students was only asked for in forced-answer questions; the students were treated as subjects who might add a little information to the course of reform. It is important to realize that Chicago students have been extremely active in forming an advocacy organization, the Student Alliance, publishing a newspaper with 80,000 copies a month, and, in the past, conducting their own survey of the school system. The surveys students have conducted show an artistic interest and are much more open, interesting, and goal oriented than that of the reformers. Reformers have assumed students were only able to make a very limited contribution in their survey. On the form, a large pencil pointed to the answers that students were supposed to choose!

In other centers of educational reform, student leaders are treated in a more paternalistic manner. In Kentucky, student leaders are asked to speak on behalf of reform and their opinions are published (Mitchell, 1996). In Alberta, though the government has ignored the students' voices in developing new policies, for several years the local Calgary newspaper helped them publish their own version of that paper, which, in turn, carried stories about student reactions to educational change. For a number of years, the Chicago newspaper, *Catalyst*, tried paying students to contribute.

Among the institutional experts, there are a few, such as Ted Sizer, who have argued for extending the privilege of participation in school governance to students. None have argued that students have a right to be involved in change decisions. Louis Gerstner has endorsed the practice of bringing students together in a day-long seminar to think about their education. The students were harder on themselves than anyone else; specifically they wanted:

an end to bonehead courses and mindless vocational courses. They were convinced that all students should be held to the same high standards. They called for an end to tracking. Instead, they argued that course completion should be determined by mastery, not time served, and that prerequisites should be met before advanced courses were taken. (Gerstner, et al., 1994, pp. 195-196)

Not everyone sees students as wanting progressive policy changes. One academic, Michael Fullan, has continued to see student response as indicated by: "(1) indifference (2) confusion, (3) temporary escape from boredom, and (4) heightened interest and engagement with learning and school" (Fullan & Stiegelbauer, 1991, p. 182). Nothing like the activities found in Chicago or other centers of student activism is suggested. An earlier criticism I had made of Fullan's position has been ignored (Mitchell, 1995). Students can be activists, people with ideas about school changes and future staff associates for reform.

CULTURE SHOCK

If institutional experts may require a shock to develop a more open position toward students, teachers have often been highly pressured by administrators to adopt innovations. In the Network study, teachers report that administrative pressure was over thirty times more frequent as a reason for undertaking an innovation than was the goal of problem solving (Loucks, et al., 1982). Administrative pressure that included strong-arming as well as persuasion was critical in getting teachers out of their daily mold (Huberman & Miles, 1982). In the same study, multiple roles for external consultants and the associated work that this entailed for them led to increased social support, work variety, new ideas, and opportunities for self development.

The transformation of any group is a social and cultural experience. As discussed earlier, reformers often work in pairs, whereas traditional teachers often rely upon teaching friends or relatives for advice (Mitchell, 1966). More recently, as stated in Chapter 3, teacher networks have emerged as a significant source for the distillation and spread of innovations. The writing project will later be discussed as a model for networking; a model that has been extended to many other teachers in different subject areas, particularly in California.

In addition, there is evidence for continuing support for innovative teachers by expert sponsors. In Chicago, for example, Bill Ayers has a number of protégés who have either started schools or been involved in them, such as Lynn Cherkasky-Davis who helped found the progressive Foundations School (Meyers & McIssac, 1994, p.88). The fiercely independent Marva Collins reports she was initially encouraged by a principal who was educated in the classics and has later been supported by the business reformer, Joe Kellman (Collins & Tamarkin, 1982; Mitchell, 1996). Nancy Atwell has always had the support of her academic husband, Toby McLeod.

In spite of these many supports, the scene for innovations is the individual school, and it is in the local school that teachers report experiences that strongly resemble culture shock. Others have referred to this phenomena as a combination of ambiguity and challenge, apparently for individuals alone (Fullan & Stiegelbauer, 1991). Culture shock involves sharp breaks from accepted cues and previously shared symbols. For the experienced teacher it is often like learning to teach all over again. Change is initially experienced very positively, similar to a tourist exploring a new country. However, like the tourists, teachers become aware of the differences between the new country and their more familiar land and get angry. Indeed, raising one's voice without realizing it is one of the first symptoms of culture shock, but later the victim is affected by extreme fatigue (Fuchs, 1969).

The later stages of culture shock can involve some alternatives. People can withdraw to be with those most like themselves or they can, supposedly more in the case of future shock, strike out in anger against those who either cause their problems or are seen as the scapegoat for them (Toffler, 1970). Teachers often appear to take the withdrawal route as they react with disbelief, resentment, and hidden fury against the experts (Cusick, 1983). As change develops, two or three different paths are often shown on flow charts of effects. From changing one's classroom repertoire, either relational changes and attitude changes occur or the emphasis on understanding and role or professional concepts change; a third route is discussed in the section on hierarchy.

Individual cases show the school effect as clearly differing between traditional and progressive innovations. At Masepa, a "highly regimented and task oriented behavior modification teaching strategy" developed for teaching language arts was produced, with scripts from grade one to grade nine (Huberman & Miles, 1982, p. 57). Since other mechanical approaches by the teachers, such as teaching grammar, had to be changed, many teachers had to adapt to a totally new experience. Most found it complicated and difficult to understand; the program was an "It" and they kept "falling down and getting up" or "getting wiped out every day" (Ibid, p. 263). After six weeks, the teachers sensed they were "getting the basics" and "being there;" as the program stabilized they were driving the car and it was one of "my own things" (Ibid).

In contrast, teachers in schools with progressive innovations failed to experience the same sense of closure and were often exhausted by the symptoms of what is called "burnout." The more open schools did not become stabilized, as occurred with traditional schools. The greater teacher involvement in progressive schools has often meant that teachers overreach what is attainable; they make increasing attempts to get the programs in tune with students or to individualize programs while also attempting to find shortcuts because of the time demands involved in relating to so many different students. From our initial description of Mr. Sprinter, many of these problems could have been anticipated.

A HIERARCHY THAT STARTS WITH THE CLASSROOM

Creative teachers are increasingly held in check by the structured approaches of school administration. Current staff training practices reinforce teachers' working under the hegemony of administrators. For the past twenty years, programs developed by administrators for guiding teachers through specific innovations have used the literature on teachers' levels of concern (Anderson, 1981). The levels of concerns approach is one part of the Concerns-Based Adoption Model discussed in Chapter 2, but it is more widely applied than the other elements: the levels of use and the innovation's fidelity in use.

Administrators often work with teachers' personal concerns about how an innovation will affect their day long before discussing the innovation's philosophy. The mechanics of the innovation are then developed between personal needs and program philosophy. The programs interestingly assume that there is a hierarchy of concerns, even if most teachers never get beyond the middle level of the hierarchy. Such a hierarchy parallels the limited achievements of teachers for whom being stuck in the middle level of bureaucracies often makes their lives very mechanical or managerial. School improvements based on the concerns literature have led to teacher evaluation efforts as well as inservice educational programs. It is possible to know that a brief program will not have proceeded beyond personal awareness; three years would be required for teachers or others to be at the middle level of the hierarchy as a whole (Hall & Hord, 1987).

This approach is biased because it assumes that only a cooperative, process alternative to be considered while ignoring an individualistic, results emphasis. The early work on team teaching perhaps led to this bias. Though influenced by the levels of concern research, the Network study, one of the largest samples of innovations, suggests a somewhat more balanced series of alternatives. The first step in this hierarchy involves changes in everyday practices and routines; these practices include either more self-directed individual activity or more structured

Chart 5.2
User Change During Implementation

1. Changes in everyday classroom organization
More individualization or more individual contact
Pupils more "in charge" or self-directed or self-paced
Less time for other activities; other subjects driven out
More accountable to outsiders; sense of being more policed
Less structure, less prearrangement
More structure; increased regimentation
Multiple materials, no longer one resource
No longer able to monitor whole class
Changes in scheduling

2. Repertoire expansion
Ability to individualize or differentiate
More 'meat' in curriculum or more approaches to call on
Greater skill in diagnostic or testing procedures

3. Relational changes
Closer to pupils or more concern for pupils
Closer to other teacher team
More egalitarian relationships with pupils

4. Better understanding or comprehension
Actual ability or skill levels of pupils
Emotional problems of pupils
How the school system operates and who has influence
Principles and procedures for mastery learning

5. Self-efficacy
More resourceful or effective
More self-confident
Either less energy, low investment, or burnout

6. Transfer
More organized in general or better at planning specifically
Using same skills or procedures in other subjects

7. Changes in attitudes
Able to trust pupils more or less need for control

8. Changes in professional self-image
Myself as a teacher

approaches where the teacher was more accountable. For people in schools, innovations are an individual stripping process slowly joined with concerns for social relationships and professional functions (Chart 5.2). When teachers see their actual classroom practices change, they often feel naked.

However, if this process continues, the same people expand their personal repertoire of teaching approaches. If they have been more traditional in using structured, whole class teaching, they become more progressive and use less tailored group activities. Yet teachers develop closer and more egalitarian social relationships with students and other teachers as they experience innovations. The relational changes are, at times, negative: One teacher told a student objecting to a new career education program, "The hell with what you want, I'm 32, you're 17" (Huberman & Miles, 1982, p. 256). Interestingly, teachers' understanding of how learning occurs includes knowledge of how power is exercised; for them, understanding learning means knowing how things actually work.

With practical understanding, an awareness of social relationships, and an expanded skill range, teachers assume control of innovations rather than succumb to them. Teachers' self-efficacy improves their ability to transfer skills between innovations and their attitude toward their pupils becomes more positive. Consequently, teachers' professional image is transformed. However, studies show that most teachers working with innovations do not get beyond the matter of social relationships, the third step.

In a larger sample of innovation sites, many of these same patterns are found, but alternative routes are suggested (Mitchell, 1992). Three routes to change emerge from the numbers listed in Chart 5.2. The progressive pattern of combining relationships (3) and attitudes (7) is one route while correlating understanding (4) and role of professional image (8) is another; a repertoire expansion is linked to both of these alternatives. However, a third path is shown, direct force rather than either form of authority. A more direct concern for power is also linked to repertoire, but follows more directly from administrative pressure and a specific attitude toward innovation which in turn ties in with efficacy (5) and transfer (6). The process is one whereby self-efficacy develops and makes possible a transfer of the innovations to other subjects or tasks (Huberman & Miles, 1982).

These three alternatives are further supported by a case study of different types of progressive and traditional teachers who were not anticipated; teachers made demands on students without any justification (Metz, 1979). The three kinds of individually guided instruction cases discussed in Chapter 2 would correspond if symbolic changes result from organizations controlling the use of force. The legitimate use of force is a realistic alternative whether teachers, administrators, or legislators are considered; unauthorized power can be used by crowds of parents, students or anyone else to bring about changes in the system. Chart 5.3 shows that, at every stage, force and the basis for understanding alternatives must be built into any use of the levels of concern approach.

In most cases, culture shock occurs from pressure asserted by administrators; this pressure leads to an awareness of the individual innovation. One's own power and ability to control an innovation are related to the personal stage, particularly as an individual's confidence has been enhanced or diminished by experiences with previous innovations. The management stage is influenced by feedback from students and support from administrators as well as the ability to control an innovation rather than be controlled by it. Another theorist has referred to these

Chart 5.3
A New Look at the Stages of Concern

Internal Developments	External Influences
Refocusing	Individual's previous change experiences, field independence, and creativity.
Collaboration—Force—Competition	Effects of incentive system on individual schools, teachers, or students, but internalized goals are more important.
Consequences	Perception of effects, relating personal and public worlds and different types of knowledge drawn upon.
Management	Feedback from students, parents, or administrators when person is in control of the innovation.
Personal and Information Stages	Success with other innovations, costs and benefits of this change, and perception of own power.
Awareness	Culture shock

developments as the "survival" stage (Nemser, 1983). Survival is said to include administrators persuading teachers of the innovation's benefits, feedback on the development of new roles, and time for the innovation. Direct incentives and punishments will more directly affect the teachers who have ignored the life force of ideology. Pursuing collaboration is only one of three alternatives suggested.

All of these alternatives are dependent upon the individuals' understanding of the field, the ways they can articulate their position, the integration of themselves with a policy position, and their view of knowledge. For example, Mr. Sprinter views knowledge relatively, related his family experiences to school, and has difficulty articulating his position abstractly. Marva Collins believes that there are absolute values and understandings that her students must acquire; she has separate expectations for her family members even when they work in the school and, in many highly publicized ways, this opinionated woman has imprinted her position on the public. In a typical public school, Mr. Sprinter and Mrs. Collins would both find themselves very isolated; they are extreme representations of these two important ideals.

The bias against one of these standards, traditional education, is altered by the reformulation of levels of concern shown in Chart 5.3. The original research attempted to jump from the study of beginning teachers to innovations involved team teaching and was based primarily on people relationships (Heck, et al., 1981). Highly structured innovations or technologically based changes require a consideration of a discipline and the way that subject is presented. It is striking that in mathematics, as opposed to reading, this research does not follow a simple linear pattern (Hall & Hord, 1987). The pursuit of the two more internalized options will be dependent upon their understanding of the reform's conceptual base, opportunities for rehearsal, administrative support, and clarity of the goals and teaching standards. The preparation required for options has been called a "consolidation stage" by Nemser.

The individual's own power and understanding are required for them to redevelop the innovation or refocus it. Individuals can skip stages or even move between innovations if their creativity, confidence, and previous experience make it possible for them to attempt such a hazardous jump. It is exactly the perception of this possibility that most distinguishes the experts from laypeople; they think laws and stages are for other people (Seeley, et al., 1956). The gap between determinism and freedom can be overcome by a specification of the learning involved. The stage of mastery is said to require conceptual learning so teachers will relate the project's practices to its principles. In addition, "mastery" requires technical assistance, time and resources, and a lack of overwhelming competition (Elmore & McLaughlin, 1988, pp. 45-46). The average teacher experiences three innovations simultaneously and some have to juggle as many as ten experiments altogether (Levine & Leibert, 1987). The work on undermanned settings is again highly relevant for teachers who struggle to develop mastery over a particular innovation (Sarason, 1982).

Most teachers, librarians, or principals have not gone beyond the middle level of the stage sequence (Anderson, 1981). Probably less than 10 percent of teachers have gone on to the refocusing stage if this stage resembles studies of outstanding or creative teachers. Generally, the teachers, like many other groups, are fragmented in their approaches to innovations. Certainly, progressive teachers are limited in developing their approaches even in schools that claim to be creative (Gracey, 1972; Berlak & Berlak, 1981). Mr. Sprinter is the only strong and consistent example of such a teacher in a model English infant school.

The difficulties of developing a consistent, articulate, and ideological view of change are substantial. Compared to individuals in such movements as Poland's Solidarity, there is no evidence that groups of teachers develop different conceptions of society (Touraine, et al., 1980). However, it is the fragmented and isolated pattern of teachers' lives, particularly the shortage of time for the many tasks, that makes broader conceptions very unlikely (Sarason, 1982). The story, discussed earlier, of teachers who originally met around pizza suggests how teachers can acquire a voice and a vision that is theoretical.

A BROADER VISION: INTEGRATED SERVICES

Specific demands on teachers and schools have led to programs to prepare students for school, activities before and after school to avoid latchkey children, and social supports for adolescents to avoid gangs, drugs, and fights. For the experts, these demands can be organized as part of "integrated" services. Such services have represented a major progressive influence, which has attempted to provide one-stop service of social and medical services schools (Mitchell, 1996). Though attacked at times by the extreme right-wing, conservative educators have not usually opposed them, perhaps because these services appeared to address the needs of at-risk students. Integrated services relate to students as clients and have all the problems of progressive-era experts trying to practice in today's schools.

Most members of school communities use such services without supporting their purposes. Students see such services as a safer place to socialize than more academic turf; the same services are largely ignored by traditional teachers because they do not relate directly to their teaching tasks. Where family centers have been created on a wide-scale, as in Kentucky, parents have accepted them; coordinators primarily handle emergency situations for some of them. Similarly, administrators have seen such centers as a convenient place to deposit their more serious student problems. All groups seem to view such centres as a separate and segregated program that does not disturb the school routine too much.

Teachers as well as other professionals follow a narrow and winding road in attempting to maintain their own autonomy. Teachers, guidance counselors, and social workers are among the better known specialists who increasingly work with schools (Sarason, 1982). Each of these groups, as well as many lesser known ones such as speech specialists, is separated from the others by the walls of professional autonomy. Teachers' concern for the general abstractions of academic learning highlights the difference between them and social workers, who are much more concerned with the particular context of family and neighborhood (Tyler, 1988).

Integrated services bring these differences inside the schools. Without the support of both kinds of professionals, only very modest steps are made toward the involvement of students or parents, particularly for early childhood and elementary education. The Comer schools, where parents have become a part of the governance systems, are the best known example of parental involvement with individual schools (Comer, 1993). However, it is Comer's colleague at Yale, Edward Zigler, who appears to have had the greatest current impact (Zigler & Finn-Stevenson, 1989). Zigler, whose current work is with the Schools of the Twenty-First Century, is one of the founders of Head Start. Zigler's ideas about changing service to young children and their families do not involve any serious change in school governance.

The Zigler effort includes programs within schools as well as outreach services from schools. The new program of child care within schools includes all-day, year-round care for children, ages three to five, from early in the morning to early evening and child care before and after school and during vacations for school children, ages five to twelve for extended hours. The outreach services include home visits from the third trimester of pregnancy until the children are three years old, a network of advice and resources for babysitters (family day care providers), and a referral service for all families in the community so that they can find quality child care. Particularly with new efforts for developing nutrition and health knowledge, the Zigler program provides a complete approach to family centers. The Zigler proposal appears to have been followed by a number of Canadian efforts, such as Better Beginnings Better Futures in Ontario (Mitchell, 1996).

A parallel effort to Zigler's work has been initiated by and has had more symbolic acceptance by the school system. The concept of a caring community appears to directly involve student-teacher relationships in a way that integrated services does not; a number of school systems now describe themselves as caring communities (Steele, 1996). The general concept has been advocated by feminists, conservatives who want the school community to replace narcissistic beliefs, and those concerned with children who experience urban crises (Viadero, 1996a). The specific program offered by the Development Studies Center in Oakland, California, teaches values together with reading and mathematics. It teaches students conflict resolution, provides parents a simple program for involvement with schools and their children, and sells teachers and schools an abundance of materials and consulting services.

If integrated services is a one-stop service, the Development Studies Center is a shopping center where all of one's innovation needs can be met. The large number of tapes, curriculum materials, and books that it distributes cover innovation, cooperative education, conflict resolution, parent participation, professional development, and specific subject areas. It has been adopted by the National Alliance for Restructuring Education as a model program, supported by a host of foundations and highly publicized by all the educational media including *Education Week*. Added emphasis is being secured by creating its own network, Cornerstones. The first conference for Cornerstones was co-sponsored by the Comer and Ziegler group as well as other national and local reform groups and their institutional entrepreneurs. The original writer on the caring community theme, Nel Noddings, was present at the start of Cornerstones, as was a smiling expert, Ann Lieberman.

The general theme has become so pervasive that a number of urban school systems, such as Calgary, now describe themselves as being dedicated to a vision of creating a caring community. Comer schools now describe themselves as "caring communities" (Teaching K-8, 1992). Statistically, the Cornerstones network is still small. Only two hundred people attended the first conference and a mere eleven schools in eight school districts have tried the approach across the country. Beginning in 1981, the original experimental programs were in San Ramon and Hayward, in the Bay Area of California. In 1991, additional programs were begun in Jefferson County, Kentucky; Cupertino, Salinas, and San Francisco, California; Dade Country, Florida; and White Plains, New York.

Compared to many other networks, the caring network is very small, but it claims to have the best research in support of its efforts. The network led by Ted

Sizer has over eight hundred schools affiliated with the Coalition of Essential Schools and has an extensive research program, which will be discussed in Chapter 9. The teacher networks discussed in Chapter 3 are much larger than Cornerstones and focused more on curriculum development than research. After being selected in 1981 by the Hewlett Foundation to change the ethical and social behavior of children, the Developmental Studies Center undertook a thorough review of literature from child development and cognitive psychology (Viadero, 1996a).

Later, under the leadership of Eric Schaps, the center carried out controlled studies of its new program. The most positive results are in the original site, San Ramon, where even into junior high, students from the program were continuing to show effects on their attitudes and involvement in extracurricular activities; there were no differences from the control groups on standardized achievement tests, although program students did better in a test of higher order thinking abilities. The results are consistent with the findings of other progressive education projects over many decades as well as more recent work in cognitive psychology (Mitchell, 1995).

As has been generally true of progressive approaches, the leaders of this center engage in striking cases of reasoning by analogy, including their literature and mathematics projects. Though attributing the remark to a sage, three of the caring prophets stress the importance of intrinsic motivation by saying that children should be rewarded for eating pizzas rather than getting a pizza for reading a book (Lewis, et al., 1996). In another example, to put off a parent who questioned the values being taught, Sheila Koshews, the district coordinator in Kentucky, says:

We would tell them: 'If your child drops a box of crayons, wouldn't you want someone to care enough to help your child pick them up and not kick them away?' People are not going to argue with that. (Viadero, 1996a, p. 104)

Values are often taught as if they were a part of science; "universal values" taught from quality literature by "synthesis, inference and hypothesis testing" (Developmental Studies Center, 1995).

In a project supported by the National Science Council for the new mathematic standards, the reality of numbers and social attitudes are intermingled (Viadero, 1996a). Numbers rather than the external world are said to be real so that students develop a "number sense" based upon "children's fluidity and flexibility with numbers." Each unit in the series, *Cooperative Mathematics Project*, published by Addison Wesley, begins with a team builder exercise so that the children get to know members of their group better and concludes with activities to help students reflect upon achievements in both mathematics and group interaction. It would be interesting to find out what happens when such students encounter different number or mathematical systems in a room of strangers!

The caring project has been particularly supported by the county in Kentucky because the state-wide changes were so drastic that this or another packaged program tended to be accepted (Viadero, 1996a). This package is one of many that California groups have been developing together with the leading experts on change. It is for this reason that California was mentioned, in Chapter 4, as the best example of the pattern for creating curriculum innovations in education. Two other examples, which have also been strongly supported in Kentucky for similar reasons, the National Writing Program and the Galef Institute's program of art integration, will be discussed in Chapter 6.

THE ART OF THE POSSIBLE

Any integration of progressive and traditional educational approaches will occur in the context of what is currently correct. In the abstract, practice is unlikely to be affected by the best program. The caring project is similar to the work and education program advocated by business in that it combines a number of different themes that are currently in demand (Gerstner, et al., 1994). Businesspeople stress parent and student involvement while claiming they are proposing organizational principles for schools, not merely business ideas. Any better program must combine choice, parental involvement, community, and competitive advantage to mention just a few that may be a logically absurd combination, but which represent a program that is currently acceptable. A new program must stress its appeal to the whole community, not just special interests.   Aside from direct appeals, a new and integrated position must start to take advantage of the unintended or unanticipated consequences of innovations. Generally, probably because of conflict between the positions of teachers and change agents, innovations boomerang, such as teachers erecting barriers in the open areas planned by experts. When teachers or another group are empowered, they may articulate their own vision and rise above the level of simple resistance. However, before the development of ideological responses, teachers can find common ground with experts in the leagues, networks, and direct social encounters that occur among participants.

With little initial commitment by those involved, the most significant effect of innovation has often been the formation of school leagues initiated to discuss and implement research findings (Lieberman & Miller, 1984). More recently, a large number of networks to support innovations has emerged; they are just beginning to develop new traditions or sagas, which appear to characterize the earliest leagues. For example, the first large-scale study of innovations by Paul Mort led to the formation of a school council in New York, New Jersey, and Connecticut. Increasingly, a common cause was sought in a writing consortium and a new computer group. The association initiated by Mort has since led to a combination of practice and research beneficial to both teachers and researchers (Lieberman & Miller, 1984).

The leagues also provide opportunities to get beyond set roles. Describing the evolution of the most famous network, The League of Co-operating Schools, a key participant says, "The 'experts' learned the limits of their expertise. All of us were experts from one time or another" (Lieberman & Miller, 1984, p. 131). In this case, informal sharing evolved from a stage at which experts gave authoritative formal luncheon talks to another stage of information sharing and social support in sessions to which everyone came with bag lunches.

The merging of teachers with experts could be a model for teachers to become organized as a social movement. The acquisition of power can enhance the importance of a position. Without power, the hierarchy of concerns is probably going to lead at most from alienation or passive resistance to the common ground of social support and progress from there, in turn, possibly to ideological alternatives. Administrative manipulation and the levels of the current school organization can promote the movement from acquaintance and personal concerns to managerial interests and possibly on to rethinking the innovation's goals. The new movement can overcome either set of options by bringing the individual and the innovation together, finding a common front among interests and ideologies, and developing a shared vision that affects everyone in the school.

Like Marva Collins and Mr. Sprinter, there must be an increase in social networks and a practice of policy decisions before a vision that in more than one way emerges. On most issues, there is neither a dialogue nor any form of collaboration evident among researchers, community members, and teachers (Noddings, 1987). A variety of other networks makes clear that experts are involved so as to encourage the exchange of ideas, the emergence of a common identity, and a new sense of purpose. Like the League of Co-operating Schools, these other efforts must show experts and laypersons maintaining less of a front with each other. The increased social distance separates institutional experts from ordinary people. Many more cases of teacher stories emerging over pizza need to be found so that the balance to summits can be found. Ideology for teachers is still too much of a personal experience and not enough of a social and political reality.

The process of innovation must become educational in order to link the individual teacher, strengthen the leadership at the school level, and crisscross between the organizations that affect school policy. The unanticipated result of innovation research leading to activity among experts and teachers is in contrast to the usual lack of dialogue between researchers and subjects. The lack of such collaboration is one reason why educational research has been argued to be so "uneducational" (Noddings, 1987, p. 394). Researchers have assumed a rational and empirical reality and have blamed teachers for becoming too adjusted to their individual perches (Mitchell, 1992). The researchers who have tried to defend teachers have proclaimed that a more personal and relative concept of knowledge is needed to free teachers, often female, from the oppression of dominantly male experts. It is, however, striking that concern for commitment among teachers and reactions against the excellence movement with its mechanistic assumptions have not led to a teacher movement displaying many of the characteristics of the high school teachers' group discussed earlier. Teachers need more than to hoist the red flag to establish their independence.

Involvement with the social forces challenging power in society does not immediately bring about the merger of individual, professional, and social concerns resulting in the formation of collaborating groups among teachers. In fact, in talking about the transforming quality of a social movement, writers on education, such as Maxine Green, are led to citing the resistance movement in France, for example, rather than progressive movements within education (Lieberman & Miller, 1979). Education needs more myths, sagas, and traditions of its own; such traditional supports will make possible the evolution of change rather than its opposite. Inspirations for charismatic teachers at the local level are particularly needed to counter the dominance of institutional experts at the national and international levels. The creation myth can lead to more active parties rather than the dream of progress that touches and changes the few. Rather than ignoring teachers who primarily use force with students, we can establish standards that allow for alternative forms of authority and that prevent the abuse of authority by any teacher. New visions for students as well as teachers can be grasped, as in the following case of a student speaking about his new peer mediation experience in a Calgary elementary school:

Being a mediator is a pretty hard job, not just the problems, but the responsibility and your emotions. All the mediators at this school are grade fours. We are a mixture of boys and girls and most of us like our job. We all take turns going out on the playground with our partner. What we do is walk around the playground looking for children doing things they are not supposed to or crying or things like that. The hardest thing is when you get a problem involving one of your friends. Your natural instinct is to take their side but you can't do that. You have to listen to both sides. Maybe even, your friend did do something wrong. You have to control your emotions too, like if you're frustrated, keep that inside your head. (Gulbrandsen, 1997, p. 7)

Chapter 6

Exemplars

As such it [French Immersion] attracted international attention and was described by one American researcher as probably the most successful language teaching program ever devised. (Tomkins, 1986, p. 337)

School site-based and participatory decision-making may well be the single most significant educational reform effort of this century. (Phillips, 1993, p. vii)

Today the National Writing Project is the most successful teacher-oriented innovation ever developed. (Mitchell, 1996, p. 185)

Perhaps the evident widespread and growing interest in *Different Ways of Knowing* is rooted in just the sense of flexibility and local determination. (Catterall, 1995, p. 11)

Though there are many claims to divine status among educational programs, the best programs are only outstanding in certain respects. French immersion has found an ecological niche in Canada among the middle class (Canadian Education Association, 1983). Site-based management has influenced managerial decisions in an increasing number of schools, but classroom instruction generally has not been influenced by it at all (Robertson, 1997). In spite of support by the federal government in the United States, the National Writing Project has not spread to as many sites as expected by the legislation (Mitchell, 1996). Different Ways of Knowing, a general program now focused on the arts by the Galef Institute, has not spread beyond elementary schools and has been rejected by art educators in several larger cities, such as Chicago (Jackie Murphy, interview, May 15, 1996).

Repeatedly, all large-scale innovations have been shown to be inferior to many small innovations, which teachers and others have found are better adapted to their local situations (Pauly, 1991). Ideology and publicity almost inevitably draw attention to model programs. Three of the programs, together with similar programs, were cited in a list by the conservative Secretary of Education, William Bennett, in *What Works* (United States Department of Education, 1986). More recently, the Clinton administration has requested support for successful innovations for poor students and has cited four specific large-scale programs, but smaller changes are not mentioned (Hoff, 1997c, September). Though smaller changes have been associated with these models, these large-scale programs are linked to experts and broadly organized positions. Each of the programs discussed, attempts to change the entire school or its curriculum; none are additions or marginal activities. The specific programs discussed in this chapter are linked to experts and are highly publicized and ideological; though ranging from conservative to progressive, the ideologies of each program include combinations of both external knowledge and justifications as well as group involvement and commitment. For this and other reasons, each of these programs has had its legitimacy challenged initially and has only enjoyed a measure of acceptance later.

THE PROFESSIONAL DIRECTION OF FRENCH IMMERSION

As French separatism developed in Quebec, both experts and parents became alarmed and developed an alternative to ensure at least continued communication between the two founding language groups in Canada (Tomkins, 1986). The experts came from McGill, which is the dominant English university in Quebec, and the parents from a middle-class English suburb of Montreal, St. Lambert, which was a part of the most important Anglophone cluster in this province. The international experts from McGill were Dr. Wilder Penfield, famous for his work on the brain and language, who claimed that the brain made possible the learning of language at an earlier age, and Dr. Wallace Lambert, a social psychologist, who argued that French immersion could be an alternative to separatism (Lambert & Taylor, 1984). The immersion program would begin with kindergarten and be extended upward in the system, but the argument that this program would be an alternative to separatism would disappear from the writing of Dr. Lambert and the linguists who came to dominate the field.

When the program first began in 1965, the interest of the parents was the place of their English speaking children in an increasingly French society. In St. Lambert, as well as later in other communities, a core group of active parents started the program, but they felt the need to persuade others. The concerns of uncommitted parents were how well their children would learn French under the conditions of a second language as the means of instruction in regular school subjects, how well these subjects would be learned, and how adequately the English language would continue to be learned. These concerns led to a wide-scale research program, which has generally supported the approach (Cummins & Swain, 1986).

For dominant groups such as the English, the second language was additive and not subtractive as it had been for most minorities who sought acceptance in their new society. The parents in the original sites as well as in the other parts of Canada became organized into the Canadian Parents for French (Mitchell, 1996). This organization became an effective lobbying group at both the federal and provincial levels and received federal support. When education was undergoing another crisis, fiscal restraint in Alberta, the obvious cost cutting possibility of eliminating this alternative program was not pursued, although the government considered it in its initial Roundtable meetings (Mitchell, 1996). The costs of bilingual education appear to be 10 percent higher than regular programs, primarily because of the higher costs of recruiting teachers (Getty, 1987). For most areas, the federal government has provided grants that cover most of the costs, but the accounting procedures of school boards consistently confuse the amounts involved and for what they are spent. However, the Canadian Parents for French has had an important role in protecting the programs and their financial support at both the federal and provincial level (Poyen, 1989).

From the moment their children enter immersion, studies and reports are regularly given to all parents in the program, such as *So, You're Worried About Becoming an Immersion Parent* (Gibson, n.d.); parents will find a large number of research studies reprinted and available to them. Those who become actively involved have an opportunity to meet with the leading Canadian linguists who usually initiated major curriculum innovations, such as whole language in the 1980s (Poyen, 1989). Parents have developed to the point that they can question the linguistic experts, and their meetings appear to represent one of the most effective links between laypeople and professionals. However, parents are also exposed to cross pressures between the English and the bilingual programs. The bilingual programs were often added to schools only when enrollment in a regular program was declining and not all parents in the regular program want to lose their school or accept a bilingual program as a partner with their regular program. Increases in regular enrollment are starting to create new problems even for schools totally immersed as "language centers" rather than an optional program.

As an option, the bilingual program is often partnered with an English program. The original formalization of the plan occurred at the end of the 1960s when alternative routes were a common solution to parental pressures for either progressive education or a more traditional route (Sussman, 1977, pp. 202-204). The actual immersion program includes many experiential activities, which have more recently been carried over in an attempt to reform second language instruction of French in English classrooms, the National Core French Study. For example, a National Film Board video asks students to find their way with French only signs in a famous Montreal amusement site. Though many techniques that are employed are student-centered, systematic approaches are also used, such as a correction supplement to whole language (Canadian Education Association, 1992, p. 15). The communicative approach that has dominated French immersion is being replaced by a language approach that emphasizes experience, learning strategies, and explicit cultural teaching in an integrated way (Yvonne Hébert, personal communication, September 29, 1997).

Many immersion classes are full of progressive activities. Beginning students are encouraged to act out concepts; the technique of "total physical response," making a surprised face, for example, represents the word "surpris" in oral French (Viadero, 1991). Class activities can include visits to bakeries, museums, and ranches, which may represent attempts to overcome the linguistic dominance in the students' education; the arts might be a supplement that could be more systematically developed. Cooperative programs, small group instruction, and active learning are reportedly used (Canadian Education Association, 1992).

The immersion program has a substantial structure and, even though students do not often begin studying English until grade three, the evidence is that they rapidly equal the language achievements of other students. The general accomplishment of immersion students has been substantial, but parents who were involved with the program wanted to be certain that their children were not falling behind others (Lambert & Taylor, 1984). In American terms, these schools would equal the best of their magnet schools, but they have, at times, introduced strong divisions within communities (Mitchell, 1992). The academic achievements of the bilingual program are perhaps best illustrated by the creation of the bilingual diploma of the International Baccalaureate at the high school level. Ironically, the regular French classes at either the high school or the university have not always been upgraded to reflect the increased competency of students in grammar and general communication.

The students' own views of their experiences have not generally been sought, though students' achievements in St. Lambert as well as across Canada have been studied and compared with others in many parts of the world. As a study of bilingual education in Wales suggests, it is the demands the curriculum makes and the discipline that is maintained in the schools, not the language instruction, that continues to attract parents to such a program (Cummins & Danesi, 1990). In most cases, this eclectic approach has worked for students who are supportive of French immersion as compared to other alternatives for learning the language (Cummins & Swain, 1986).

One of the most interesting answers as to why the program works with students is the finding that students must pay much closer attention to instruction because of the different language (Morrison, et al., 1986). Any language would presumably have the same effect, but the study skills developed for learning the language are substantial in the early elementary grades. In addition, students need to acquire substantial experience in a French community and, until they have such a period of exposure, understandably lack confidence in their French speaking ability. Without such extended living experiences, immersion graduates do little reading in French and do not seek out opportunities to use French (Edwards, 1984). Success in school was expected to require supplements, and a federal exchange program was provided for the student's airfare to Quebec.

Moreover, the creation of late immersion in the junior high school, which in Calgary rapidly showed French achievements equal to those who had French since kindergarten, does suggest that not enough is done to maintain student interest in the program. Students should have continued their progress (Mitchell, 1992) and the extent to which late immersion students can catch up with those who have studied it since kindergarten seems to reflect the distractions of adolescent interests and the expectation of administrators and parents, unsupported by research evidence, that success will be more easily attained in English. It is probably for similar reasons that substantial numbers of students drop out of bilingual studies during or after junior high. Perhaps as many as 70 percent of students in Alberta who start the program in grade one do not complete it in grade twelve; in the same province, 34 percent of the entrants drop out by the end of grade six (Judy Gibson, interview, August 26, 1997). The completion rate is higher in areas of Canada that provide more support for the program, such as near the federal capital, Ottawa, or in British Columbia.

In addition, the school environment itself remains limited because most announcements, recorded music, and playground chatter are in English. French-speaking families have wanted their own schools as their community became more vocal and organized, but their withdrawal reduced exposure of Anglophone students to French speakers. The initial enthusiasm for parents to learn French along with their children has also abated over time or at least the program for parents is less often offered in Calgary at the local elementary schools. Some small supports do exist to keep the program alive in dominantly Anglophone areas, including a federal government program that pays university students to work as teacher assistants or monitors.

The spread of the immersion program has stalled and even declined in a few areas of Canada; between 5 percent and 50 percent of all students in urban areas participated in the program (Canadian Education Association, 1992). School systems differ drastically in the support that they provide for immersion, including such specifics as the information provided to parents on their options in enrolling students and the provisions that are made for busing students (Judy Gibson, interview, August 26, 1997). The demands that the program makes on parents is one stated reason for some parents not wanting to be involved (Mitchell, 1992). Surveys suggest the original middle-class clientele wanted French for their children more for cultural development rather than vocational success (Burk, 1989). Attendance and involvement in the bilingual schools is extremely high and only the most devoted parents in other programs can match them. An interesting extension of the immersion program in Montreal is trilingualism, where French and English together with either Hebrew, Greek, or Italian are learned. Trilingualism, in spite of the students learning to see the relationship between thinking and language more clearly than in bilingualism and approximating the European standard of students learning three languages, has not spread in Canada; supporters for such a program have not become organized as a way of unifying ethnic minorities with the two founding groups.

A number of Canadian constituencies have not been involved with French immersion. In western Canada, bilingual schools have been established for Ukrainian speakers and, after regular school hours, heritage language programs for other immigrants have been extensively offered. Still other language programs have appeared as alternatives across Canada. Other groups have been more directly neglected by the program. For a long time, students who needed the services of special education had to withdraw from the French immersion program, but recently this barrier has been partially overcome (Morrison, et al., 1986). Since budget cuts are occurring, the availability of special education is again very questionable for immersion students; 26 percent of the school boards indicated some special services were available (Canadian Education Association, 1992). Rural areas and small towns have difficulty supporting bilingual programs, in part because of the difficulties of having enough students for a dual or separate school and in part because of a lack of interest in the cultural objective. For working-class students, the social distance between the program and its academic or vocational benefits appears to account for the lack of support.

English politicians and school administrators often speak about these French programs as a way of showing their support for French Québec, but Québec does not see immersion as their program. The French in that province are resentful of the federal money that is spent on teaching English students French when comparable funds are not spent on teaching English to French students (Mitchell, 1992). Québec supports English instruction for only a closely defined minority, established Anglophones; for Francophones, until recently English could not be learned in school until after grade four.

The links between the program in English Canada and the French-speaking province are indirect. During the period of rapid expansion, Québec teachers were frequently hired for the program, inadvertently given preference for jobs over those in the province because of administrators' usual inability to evaluate applicants' abilities in the language or in pedagogy. It is ironic that parents and educators want native speakers of the language, yet resent their hiring and criticize them (Yvonne Hébert, personal communication, September 29, 1997). The original planners of the program had envisioned the retraining of English teachers to teach French, but this has not generally happened (Lambert & Tucker, 1972).

Like minorities in the United States who were hired for ethnic schools, French teachers from Québec have received jobs that, under previous school programs, they could never have expected (Swindler, 1979, p. 156). The socialization of these teachers has not always prepared them for the tasks. An extreme example, which I observed, involved one teacher trying to teach the language through correcting the mistakes of pupils.

The use of a French language test has slowly spread among administrators as a basis for hiring teachers (Gadoury, 1991). When the immersion programs were expanding rapidly, Anglophone teachers and parents preferring traditional education both felt threatened (Canadian Parents for French, 1979). English parents who supported traditional schools have at times blamed Québec for the program (Mitchell, 1992). Parents outside the program have remained suspicious of the quality of the program and the ability levels of teachers in the program (Bienvenue, 1986). In Catholic schools, where there are more minorities, including those speaking the ancient French of Acadia, there is even more of a juggling act to pacify different groups; in Calgary, the original French immersion Catholic school moved three times as a way of trying to satisfy different groups

(John McCarthy, personal communication, 1994).

The success of the immersion program in either system is due to the dedication and confidence of the teachers. This program is one of the few where the most experienced teachers have been the ones to adopt an innovation; almost all other innovations are adopted first by younger teachers, whereas the older teachers hold back because of previous experiences with changes (Barbo, 1987). The teachers have been very adaptable; the original materials used in the program were intended for teaching French students their mother tongue in Québec, not English students in the rest of Canada. In addition, the planning of the expert linguists has, in the view of teachers, presented them with materials that were several grade levels higher than their students, such as in the adoption of whole language in the 1980s.

However, there is not an extensive network of teachers to aid others in the program, such as in the National Writing Project, which will be discussed later. One study in Ontario found that immersion teachers often developed their own materials in isolation: for a long time, the limited inservice education was a major problem (Canadian Education Association, 1983). Later on, the needs for inservice education for immersion teachers are still one of the most important needs (Canadian Education Association, 1992). At least second language teams in large urban school systems helped provide resources and inservice education for many teachers (Burk, 1989). Either alone or in groups, the teachers have overcome many difficulties, and many Anglophone teachers who often share the teaching of a class with French teachers have been among the stronger supporters of the program. Unfortunately, after many years of teaching in the bilingual program, Anglophone teachers have not been provided with opportunities to become fluent in French, comparable to the immersion opportunities for administrators or politicians, so that they could contribute even more to the immersion effort.

The task of reconciling the different interests of teacher groups and community divisions has fallen to administrators who have often lacked any substantial preparation to work with these schools. Within the bilingual schools, principals and other administrators have occupied a curiously ambiguous role. Higher administrators have been responsible for hiring the French teachers, but neither they nor many of the principals usually became fluent in the language. It has even been argued that supervisors do not need to understand the language of instruction to determine the competency of teachers because they can not understand sign language and they must oversee teachers of the deaf (Gadoury, 1991)!

Certainly, the expectation of the principals is that they should maintain a highly academic program with good discipline. However, when they understand little and can only sing in French, instruction is questionable or, at least, something the principal only knows about. In Calgary, the elite International Baccalaureate program, including the French version, is still administered by coordinators who do not speak any language other than English. This program was originally intended for the sons and daughters of diplomats but, in Calgary, manifests itself as a gifted program where multiple-languages are not a critical component. The

Canadian Parents for French has sought to have French immersion teachers promoted into administration so that, similar to women, they would be among those with power (Burk, 1989).

Outside of the schools, the interest of administrators and linguistic experts has been to obtain international recognition for this program. The educational media in the United States continues to report on immersion as if it is a new development that is never integrated with bilingualism for immigrants (Conover, 1997; University CARLA, 1996). The United States Department of Education has listed the program as one of the most effective ways to learn a foreign language on the basis of research in "the United States and Canada" (United States Department of Education, 1986, p. 57).

The Canadian immersion program has been followed a little more than the Canadian medical system, but there are enough examples to cheer Canadian research on, particularly considering how dominant American innovations generally are in Canadian education. In 1991, less than 5 percent of all American elementary students were estimated to have any form of language instruction and only about 2 percent of all U.S. language programs were of the immersion variety. Currently, there are over 180 programs, compared to 67 in 1987, though the partial immersion in 140 elementary schools appears to be most popular (Conover, 1997).   Canadians cite their influence as model programs for Americans in Cincinnati, San Diego, Milwaukee, and Culver City (Genessee, 1983).

The preoccupation with Americans leads to a failure to enlarge upon the program at home. Within Canada, there has been no serious attempt to use involvement in the immersion program for a political purpose even when in 1995 large numbers of Anglophones descended upon Montreal as a way of persuading Quebecers to stay in Canada for the most recent referendum vote. There have been only cultural and individual exchanges developed in relation to a program that originally had many stated political purposes. A later survey finds support for a united Canada, but only a call for more cultural encounter groups and increased federal funding for immersion education resulted from the study (Van Loon, 1996).

Most criticisms of the program have only led to a continuing stream of research to justify its existence, but there has been no attempt to relate the program to broader questions. Why is French culture recognized in bilingual programs, but not one word of a native language is known by teachers in many English as a Second Language classes? How can the social conditions that make learning subtractive to learning English for many immigrants be changed, instead of additive as in the French immersion effort for Anglophones? Why aren't the discriminatory policies that Québec teachers have faced in the program seen as a problem to be changed? And why is professional knowledge *not* related to political concerns, at least to the extent of knowing about the successful but pressuring approach to teach French to immigrants in Québec, "classes d`accueil" (Ansam, 1988). The French immersion program, which emerged from the interests of parents due to political changes in Quebec, needs to find a broad basis to renew its commitment. The preoccupation of the planners has been in proving which approaches are effective and how different professional approaches can be adopted. The limitations on growth in the program involve finding a larger constituency and seeing how attitudes and social practices must be changed to reduce the dropout rate and improve the lot of those involved in the effort.

THE MANAGERIAL SOLUTION

French immersion represents a curriculum response to a crisis that has underestimated the need for administrative and social changes. Many other changes have prompted managerial and community responses. In Chapter 4, three crises of the multitude of crises are mentioned. Racial and community conflicts dominate in Chicago, an educational failure has forced action in Kentucky, and a perceived financial crisis has produced sweeping changes in Alberta. In Chicago, the racial problems were augmented by repeated strikes, an inflexible bureaucracy, and a history of community advocacy, which together added to racial and community conflicts as sources of change (Mitchell, 1996). In Kentucky, the educational revolution developed as a result of the supreme court decision, the creation of a state-wide and inclusive organization that supported reform, and community members who rejected the past pattern of nepotism for selecting school personnel and restrictive budgets for education that were far less than surrounding states. In Alberta, the government's intentions to curtail the independence of schools boards, establish tight provincial controls, and have tough decisions about the division of smaller expenditures made at the local level were intertwined with financial cuts in expenditures for education (Mitchell, 1995).

In each of these cases, as well as others, the initial answer has been school-based management. In Chicago, school-based management has been combined with school councils so that laypeople, who are the majority, can select untenured principals and help establish educational plans; in most cases, particularly elementary schools, parents are increasingly active and management of the schools has changed (Editors of *Education Week*, 1993). In Kentucky, parents are a minority on the councils and only the use of integrated services has seriously touched traditional parents; school-based decision-making preceded the legislative act for the state in urban areas and appears to involve primarily principals (Appalachia Educational Laboratory, 1996, p. S2). In Alberta, school-based management goes together with advisory councils; the government tried to make the councils decision-making agents, but the public showed no interest in such an active role. A recent case study in Calgary found no influence in the decision-making process by parents and teachers who were, at times, unwilling partners for principals (Robertson, 1997). Edmonton, which is a model for many schools in the province as well as in North America, has always been school-based program where principals make most of the decisions (Rothman, 1995). Of the three types, only Chicago has been a clear example of democratic involvement.

However, there are many other communities that show substantial participation and select school-based management for many other reasons. Boston has recently attempted to use school-based management as a way of integrating programs for poor families, Title 1, with the school's other functions (Hoff, 1997b, April). Chattanooga, Tennessee has attempted to extend local decision making together with a clustering of schools as a basis of integrating its city system of schools with a county pattern, a situation that is complicated by the dominance of Blacks in the city and Whites in the country (Bradley, 1995b). Los Angeles has experienced conflict between school-based management and its program for broad-based reform financed by the Annenberg Foundation, LEARN.

A number of states, including Colorado, Florida, Kentucky, North Carolina, and Texas, have mandated participatory decision making in a variety of ways (Editors of *Education Week*, 1993). For almost every state or city, the reasons for developing new forms of governance are different. As will be discussed in Chapter 9, there are a number of national programs that include site-based management; today, there are very few programs that do not include it.

The diversity of programs reflects the pervasiveness of multiple crises in education. Though the other exemplary programs are affected by a crisis, school-based management is almost consumed by them; it is one of the changes that develop from "intense stress" (Malen, et al., 1990). Chicago was one infamous stress scene, which the then Secretary of Education, William Bennett, proclaimed was the worst school district as demands for reform mounted there; other areas who feel the some stress tend to adopt the same solution . Ambiguous responses, little more than slogans, can be developed as responses to apparent consternation among the public. Unlike classroom changes, managerial revolutions can be proclaimed with almost no cost and little possibility of measuring effectiveness. Again, an underdeveloped plan may spread to other places with different problems.

It is probably not surprising that there is no proof that the cure will actually work in so many different situations. In fact, by the usual ways of viewing education, local decision making is a failure. There is no evidence that it increases academic performance in schools (Lawton, 1996; Robertson, 1997). However, almost all of these studies involve only teacher participation, not parents or students. Many teachers are somewhat unwilling contributors who complain about the innumerable meetings that take time away from their focus on the classroom (Robertson, 1997). Teachers must want to be involved in management and extend the program to classrooms. Projects, which have been inspired by experts, such as the psychiatrist,   James Comer, have not been any more successful when they have been applied to a larger area or when Comer is not present; an error made by Comer is apparently having the principal continue as Chairman of a governance system of parents and teachers (Carrano, 1990).

School-based management must deal with the enduring resistance of traditional authority in schools:

Principals tend to take the lead role, parents play a supporting one, and many teachers remain hesitant to question established practices. More rarely still has school-based management made any inroads into changing the authoritarian relationship in the classroom between teachers and students. (Editors of *Education Week*, 1993, p. 47)

There is evidence of change as a result of local decision making. A more horizontal or matrix organization spread in several schools (Robertson, 1997). A larger study found evidence that teachers dealt with problems such as student tardiness and course alignments, if not large scale reforms (Weiss, 1995). The options to change are less involvement, which has often caused student and teacher alienation in schools; like democracy in general, the problem is that the alternatives are all so much worse. However, the problem requires more concrete ways to make collaboration essential, similar to the development by teacher teams who work together for individual student programs in special education. Teacher individualism is deeply embedded in the institution of education and a variety of attacks will be necessary before a frontal assault can ever be launched.

Considering how underdeveloped the current approach is, why do people in so many different situations buy into this solution? In Chapter 4, it was shown to be one of the major solutions that institutional experts were offering for education. Many innovation solutions are waiting for a problem to come around that they can solve. When crises occur, only the computer and the Internet are touted more favorably for any problem than managerial solutions. Bill Clinton, who wants to lead the technological revolution for schools, does not even type; he relied on his daughter to learn about e-mail (Hecht, 1997). Other than typing and writing, there are few known educational benefits from the computer; the school as an institution and groups within schools have determined the use that is made of it (Mitchell, 1992). Because students like computers, they have been compared to the students eating candy in terms of their dangers and limited benefits (Schmitt & Slonaker, 1996).

As a supplement to technology, North Americans have repeatedly tried managerial answers to overcome educational and related crises. Many business groups have sought to overcome their perception of education as rigid and stereotyped in its response to change by adopting decentralization (Mitchell, 1996, p. 106). Business has *not* seen the schools as needing an increase in democracy. More conservative city administrators have been so concerned about performance they have attempted to reconstitute schools, as discussed in Chapter 4. Business executives are supportive of such takeover moves.

The link between the democratic achievements and the control focus, is the entrepreneurial action of some administrators and a few teachers. One of the oldest examples and most extensive school decision-making schemes is in Edmonton; well over 80 percent of budget decisions, the first focus for change, are at the school level (Rothman, 1995). However, the most striking result of the change in the northern Alberta city is the extent to which the administration promotes the educational service that they offer to their schools or schools far from Edmonton. Unexpectedly, when tasks were divided between district and local schools, some schools began offering services to other schools, (O'Neil, 1996). The knowledge of staff training and consulting as well as more specific skills was not confined to the central office!

In Chapter 4, the occasional appearance of local charismatic leaders was noted as an antidote to the institutional experts. However, the significance of local leaders crossing between schools has not been appreciated, apparently because the study of school decision making and school councils has been largely limited to individual schools. In Rochester, New York, Eastman Kodak provides the schools with such a facilitator, and school systems have been urged to appoint such coordinators from their own ranks (Editors of *Education Week*, 1993).

Unless both councils and decision making are to be tools of ever more powerful central offices that establish their objectives and evaluate their performances, such intermediaries and confederations are essential. In Chicago, the school councils have formed a confederation that has attempted to coordinate the progress of reform, but this federation is still in its infancy under a Latino parent and active council member, Sheila Castillo (Mitchell, 1996). In Kentucky, a lawyer and educational expert, Susan Weston, has tried to act as an agent to bring the councils together with limited success; she has not played a very active role in the state-wide parent empowerment program that the large advocacy group, the Prichard Committee, has conducted. In Alberta, only the Department of Education has linked the different councils through materials it has developed and training it has provided, which is not likely to encourage democracy.

The question is how the professionals in schools and professionals and laypersons in councils can encourage greater participation with a broader focus. School-based management may encourage other forms of management behavior that can affect student achievement and may develop together with forms of advocacy for at-risk families. There is some evidence that a program of decentralized decision making will encourage effective schools that are defined by the contribution they make to student achievement (Malen, et al., 1990).

Effective schools have principals who set goals primarily through the examples they set, teachers who emphasize instruction, and parents in middle-class schools who are highly involved (Mitchell, 1992, pp. 112-114). When school-based management is combined with parent councils and school improvement plans, as in Chicago, the original plan was to create effective schools (Moore, 1990). However, the problem is to find other reforms, such as Title 1 changes in Boston, for which local decision is also an effective supplement.

Just as effective schools in Great Britain and Canada became progressive in the encouragement they provide for self-realization and participation in the group, school-based decision making needs to expand the images that guide its agenda (Mitchell, 1992). The language of school-based management is currently very task centered. Wohlstetter and Mohrman (1993), for example, see the elements as power, knowledge of organizational performance, information, and rewards. However, almost all school-based management includes the development of vision statements and commitment. A recent study found that, in two high schools, the vision statements represented a difference that had always been there, but teachers and administrators thought that they were still very important for the development of the sharing of managerial responsibilities that they had achieved. Greater commitment is dependent upon student response to teachers. A consistency of a managerial approach has been shown to improve academic performance (Editors of *Education Week*, 1993). Parents and students are the ones who can remove the

(Viadero, 1996b). The most dominant figure in American educational reform, Theodore Sizer, who headed a number of advocacy organizations that are discussed in Chapter 8, called on NWP to conduct a writing seminar for teachers in schools who are undergoing change in order to give voice to their experiences (Olson, 1995a).

Overwhelming numbers of teachers have also expressed their support for the program informally as well as in studies. The teachers who have been involved in the program, particularly in rural areas, report a virtual religious experience, which is discussed in more detail in Chapter 7. In addition, as will be further discussed, NWP became the model for a number of teacher networks, particularly in California (Viadero, 1993). However, objective problems of achievements and traditional conceptions of education continue to disturb harmony at this love-in (Wilson, 1994; Gomez, 1990). The opposite position, which stresses students writing from a model of good writing, even copying its grammar in copying a text, has been advocated by cognitive psychologists, such as Arthur Whimbey (Viadero, 1993). This more traditional position has not received much professional support among the teachers' organizations.

Neither the problems nor the achievements could have been anticipated when the program was developed in 1973 by James Gray and an associate, Albert "Cap" Lavin, in 1973 in Berkeley, California (Goldberg, 1989). A few years earlier, a three-year study of the causes of California students' declining ability to write identified the teachers' lack of expertise as a crucial variable; the study believed this was an objective problem and, as a result, external student achievements were measured. The subjective process view of writing was developed to bring about "a revolution in the treatment of teachers" (Goldberg, 1989, p. 65). In this radical plan, all teachers, regardless of subject, from elementary school to the university, could relate to a common model to improve writing.

In this unorthodox view, practicing teachers were the people who knew the problems and some of the answers to the problems. Experts were not to be trusted because they were distant from teachers and usually believed there was only one answer to writing improvement. To take the learner's perspective, all teachers in NWP training sessions go through the writing process; they write, interact over each others' papers, and work to publish their work (Krendl & Dodd, 1987). Aside from the combined student publications, a substantial number of writers have emerged from the program and have been commercially published.

However, the approach of teachers teaching teachers is guided in a number of ways. Early identification of teachers, particularly for the initial classes, is made so that they would be more reliable resources than the transient experts. Outstanding or master teachers are identified; an elite group of experts within teaching is thus recognized. Links with the world of experts are also made in a number of ways. A prestigious setting at a university is used for a first meeting and research and theoretical papers are read, usually during the morning sessions of the summer program.

As in all of the programs that are discussed, academics do the studies that give the program legitimacy though, in this case, many of the studies are carried out by committed members of the NWP community of teachers. The summer program is directly supported by a number of rituals, such as faculty or students serving a common dinner and the development of designs for NWP T-shirts. Such rituals create a common identity or temporary culture (Wilson, 1994; Sunstein, 1994). The outside researcher is easily overwhelmed by the many efforts, including extensive writing, that so many participants have undertaken.

The program usually begins with a three-week or five-week graduate course in the summer, though a Chicago group has developed courses throughout the year to make the program more available to teachers in a large metropolitan area (Steve Zemelman, interview, October 22, 1993). There are usually three levels in the program so that participants can return for annual celebrations. Though not officially endorsed, Zemelman and Daniels, leaders of the Illinois Writing Project, created a detailed prescription of how to conduct the program, which was never accepted or rejected by James Gray (1985). From many successful practice sessions in the courses as well as their class efforts, which are always published in some form, some teachers are chosen and dubbed with the title of consultant; such consultants are expected to conduct similar programs in their schools for other teachers. Some of the select teachers may also be chosen to attend a special program at Mecca, the University of California campus at Berkeley. All teacher-participants can increase their competency by follow-up training and by assistance from teacher-consultants. Identification of participants is currently not as rigid as when the program began in Berkeley in 1974 (Batiuk, 1993), but Gray or his successor still attempt to visit and inspect each site.

Today, the NWP is a dominant model of innovation for the professional education of teachers. From Chapter 3, it might be recalled, on the one hand, how pedestrian many inservice classes for teachers are and, on the other hand, how even more exceptional aesthetic classes at NCCAT were. NWP is very widespread as well as reasonably effective. In 1996, it had 160 sites in 45 American states. NWP has also spread to six Commonwealth countries and four other countries (Pritchard, 1989). In Canada, there are NWP sites in Calgary, Vancouver, Regina, Yellowknife, and Halifax (Washburn, 1991).

In the United States alone, NWP claims to have trained over 1.4 million teachers and administrators between 1973 and 1994 (National Writing Project, 1995). In 1991, federal support was enacted to spread the innovation to as many as 250 sites; at that time, the appropriation was $3,211,000. NWP claims that it is an extremely cost-effective program because its courses serve teachers for $22 each and generate $4 for every federal dollar received.

Aside from the money and numbers served, NWP allows participants to overcome social isolation, develop personally, and become members of a community composed of teacher-writers. In turn, the participants frequently become advocates for NWP (Gomez, 1988). Currently, the stronger effects of the program seem to be evident in more remote cities and towns. Earlier, one entire Calgary class reported totally positive evaluations by all members (Calgary Writing Project, 1986). Unexpectedly, a study that employed the more structured approach of levels of use for innovations found striking changes in social and personal orientations (March et al., 1987).

The levels of use is one of three parts of the research conducted by Hall and Hord (1987); Chapter 2 described one other part, the components of an innovation, and Chapter 5 discussed the levels of concern as a progressive project. Both the focus on components and the levels of concern were used in a study of the writing project (Bratcher & Stroble, 1994). The components were rhetoric (purpose, audience, form, and voice), planning for writing, revising and testing against a criteria, and publishing or sharing the work with a wider audience. Three different groups of summer institute teachers found difficulty in adopting all of the components even after three years. Sharing, planning, rhetoric, and revising, in that order, were adopted by teachers, but the number of teachers using each component steadily increased over time. With respect to conclusions about the levels of concern approach, teachers moved from self-concern about their adequacy with the NWP stance to thinking about the effects of the program on students. Teachers, like students, were described by the interaction of "comfort, confidence, competence," coming from "fear of writing, to great fluency, to skilled writing" (Bratcher & Stroble, 1994, p. 82).

Teacher anxieties blocked their complete implementation of the program and previous, more controlled research, had shown that significantly better writing by students was dependent upon the implementation of the entire process. Getting complete implementation of the approach is a problem because the NWP has been opposed to any compulsion about adoption, preferring that teachers adopt the program voluntarily because the professional development of teachers is NWP's primary goal (Goldberg, 1989). In 1990, a survey for the National Assessment of Educational Programs found only half of the teachers were using the process approach to writing; the test scores of students were not improving, though "the students are feeling better as they are writing more in school" (Viadero, 1993). For at-risk students, who make up the majority of those in Chicago's schools, the process approach has improved standardized scores. To hurry the process along is to recognize that the NWP is a "professionalization project," as ironically stated by Miles Myers, the executive director of the National Council of Teachers of English (Ibid).

Reform increasingly involves many parties other than teachers who are engaged in making controversial decisions in a fishbowl of publicity. Though the first executive, Jim Gray, has received a great deal of recognition for his efforts (he initially lacked a Ph.D. or tenure at the University of California) and the program has been recognized by educators, there has been very little publicity about the program. Marva Collins has probably received ten times more television and newspaper coverage than has the writing program.

Though connected with professionals in government as well as outside of it, NWP has had very few political connections and limited publicity. For NWP, there is nothing like the political ties that Ted Sizer has developed with state governments (see Chapter 9). Materials that one receives from branches of NWP are often extremely low key; a teacher walks one through the program rather than achieving this through a public relations' effort (Majorie Kaiser, personal communication, October 1, 1995).

As a result of the political and public relations vacuum, I have, on a number of occasions, found many influential people on the fringe of the writing project who were totally unaware of the program or of its relation to reform. A number of art educators who also carry on state-wide programs in writing are unfamiliar with NWP (Engen-Wedin, interview, June 10, 1996); there are still many states that do not have local sites in spite of its support by federal legislation. Even the extensive academic literature on the program appears to be mainly writing by NWP professionals for others already involved in the program, rather than an attempt to reach outsiders.

As discussed in Chapter 4, there are substantial variations in NWP depending on the type of state or province in which it is located. There has been the greatest activity in Chicago, and NWP staff and consultants have picked up the challenge that the early reform there presented. The consultants for the program helped bring out an initial publication about education reform in Chicago, *Best Practices*, and subsequently supported student publications (Mitchell, 1996). There has been little public recognition of the role that the Illinois group played there.

In Kentucky and Alberta, the writing program is even less known and recognized. In Kentucky, the program has helped support art education and other educational reform and is itself housed in the Department of Education. However, the executive director of the dominant reform organization in Kentucky, Robert Sexton with the Prichard Committee, was unfamiliar with their efforts (Interview, June 5, 1996). In Calgary, the program has never been a subject for a major newspaper or television story; though it was one of the first Canadian sites, the Calgary program has had no political influence (Mitchell, 1996).

The program may have writers, but it clearly needs to go beyond its professional pillars and confront a number of dilemmas. Because of problems in getting the supportive environment for teachers that Gray wanted, it has not been possible to expand the program to the 250 sites called for by federal legislation. The project has never attempted to change the structure of schools and universities, but both types of organizations are involved in providing the joint writing programs. The major question has been whether students are changed. Students have not been involved in the decision to undertake or to continue with the programs. However, student leaders do mention the support of leaders in NWP for their own writing efforts (Mitchell, 1996). In general, students write more and have more school time for their writing after NWP is adopted (Purves, 1992; Putka, 1992).

The program has begun to expand so that it reaches parents, and a number of different types of programs are aimed at students. In the Milwaukee area as well as elsewhere, writing programs have been planned for parents (Vopat, 1993). However, since the initial programs in Oakland, California, parents have always been involved as monitors of students' work. Though the original program was meant for all subject areas, separate courses have been developed in a number of specialties, including science. In the original home of the NWP, California, the success of the program has led to nine additional subject areas developing similar programs coordinated by the University of California in Oakland; this cluster claims to reach 65,000 teachers every year (Richardson, 1996).

Other unrelated teacher networks have emerged that develop similar ideas to NWP. Project Zero at Harvard is using similar ideas about process and criticism to develop programs in art, music, and literature, as illustrated by a video (Harvard Graduate School of Education, n.d.). Though much smaller than NWP, a mathematics network seems to have a similar effect on those involved in its 14 sites, which include Los Angeles, Minneapolis, and New Orleans. The networks discussed in Chapter 3 are, of course, further examples. There may currently be hundreds of networks in the United States and these include teachers interested in portfolios, other writing programs, and historians (Richardson, 1996).

The network of mathematics and science teachers are each influenced by the writing program (Rothman, 1987). NWP's focus on writing across the curriculum had meant that, according to its founder, James Gray, over a third of those attending the programs were entire faculties, not just English departments. However, research in science and mathematics showed improved learning if students undertook informal writing. One guru, Paul Connelly, director of the Bard Institute, saw writing as a way to get away from teacher talk, increase student understanding, and get both teachers and students to think like mathematicians or scientists.

The emphasis of this expert's approach is on informal writing with "free writing" by students for five minutes at the beginning of a lesson; "learning logs," records by teachers of what students knew about a subject, such as geometric numbers before and after a lecture; and "dialectical notebooks," which are comments on a text that one subject teacher exchanges with another one (Rothman, 1987). The exchanges among teachers are models for students to question their textbooks. NWP teachers always have students express their ideas, write logs or journals, and discuss the contrasts among approaches. Teachers frequently object that they do not have enough time to cover their subject and use this approach; they do not directly object to the more progressive education ideology for their subject, which is being imported to their field along with the writing approach.

ART AS AN ESSENTIAL

The arts are so exposed to political pressures that those involved in this field cannot pretend that art education is only a professional matter. Art has been one of the approaches that are organized as a teacher network in California as a result of the dominance of the NWP model among administrators. However, art networks and, more generally, art education are exposed to larger pressures. Art teachers have been eliminated from elementary schools in many cities, including New York and Chicago. The back-to-basics movements is a threat to art education everywhere. As a result, often because of these cuts, artists have been brought into the schools and many art educators believe that the integration of arts is the safer strategy to pursue.

Programs for art education have had to struggle for recognition as well as basic support. Recently, art educators have fought to be included in the U.S. statement of national goals as well as having art exams included in the national assessment of education. The arts educators feel they must prove their efficacy; findings supporting art education are summarized (Welch, 1995) and the summaries are used to develop pamphlets for wide distribution (President's Committee on the Arts and the Humanities, n.d.). Videos are produced with movie stars to further promote these programs. The argument is also made that art education is important for business, particularly in high-technology areas, and a number of businesspeople have made strong statements in support of the arts.

There have been signs of increasing acceptance for art education. No arts program was included in the conservative list *What Works*, but art was found to be a basis for developing reading among difficult students, which the National Diffusion Network certified. Massive statistical evidence has been mounted to support the contention that the academic performance of students is higher when they are enrolled in the arts (Welch, 1995). Ironically, it has been the theoretical position that the arts represent some of the fundamental forms of intelligence that has perhaps been more influential than all the research evidence. Who wants to be stupid even if there are seven different ways to accomplish it (Louis DeLuca, interview, June 4, 1996)?

In addition, support for art education comes from a number of very wealthy benefactors and many volunteer supporters for art education. J. Paul Getty, at one time the wealthiest man in the United States, founded the Getty Center for Education in the Arts. The Getty Center has an extensive staff and resources at its lavish main center in Santa Monica, near Los Angeles, and six modest regional centers throughout the United States. However, critics assert that the Getty Center has had no effect on increasing the amount of art education in the schools and has mainly had prima donnas with superb materials (Louis DeLuca, interview, June 4, 1996). Certainly, the Getty Center has taken a professional and expert path; the resources of many devoted volunteers that keep many underfunded programs operating are ignored (Mitchell, 1997).

In contrast, the Galef Institute works with a variety of community sponsors and parents to provide "art enhancement" for a program of crossdisciplinary themes at the elementary level (Viadero, 1994a). In the initial program, parents are involved so that they could later help promote the program. Subsequently. the few interested parents were allowed to attend training sessions with teachers free. As the program develops in each community, a range of sponsors, such as Parent Teacher Associations and the Deposit Guaranty National Bank in Meridian, Mississippi, has supported the program. Kentucky has become a major supporter of Galef and, nationally, Galef tried, though unsuccessfully, to become the administrative agent for a series of art and related centers, including the Minnesota Center for Arts Education and the NWP (Galef Institute, 1996a).

The founders of the institute are Andrew and Bronya Galef. Mr. Galef is Chairman and President of The Spectrum Group, which includes such major corporations as MagneTek, Warnace, and Petco Animal Supplies. He had been involved with business education and job training and was one of the select business groups invited to the summit of business leaders and governors convened by IBM CEO Louis Gerstner, which was discussed in Chapter 4. Mr. Galef's aim in founding a new program was different from that of the summit. He proposed to "lessen the widening gap in society between the haves and have-nots" (Galef Institute, 1996a, p. 25). Mrs. Galef, a photojournalist who left school at age 15, believed the arts could provide a place for students who are similar to the kind of student she had been.

The Galefs left it to experts to help shape their intentions when the program began in 1990. The program, which was centered in Los Angeles, was developed by drawing on Howard Gardiner's theory of multiple intelligence and on constructivist psychology, although the planners borrowed widely from a number of other sources, including NWP. The initial program featured thinking about social themes; it also "featured bibliographies and sample letters explaining each unit of study to parents" (Galef, 1996a). Between 1991 and 1994, the new program, Different Ways of Knowing (DWoK), was offered at four elementary schools in mixed social class areas (Catterall, 1995). Though the program, including six modules for study between kindergarten and middle school, was still focused on social studies, a joint focus on art with social studies had developed by 1994. The evaluation probably suggested a greater emphasis on art because it showed substantial improvement in language and art work together with the program's success in preventing student alienation, denying that student efforts in school determine their school success.

Though the trial schools were in California and Massachusetts, the program has developed a substantial connection to Kentucky, which had simultaneously been undergoing massive educational reform. In 1993, Donald Ingwerson, a leading reformer for twelve years as superintendent of schools in Jefferson County (Louisville), Kentucky, became the institute's president. When Dr. Ingwerson left in 1994 to become superintendent for Los Angeles County, Linda Adelman, the director of programs, succeeded him as president. Mrs. Adelman had extensive experience in publishing as well as education: she is the senior author for some of the program's modules on families, the environment, geography, and history.

Mrs. Adelman rapidly found herself spending a great deal of time in Kentucky because that single state, among the more than eight others with schools in the program, became the largest and most important supporter of the program. Since 1990, when Kentucky was required by the state legislature to revamp its entire system of education, the elementary teachers have needed guidance for a child-centered effort with multiage groups and portfolio exams. In 1993 and 1994, fifty teachers from twenty-five schools participated in a trial effort with this program (Hargan, 1995). The response to DWoK was very positive because the teachers were at last getting direction (Robert Sexton, interview, June 5, 1996).

The numbers of schools involved rapidly spiralled as did the number of significant grants. By the 1996-1997 school year, all eight districts of Kentucky were involved in supporting the program with 75,125 students, which was 72 percent of all the students involved in the program in nine states. In September

1996, it was announced that the Galef Collaborative in Kentucky was to receive a large share of a grant from the Annenberg Foundation. Earlier, the Kentucky program received large grants from the Knight Foundation. The number of small grants received by Kentucky also appears to be larger than those given to other states.

Furthermore, the program was officially recognized by the state as the Galef Institute-Kentucky Collaborative for Elementary Learning; this legitimacy has not been given elsewhere. Linda Hargen, who became the program's executive director, had been associate commissioner for the Office of Learning Programs Developing in the Kentucky Department of Education, which meant she had substantial responsibility for elementary education in that state. This public/private partnership initially was to be under a state board, but is currently administered by Galef (Linda Hargen, interview, June 3, 1996). The Lexington newspaper, *Herald-Leader*, regularly provides free space for representatives of Galef, teachers, or administrators to tell their story. The paper is owned by the Knight family whose foundation had supported the program. The educational television station for Kentucky has made a series of videos about the Galef program.

The organization of this program is extremely demanding. The initial training of teachers was primarily handled by teacher facilitators from other states, but in 1996 Kentucky had eight coaches throughout the state with an annual budget of $1.4 million. The money is used to provide an extensive program of teacher training and materials. Each teacher receives fifteen days of professional development and five days per year of technical assistance, two newsletters, and the teaching materials. Part of the professional development is a series of three arts strategies workshops, which, by 1995, had been attended by over one thousand teachers in one hundred workshops in twenty-two counties. The cost of the entire program is $3,200 per teacher over three years. Moving materials around between the 40 different sites and over 140 schools is so substantial that they have hired a moving van (Linda Hargen, interview, June 3, 1996).

The program is an extensive structure from which teachers are encouraged to deviate. The aim is to develop the teachers' expertise, and students are expected to become experts as well. Learning for teachers and students is thought of as a series of wheels rather than linear patterns (Galef Institute, n.d.a). Wheel 1 involves exploring what students already know, whereas Wheel 2 involves becoming an "expert" through the use of materials where learning events, which may involve poetry, stories, or music, is called "research." Wheel 3 involves working collaboratively to expand knowledge through projects, and Wheel 4 revolves around the application to their own lives, which helps to synthesize knowledge and create opportunities for reflection.

This nonlinear approach to learning is as evident in the art workshops for teachers as it is in the primary grade work of students. As teachers experienced writing in NWP, those in DWoK are involved in experiencing many of the art activities that students will later develop. With other, more experienced teachers as facilitators, teacher-students form cohesive groups and experience arts in a nonthreatening way. In one case, teachers learn to see colors as shading by working together on a single work of art (Chapman-Crane, 1996). The teachers enjoy having plenty of materials to work with whether they are "paints, colored markers, glue, and paper to scarves and musical instruments" (Galef Institute, n.d.a). The experiential activities are supplemented by group work and opportunities for individual reflection. Many of the facilitators speak of learning from their teacher students even while they are missing their own children while they are away from them (Wysinger, 1995).

Because of the reciprocal relationships among teachers, artists, and facilitators, an incredibly high percentage of teachers use the program in some way, over 90 percent in the evaluation (Catterall, 1995). The Galef newspaper is full of testimonials by teachers, regular columns by artists, and reports by facilitators on their experiences in encouraging teachers to develop their expertise. A series of background books are prepared for teachers, such as on drama, music, and mathematics, which regularly provide opportunities for teachers to dialogue, learn the experiences of other teachers, and learn about even more specialized studies or "shop talk" (Heller, 1995). However, three different technical consultants to the program reported to me that teachers often use DWoK as material for their preexisting programs.

The publications for teachers convey a respect for them that teachers appear to carry over as respect for students in their classrooms. A surprising number of students express their appreciation for the education they are receiving. One primary student drew an engaging and imaginative bird to show what a DWoK looked like. Others have submitted articles by themselves or with their teachers for the Galef newspaper. One example is an interview with Sir Francis Drake with a dramatic recreation of the experience of being at sea (Fourth grade students at Mildred B. Janson Elementary School in Rosemead, California, 1996). Another report by teachers shows students founding an imaginary community and becoming "plant experts" who try to convince the citizens to stop polluting their environment (Graves & Coffey, 1996). In one school in Shelby, Kentucky, which I visited, students thought of themselves as speakers for DWoK.

The teachers role, whether in teaching students in the classroom or other teachers in a leadership institute, is to get out of the way, similar to the creation myth, and let others develop their expertise. One teacher-facilitator says, "I kept wanting to stop the session to take notes on what the participants were saying" (Wysinger, 1995). Another person in the same role says, teachers need to "lead students to self-discovery without overpowering them so the student can take all the credit" (Bornstein, 1996, p. 5). Similarly, teachers are advised to study the natural play of students as the basis for developing both their individual strengths and greater understanding of drama as a creative event before an audience (Heller, 1995). The program is dependent on art and humanities being tested as they are in Kentucky. For both teachers and students there is an interesting role reversal from the dominating sage on stage role.

In some interesting ways, the program itself has tried to become a teacher for other reformers. Henry Levin, who founded the Accelerated Schools Project at

Stanford to provide the same enrichment for at-risk students that gifted students have received, has become an enthusiastic supporter of DWoK (Levin, 1996). Dr. Levin reports on one of his schools with mostly at-risk students, which had been established only two months before, but has already developed a music conservatory for their children in the afternoons and on Saturday. One teacher started to think about a dream school that the parents wanted and realized that "underemployed" Russian emigrants were available and would gladly teach the children. So a very poor school obtained accomplished musicians who were trained in the top conservatories of the former Soviet Union for either $6 an hour for group lessons or $8 an hour for semi-private training. Music rapidly became an essential in education because it was perceived to be possible.

The contact between the Accelerated Schools and the Galef project was expected to be a forerunner of some exciting cross-fertilization with other reform groups. For the time being, the cancellation of the Annenberg grant has polarized Galef from some of its prospective partners, such as Leonard Bernstein Center in Nashville, which is attempting to form a national league of schools; Chicago Arts Partnership, which is one of eight programs that follow Arts Vision model from New York City; and North Carolina A+ Schools of the Kenan Institute which resulted from an extensive state-wide program in South Carolina. The mixture of art education, innovative activities, and many different organizations might have provided a creative synthesis. The people involved did not understand each other and DWoK will have to find other partners (Linda Hargen, interview, January 13, 1998).

Aside from its current problems, the Galef program remains critically flawed. Its emphasis in all forms of education is on the development of expertise, not wisdom, judgment, or creativity. Similar to gifted programs, the possibility of developing broad intellectuals rather than the narrow specialists has not been sensed as the objective in education (Mitchell, 1992). Unlike the NCCAT program for teachers, a balance among teachers or students for a liberal or liberating education is not foreseen.

In addition, the program seems to adjust to whatever is asked of it rather than developing any autonomous function. When a report on the work needs in the next century was developed, A Scans Report for America 2000, DWoK developed a statement that showed it already met all of these needs (Galef, n.d.b). Similarly, Linda Adelman, the president of the Galef Institute, said in defining DWoK:

To prepare children for the workforce of the future, DWoK encourages self-directed, collaborative thinking and doing. One of the purposes of DWoK is to expand awareness of what it means for a child to be literate. A truly literate child does more than read sentences and add numbers. (Bornstein, 1996, p. 7)

Apparently, DWoK can do anything that is demanded. An elaborate justification was prepared to fit all of their activities to the specification of the 1990 Kentucky Education Reform Act (Huffstutter, 1996). This rationalized approach enabled Galef to be a leader among art education groups in obtaining a large number of Goals 2000 grants (Sara Goldhawk, letter, July 10, 1997); Galef is currently involved in the hunt for new federal funding. Galef is certainly open to new approaches, such as a web site to connect educators with a grant of $1.525 million from AT&T (Galef Institute, 1996a, p. 6).

Even the increasing commitment to art education appears as an expedient response to changing conditions. Sometimes, Galef has secured grants and developed programs, such as one on Egypt Connections with some eminent experts, which appear to lead nowhere (Galef Institute, 1996b). Other times, a promising program has a questionable sponsor, such as one at the University of Louisville, which provides future teachers with field experience with DWoK, and which is supported by $135,000 from Philip Morris (Galef Institute, 1996c). Some grants should not be accepted, but Galef, in terms of general direction, does seem to be lost in a smoky room.

More than the other programs discussed, DWoK is just developing. French immersion needs to renew its period of development, and school-based management needs to develop far more so that classroom behaviour will be a clearer focus. DWoK, French immersion, and NWP provide that focus. However, French immersion and NWP are both caught up in their professional limitations. Together with school councils, school-based management and DWoK are more open to society and the changes happening within it. School-based decision making is almost overwhelmed by the crises that it is thought to answer, whereas the linguists and the writers are more threatened by being marginalized and, as a result, found irrelevant to mainstream education. In these as well as a variety of other ways, each of the exemplars can be said to compensate for the limitations of the other, and we can combine all four together for a larger discussion of many other changes. At the end of Chapter 6, a further discussion of these four programs is presented, following a more detailed examination of the process of change and the presentation of a pattern against which these processes can be evaluated.

We receive the lesson that our advance to knowledge is of asymptotic type, even as continually approaching so continually without arrival. The satisfaction shall therefore be eternal. (Sherrington, 1953, p. 291)

Chapter 7

Action Research

Here, courses are constantly revised, the amount and quality of learning is constantly examined, we're always looking for effective ways to offer support to kids. The grading system, the approach to colleges, voluntary community service have all changed. In traditional schools, changes are implemented and if they don't work the kids are blamed. Here, it's back to the drawing boards. (Louis & Kruse, 1995, p. 68)

Teacher leaders seem to position themselves on the cutting edge of the pedagogical frontier: they like to plunge, go for broke, boldly explore the realm of possibilities, and take action in the spirit of exigency rather than waiting for any problem to present itself. That feat, however, requires new and sudden insights, active learning, belief in a technical culture, and long successful practice. The beatitude of helping other teachers with a leap of intuition and knowledge is a form of inspiration, an elixir that can permanently stymie the recipient's self-doubt with a high, hopeful spirit. (Rosenholtz, 1989, p. 66)

I think art is important because it is part of learning. If there was no art there wouldn't be science, social studies and music—Jason Tang, grade 2 student. (Artsconcept, 1997, p. 2-3)

Specific programs fail to suggest how crucial the involvement of people is for the development of any innovation. The most successful schools believe that any school can influence a program. Art programs may be crucial for students, just as networks are very important for teachers, and new forms of decision-making challenge administrators. Each of these actors must believe that the change can be effected in a particular place. Conversely, school faculties can blame children's background or the character of a community for failure (Joyce & Calhoun, 1996) or faults can be found by parents and students with the teachers and the schools.

The decisive role of attitudes is revealed by following a school that initiates a new program, particularly in a new building (Smith, et al., 1986). For the first initiators, the transformation is a change in culture, a way of thinking about and valuing people and things. The traditional culture of teaching is perhaps the biggest obstacle to reform. Thus, it is important to examine the "cultural frameworks—the perceptual lenses—that teachers and administrators use as they approach school improvement" (Joyce & Calhoun, 1996, p. 138). Schools do not exist in a vacuum; they are part of a socially constructed web of relationships and shared meanings that are held together by strong internal and external forces. Action research includes both the specific content of change and attitudes toward these reforms.

Informal group experiences can continue the experience of creating culture. For action research, such changes are both created and studied. These changes can be promoted in oneself or others, but the direction for the innovation must be understood and plans must be made to support its realization. A series of interrelated changes may lead to learning organizations that are strikingly different from teaching in traditional schools. The pattern of these series can be partially delineated, but such innovative schools still appear, at times, where one would not expect them.

EFFECTIVE PEOPLE

Teachers have been shown to take their first step toward greater professional effectiveness by focusing on getting students to class (Lieberman & Miller, 1984). From a study conducted by the attendance committee, teachers in one high school determined that lateness was a period-by-period problem, not all day, and specific periods with high likelihood of late appearances could be graphed. Tardiness was as much a problem as absenteeism. The teachers developed a new policy, with the support of their administration, based on reestablishing their convictions that all students should be in class on time.

Both administrators and teachers emphasized the new policy, which was announced at the start of a new semester. After three absences, the teacher prepared a contract for the student and any further absences meant that an administrator was called in. After the big fifth absence, students had to make up the absences with the concerned teacher or in a supervised study hall. This modest but clear policy change had results for most students. The authors of the plan write:

We explained the policy to the students by handing out copies of the rules and conse-quences in each first-hour class, having the teacher go over the rules, asking the kids to sign a statement saying they understood the rules and consequences in each first-hour class, and having this backed up with a statement by the principal. From the first day, the results were phenomenal. Almost every teacher in the school was out in the halls. They were friendly and walked students to class encountering little, if any, resistance. In fact many teachers commented that the kids liked the attention and jokingly asked to be "escorted to class." (Lieberman & Miller, 1984, pp. 116-117)

After two weeks, the policy was working for all but the most intransigent students. Teachers in successful schools for at-risk students would have tried to find out from the students what policy would work for the school's attendance aim (Louis & Kruse, 1995).

For both teachers and students this new policy was an important step. But many highly experienced teachers in the school were cynical and suspicious (Lieberman & Miller, 1984). The majority of teachers in this case, as well as elsewhere, believed that attendance was within the sphere of the administration. However, as is probably also true of schemes for labeling and tracking students, teachers were concerned. They were caught up in "a neat contradiction: 'I don't care—I do care'" (Ibid). This policy change used the opportunity provided by action research and professional education to expand the teachers' sense of efficacy; many students also seemed to have benefited, because for self-efficacy there is nothing worse than being ignored.

The realization of what one can do in a situation and the effects that one's actions can have causally is crucial for the performance of both teachers and students. In very large studies of teachers, efficacy is either directly or indirectly the critical variable for their reaction to change (Ashton & Webb, 1986; Huberman & Miles, 1982; Loucks, et al., 1982; McLaughlin & March, 1979; Rosenholtz, 1989). The teachers' sense of making a difference in schools results from being selected for education in the first place, involvement in a special project, student responsiveness to teaching, and teacher recognition from administrators. Teachers must think that their actions lead to improvements, but the ambiguity surrounding education makes that very difficult.

Similar to teachers, large-scale research studies have shown how important efficacy is for students (Coleman, et al., 1966). These studies of student reactions to inequality led to work on effective schools as a way of showing that, in spite of the original study, school could make a difference (Mitchell, 1992). Attendance and tardiness have been shown to relate to the opposite of personal effectiveness, alienation (Stinchcombe, 1964). Students from poorer and more erratic backgrounds have been found to stumble and reveal little sense of direction in their educational or career decisions (Mitchell, 1992). One classic case of young men showed them turning down an offer to do exactly the same work of painting and making repairs for more money as independent contractors than they had been doing as employees (Liebow, 1967). Everyone seems to need a vision about their own destiny.

FROM CLASSROOM THEMES TO SCHOOLS-WITHIN-SCHOOLS

Those whose vision is limited are particularly likely to reinvent the wheel if they engage with innovations at all. Limited or local perspectives is a sign of very localized problem solving and many teachers continue to rely on their own experiences and those of whom they know best in their schools (Weiss, 1995). At the elementary level, such teachers have reinvented resource centers and team teaching without being aware of it (Sussman, 1977).

Both traditional and progressive teachers can benefit from finding new starting points for their education. Traditional teachers might prefer parables or morals as a guide (Collins & Tamarkin, 1982). The progressive phrased themes are used in a nonthreatening way in some interesting research from Great Britain:

1. First, a theme was chosen. Teachers were asked to consider conditions under which unfamiliar ideas would be used in the classroom. The concept of "Living Space" was the organizing focus.

2. Teachers were encouraged to try something they didn't ordinarily do. The trial period was one hour.

3. The theme of Living Space allowed different teachers to come up with different versions of how to deal with the topic (e.g., posing questions, designing a house, opinion polls, poems, stories).

4. Teachers who normally used group project methods tried whole class teaching. Those who usually did whole class teaching tried project methods. (Gibson, 1973, pp. 264-267)

In this study, a whole school developed an initial three-week project around a common theme as a way of developing integration among faculty, teachers, and new students. This project launches each semester as a way of using inquiry methods with at-risk students. Working in groups of eight to twelve, students discuss such themes as "What makes a good subway system?" or "How does architecture affect lifestyles?" For full days, students and teachers work together in and out of school. During the three weeks, they develop either a common definition or a way of talking about their problems; later, coordination occurred though the classes were separate.

Using the themes either for individual teachers or as a focus for an innovative school, leads teachers to discover for themselves that some of the most effective modes of learning depend on relationships more than techniques or specific knowledge. To go much further in developing innovations as individuals, teachers need the support of a team or, at least, a critical friend (Sussman, 1977). In an innovative school, teachers and outsiders can participate together in an expert panel, a debate to show students how teachers disagree, and how such disagree-ments can be handled and sorted out into a number of different alternatives. The issues the teachers discuss range from parenting to interpreting American history (Louis & Kruse, 1995).

Teacher participation, together with parent involvement, has been the basis for developing progressive school programs. In 1974, Deborah Meier created an exceptional elementary school in one of the poorest areas of New York City (Schorr, 1988). Protected by the Superintendent, Anthony Alvarado, the program prospered and achieved fantastic results. Among the reasons given for this success are integrated services, parental allies, teacher autonomy for planning, and community support (Schorr, 1988; James, 1992). The elementary curriculum was based on themes, such as families, the Inuit, the solar system, and skyscrapers, with basic skills integrated around the themes.

In 1985, when Debbie Meier expanded her work to found a secondary school, themes became the basis for the organization of schools, particularly since its expansion was part of an alternative school program. Though Meier's own school emphasized individual support in an open environment, a variety of programs was rapidly developed that provided choice for students and their families including the arts, community action, health sciences, and a number of academic divisions.

The program spread to a number of other cities. In 1989, it was the inspiration for charters within other schools in Philadelphia (Weissman, 1992). By 1990, Chicago had developed small schools within its large elementary and high schools; by 1992, the progressive Foundations School (grades one and two) stressed whole language, the Journalism School (grades four to seven) taught all forms of writing, the Classical School used the theme of "Discovery" to relate different fields of knowledge, the Environmental Sciences School (grades four through seven) drew an "environmental thread" through all courses, and the Prep School (grade eight) prepared students for entry into high school. In 1995, Annenberg grants to a number of large cities rewarded proposals that followed the "small school/special focus model" (James, 1992, p. 5).

By then, Deborah Meier was a senior fellow at the Annenberg Foundation and she was planning to teach at Harvard and was presenting an expert proposal to Boston (Gamble, 1996). Ms. Meier had affiliated her original school with the Coalition of Essential Schools (CES), which became the dominant form of small schools in New York City, called "Coalition Campus schools" (Bradley, 1995a). Most of the CES schools were fairly minor variations on a core curriculum, such as an emphasis on community service by Landmark school. Because "politics intervened" much more drastically, different schools were housed together with the CES school. CES is discussed more extensively in Chapter 9.

Regardless of the limits placed on cohabitants of a school, the concept of schools-within-schools is ambiguous. At times, divisions between traditional and progressive teachers have led to the division of programs. Many of the themes do not provide very much information. Schools-within-schools may be nothing more than a halfway step toward separate charter schools. The programs are only distinct from some charters by their emphasis on equal admission of all kinds of students (James, 1992). The program advised by Meier primarily attempts to create a sense of community for teachers and students so that both can identify with schools and develop within them as people.

LEARNING ORGANIZATIONS

Colleague relationships are difficult to transform within schools, in part because teachers' relationships become so invidious (Waller, 1967). But in those schools where consensus is valued and staff learning is promoted, the needs of innovative teachers for support and advice are recognized. In one such school, a new teacher speaks revealingly about her experience:

I had worked all summer making materials for the year and at the last minute I was given a sixth grade. What an adjustment! [How did you make it through the year?] Well, people on the faculty—other teachers—pitched in and helped. One teacher gave me a bunch of material on synonyms and antonyms, another gave me math materials. I went to many people with teaching problems. [Do you think that "pitching in" is a regular occurrence at your school?] Oh yes. We all work together here. (Rosenholtz, 1989, p. 36)

However, in more conventional schools, teachers who march to a different drummer are afraid of being shown up in front of the principal. More to the point, such teachers come to see that, even if they are successful in terms of student learning, they must act, dress, or express opinions that correspond with those of the dominant clique (Rosenholtz, 1989). One new English teacher, who had students writing and publishing their own journal, was not around the next year because she was too different from the established teachers (Cusick, 1973). A leading study of learning-centered schools states:

A teacher's effectiveness . . . depends heavily upon the specific situation into which the teacher is placed, the expectations and behaviour of one's colleagues, and the goodness of fit between the teacher's own behavior and the norms of the school. (Rosenholtz, 1989, p. 38)

In learning-centered schools, teachers found time on the fly to talk; they talked about instruction and engaged in problem solving and planning. In more conventional schools, teachers claimed they could not use the time between classes to talk; instead, they exchanged war stories when they did talk and, because of their isolation, leaders for curriculum change did not emerge (Rosenholtz, 1989).

In classic studies of traditional teachers the teacher group's norms are shown to be the criteria that teachers use to maintain their dignity (Waller, 1967). A new teacher knows she is established, for example, when she makes an "s" sound to keep elementary students quiet (McPherson, 1972). After accepting standards from the group, the teacher learns to avoid being labeled as an easy mark (Waller, 1967). Even though they become very competitive with each other, particularly after ten years, the teacher group becomes the exclusive reference for individual teachers. At the outset of their careers, most individual teachers, understandably, wanted to be very different from the older teachers; they change their orientation after teaching (Mitchell, 1968).

The structure of learning-centered schools is dramatically different from traditional ones. In the other type of school, the relationship of the principal to teachers is often described as bureaucratic. However, in contrast to learning-centered schools, traditional schools show a structure that is more feudal than bureaucratic. In stable situations, teacher acceptance of school-based management is probably related to the long awaited respect that administrators are showing them. In learning-centered schools, principals encourage every teacher to be a leader, and they help support relationships among teachers who, in turn, develop new ideas.

The two types of schools contrast in whether the mask and externals are the only reality or if the individuals can remake the play in their own image. In the feudal structure, principals use the rules as a basis for making exceptions for the teachers who have shown their loyalty to them (Cusick, 1983). In progressive schools, teachers are encouraged to be individuals and they, in turn, encourage their students to realize themselves (Louis & Kruse, 1995).

Leadership for learning-centered schools can come from parents and artists who join together with teachers and administrators to support new programs. In contrast to the expert ideal, one parent says:

In other words, we do not need "flat" professionals, but "round" ones who are not slotted into one area of expertise but are capable of seeing with perspective all of the possibilities in their work environment. My expectations of the education system, as a parent, is [sic] that they [sic] should provide children with the necessary skills and confidence so that they are capable of self motivated learning throughout their lifetime in order to compete successfully in the area in which they have the most aptitude. (Artsconcept, 1997, pp. 2-20-2-21)

The focus on learning has meant that the teachers have had more professional training than before, although this particular school has not undertaken the entire revision of concepts of teaching that occurred in another site (Artsconcept, 1997). With the support of an outside arts organization, the administrators in both of these schools have been able to implement their ideals for arts instruction in elementary schools. Teachers have conveyed their enthusiasm to students and believe that they will be able to work with "big ideas" for planning in the future.

In contrast, in traditional schools teachers and administrators are concerned with the limits they confront and principals are geared to keeping control over their kingdoms. Traditional principals typically relate to teachers individually in their office, rather than working with teacher groups, as a means of maintaining power over them (Sarason, 1982). Similarly, principals in the traditional school use flattery to mollify the discontent of teachers together with appeals to a transcendent world of laws, regulations, and budgets, which they claim teachers cannot understand. There is no working with community groups or expanding the horizons of teachers and students in these settings.

In more open schools, all of the external controls are subject to change. Teacher groups limit any possible assertion of power by administrators (Sussman, 1977) and teacher leaders represent the freedom that principals can give teachers (Rosenholtz, 1989). School-based management is changing the budget with the help of teachers. In charter schools, as well as in other cases, exemptions to the laws and regulations are granted. In one California charter school, teachers did the principal's job and students replaced the janitor, in both cases because of the costs. In many other schools, the schedule is no longer sacrosanct and it changes for students as groups of teachers increasingly act together (Louis & Kruse, 1995). In traditional schools, principals must foster the dependency of new teachers who largely remain isolated from others on staff.

The culture of teaching can come to involve collegiality, particularly through the implementation of action research. Though such research runs counter to traditional views of teaching and education, teachers generally welcomed the opportunity for adult interaction and study groups. Action-research offers teachers a new adult peer experience. Teachers had many surprising concerns about the new approach; one of which was "whether cooperative teacher work was legitimate and whether the principals should be giving them cooperative planning time during the day which was suppose to be devoted to their teaching" (Joyce & Calhoun, 1996, p. 32).

The very process of collective lesson-planning was seen as "cheating" and a violation of professional integrity, unlike spontaneous get-togethers for sharing information or exchanging war stories. Such joint planning is the extension that is most needed to make school-based management more meaningful. Action-research brings shared decision making into classrooms, where for most teachers privatism has been the practice. Furthermore, there is traditionally little time for collegial inquiry and collective decision making. The aim of action-research was to "increase teacher interaction about curriculum and instruction, and to reduce the norms of privacy and isolation" (Joyce & Calhoun, 1996, p. 45)

Though administrators and other teachers can influence innovative teachers, the greatest effect on teachers is their own conception of their role. In learning-enriched schools, teachers believe that learning to teach is ongoing, that teachers become better as a result of a variety of experiences rather than because of their innate disposition, and that teachers can even affect student learning on standardized achievement tests (Rosenholtz, 1989). However, such schools can be quite varied in their approaches. Many are more concerned about their students than they are about achievement results. Others try to relate their teaching to current events, changing styles and trendy ideas so that education is in constant change rather than a yearly version of the same old yellow notes (Louis & Kruse, 1995).

In more traditional settings, teaching is a fixed state where through voice, standards, and procedures, one shows how totally one is "all business." Because of their own values, teachers support the high achievers among students rather than the creative students (Getzels & Jackson, 1962). Traditional teachers accept stereotypes about themselves and even identify with those who have more power than themselves. They may use the teachers' union as a guard or directly identify with the system; in contrast, innovative schools or projects are the focus of the teachers' view of themselves and their craft. Teachers in stable situations admire the doers rather than the thinkers in society, often plan on leaving teaching for business opportunities, and frequently become the worst critics of teachers (Waller, 1967). Teachers are one of the few occupational groups who place themselves at a lower level than the public does (Hodge, et al., 1966).

However, the most devastating effect of teaching upon teachers is that they can lose their creativity within teaching or their ability to understand the learner's perspective (Waller, 1967). Security concerns have been associated with teaching since the original job choice, but the need for security was always balanced by a belief that there were some opportunities in daily work to develop new methods and different approaches. As teaching becomes separated from the rest of one's life, concern for discipline and a search for an appropriate response to grading eliminates an openness to student views. A preoccupation with the perfect result replaces the capacity to relate the world to the content. An understanding of the learner's perspective and concern for the process of learning is obliterated by a view of students as a class to be conquered. Involution among teachers can make teachers unfit for teaching, and schooling becomes a rack on which students are stretched.

Though not reversing this entire scenario, action-research seems to tap into the needs of experienced teachers for development. Regardless of age or experience, teachers responded to it with "increased receptivity to innovations" (Joyce & Calhoun, 1996, p. 11). All teacher groups needed support, time to develop their ability to work collectively, and find resources with which they could carry out their new tasks. The total environment of learning-centered schools seems to be required. Specific programs, such as French immersion discussed in Chapter 6, where teachers have had a series of successes, are also important. Teachers have got to feel that other teachers, administrators, and community members want them to be better, that they can do it, and they want to change themselves. Older, more experienced teachers can avoid cynicism about reform when they are a meaningful part of it.

INDIVIDUAL RESPONSES

Creative schools can alter the fate of those within schools. Complex innovations can lead to a variety of consequences (Huberman & Miles, 1982). If the innovations involve people in networks, the social supports generated can lead to the transformations, which otherwise only occur for leading educators individually. Individuals in teaching always become known for their separate, even eccentric approaches (Swindler, 1979; Louis & Kruse, 1995). Groups allow them to find themselves as much by contrast as imitation.

Individuals appear to change and become supporters of innovations in rather unsuspected ways. As was generally recognized in the nineteenth century, such changes are like religious conversions. A series of studies has found that teachers continue to change in largely the same way today, but that it is less recognized (Smith, et al., 1986; Sussman, 1977; Wilson, 1994). These changes, which occur after the first year in teaching, are often followed by another similar change to a different ideological position and are a part of a wandering life where different situations are explored before returning home.

One of the teachers who had gone from being a progressive educator to a born-again Christian educator speaks of his changes:

I had a very liberal attitude toward discipline at the time which was one of my biggest mistakes, but if I was to take over a school today or take a school on like Kensington, my style as a leader would be very—not highly structured—it would be structured but it would be a strong, aggressive role as the leader—leading a staff and try to get them to work together as a team, you know, not being a total autocrat but making decisions—and making things happen and not being a reactor. . . . Children need discipline they need guidance and structure to be secure. And I think one of the major things that changed me in addition to my spiritual change was having a family. . . . You know, we have three beautiful children, God has blessed us—it's been beautiful and they are all just—they're doing super in school. . . . The change and what I discovered as a parent was that the Rousseauian concept was just totally unacceptable for me. (Smith, et al., 1986, pp. 152-163)

This changer continues to vacillate between traditional and progressive education as he pursues his new job as a training director in industry. For others, change may be a combination of opposites, but, in some of these extreme cases, the conflict is exposed.

Within teacher networks and other support groups, this change does not leave the individuals to wrestle with their own identity. Though many teachers may join the increasing variety of teacher networks for advice, others come to practice leadership. For either reason, teachers become involved. Professional association together with additional resources, which the school system can provide, is the best known reason for teachers seeking innovations (Huberman & Miles, 1982). Teachers have long found similar opportunities in team teaching (Sussman, 1977). Informal groups based on readings, oral presentations, or problem solving can serve the same function. Colleagues can provide an audience for trying out changes for the classroom before presenting them to students. Some teachers can serve as models for others, while other teachers need to "give orders" (Sussman, 1977, p. 230). Such emergent forms of teacher organization can provide autonomy from administrators (Sussman, 1977) and more authority than traditional competition with peers or control over students (Waller, 1967).

The traditional isolation of teachers is dissolving as computer and social networks provide an increasing number of opportunities for teachers to interact. Aside from the NWP with its 160,000 teachers and IMPACT II with national support, there are hundreds of small networks in almost any subject imaginable (Richardson, 1996). Teachers find that networks provide an opportunity for them to develop both their social links and their unique preferences. Like members of an immigrant group who prefer to practice behaviors for the dominant society within their ethnic associations, teachers find the support within their own networks that is usually missing in professional development controlled by administrators or graduate training dominated by the university experts.

Teachers in the networks are grappling with decision making under conditions of uncertainty and learning how to make political moves, including finding financing to keep the networks themselves going. The typical program includes a "Chinese menu" of opportunities for teachers. A small mathematics collabora-tive in Georgia called its assembly "Birds of a Feather" and offered a statistics workshop, a summer camp for girls, an institute to integrate mathematics and science in the middle grades, a school-to-work meeting intended to relate mathematics to business, and training for elementary teachers on the uses of science labs. The teachers were determined to develop their own practical answers to the problems they knew and experienced. One high school mathematics teacher says: "Sometimes, administrators aren't sure about all these crazy ideas teachers have. So it really helps to have a critical mass that supports experimentation" (Richardson, 1996).

However, teachers also develop their own individual reaction to both teaching and network projects even when universities are involved, as they are with NWP. Though a long series of studies has shown four or five patterns among students and teachers, many studies have shown complicated reactions to a single program (Mitchell, 1971). The four typical patterns are a creative interest in ideas, a search for status recognition or achievement, a need for people interested in them or to stimulate their interests, and several forms of reactions to power including alienation, striking out, and erratic change.

A British study showed most of these differences among both teachers and students (Galton & Willcocks, 1983). A class inquirer who asked more questions than other teachers in order to stimulate thought, corresponded to solitary workers among students for whom the school work is the primary consideration; both achieve with a common focus on ideas (Galton & Willcocks, 1983). However, virtually equal achievements occur from teachers and students who allow some sociability within their school roles. Other configurations concerning power and status did not seem to connect teachers with students, but the most effective teachers move among all the options as circumstances require, whereas others never change their dominant pattern in the British setting.

An intensive American study of teacher-students in a summer NWP program revealed that all varieties of people found meaning in this program (Sunstein, 1994). One woman was so affected by power and alienated that, when asked to share her experience after returning to school from the summer program, she returned pictures of the school without any people appearing in them; however, she developed a strong commitment to writing. This woman needed leadership in order to follow through on the writing program in her class and she was still insensitive, but the program had changed her substantially. Another more idea-centered participant "met her students with the same paradoxes she had explored in herself" (Sunstein, 1994, p. 221). A student who was more affected by people almost left the summer program until she discovered a community of several returning students; she later approached her students as a mentor, just as she believed she had been mentored to overcome her fear of writing; she taught writing more confidently to her students after the NWP program. Those who sought a place as consultants probably revealed a status or achievement orientation more than these three women did.

PROFESSIONAL DEVELOPMENT SCHOOLS

Though a long way from recognizing different ways of knowing and relating to school, faculties of education have tried to take some giant steps in transforming themselves. One of the leading individual reformers, John Goodlad, tried to change teacher education so that it would be relevant to the work realities and at the same time make the student-teacher a moral agent for schools (Bradley, 1991). Institutional experts associated with research-centered universities formed the Holmes group, which called for an inquiry approach and a partnership between faculties of education and public schools (Bradley, 1990). The Holmes group coined the term, "professional development schools," but many others have followed with similar ideas. The Ford Foundation sponsored eleven such schools; in Louisville, Philip Schlechty claimed twenty-four schools for his Center for Leadership in School Reform (Olson, 1989).

Following extensive studies of education schools, Dr. Goodlad transformed his earlier research league of universities associated with his change studies into a group that attempted to change the "weakest link" in the chain of reform, universities. Faculties of both education and arts and sciences would join together with school districts to form "centers of pedagogy," which might help teacher training to overcome its "chronic prestige deprivation" (Olson, 1990, pp. 7, 9). A key to Goodlad's position was abandoning individual supervision of students; groups of them would be supervised by representatives of all the partners.

After a prescribed initial curriculum, students would enter a three-year teacher-preparation program where the last year would be largely an internship in partner schools. The partner schools would provide a program for all those involved in offering "reading, writing, field projects, and intensive conversations (22 days in a residential setting)" (Goodlad, 1994, p. 635). Cooperating teachers, together with faculty members in education and arts and science, and with the support of the Exxon Corporation, rethought their tasks. Goodlad urges that the student courses in the arts and sciences should be organized in broad areas so that general understanding rather than specialization would be provided for prospective teachers (Olson, 1990, p. 9). This, like many of his other ideas, including an emphasis on the moral purpose of education, is similar to the practices of the University of Chicago under Robert Hutchins where Goodlad was educated and taught. Goodlad has selected some twenty-five colleges and universities to participate in his National Network for Educational Renewal (Goodlad, 1994, p. 637).

Lacking the roots that Goodlad has as a person, the Holmes Group became involved in a search for group status. In 1986, they formed a select group of research universities calling for improvement in the quality of teacher education and adding demands for more than the traditional four years to become a teacher. The Holmes Group initial report, *Tomorrow's Teachers*, appeared at almost the same time as a report from the Carnegie Foundation's Forum on Education and the Economy, *A Nation Prepared*, which called for clinical schools. It was not until 1990 that the Holmes Group actually called for professional development schools under the same general rubric, *Tomorrow's Teachers*; this proposal was related to the group's most general goal, increased professionalism (Bradley, 1996b).

Though by 1993 there were ninety-seven universities in the Holmes program, some, such as at Michigan State, continue to be very dominant. This program is called the Michigan Partnership for New Education and, in 1990, had a budget of $48 million (Bradley, 1990). Students enter in cohort, as Goodlad wanted; their program takes five years and they are expected to have both a major and minor outside of education with a year's equivalent of practice teaching. In some instances, university faculty team teach with school teachers, but the faculty are more likely to be involved in curriculum planning and research within the schools. The program at Michigan State involves a redirection of faculty research to the clinical classroom setting, where teachers can contribute as much as researchers to the process. The faculty find that there is a reduction in the time that they can spend on any kind of research, and teachers have not typically become co-authors.

Under various sponsors, professional development schools train new and experienced teachers as well as other school-based educators (American Association of Colleges for Teacher Education, 1997). There are 344 individual schools involved in 84 partnerships, which include 96 colleges and universities in the United States. Almost three-quarters of all such schools have been founded since 1991 and a similar percentage exist only at elementary schools. There is strong suspicion that many of these schools represent only symbolic changes and that many others may not last because they exist through a combination of soft foundation money and voluntary efforts. In Louisville, action research remains an academic exercise for students in professional development schools (University of Louisville, 1997). Unless the separate worlds of schools and universities are integrated, these schools are expected to remain permanently at the margin of education; a woman who is paid both by a university and a school district is called a "paradigm pioneer" (Bradley, 1993).

Outside the United States, such schools as a part of partnerships now exist in Canada, Greece, Israel, Japan, and the United Arab Emirates. As discussed in Chapter 4 concerning other innovations, Canadian professional programs are not usually a part of a large American network, as with other Canadian uses of American innovations. More than any other institution, Canadian higher education is distinctive from its counterpart in the United States. At the University of Calgary, the new program to train teachers is an imitation of a plan to educate doctors at McMaster's University. However, this program requires a Bachelor's degree before entrance to its two years of largely clinical activities in schools. American writers are cited and similar directions for educating teachers are suggested (Faculty of Education, 1996-1998).

Though there has been a seemingly spectacular growth in professional development schools and their parallels, the partnerships have corrected at most one limitation of the exclusive emphasis on professionalism and expertise; the experts have tried to link up with the classroom teachers. However, the communities in which schools are located are still not a part of these partnerships. In the two Louisville schools I visited, neither university person had ever spoken to parents who were also in the schools. One critic of the other experts, Peter Mureel, director of the master-in-teaching program at Northeastern University in Boston, argues for an "anti-bureaucratic collaborative that also gives parents and community members a voice" (Ponessa, 1997).

There has always been a major difference among the networks that promote these schools in terms of their emphasis on equality among minority groups. As a result of initial criticism of its elitism and failure to represent colleges training minorities, the Holmes Group developed a careful position; it tries to "prevent tests from discouraging minority candidates," "identify" and "finance and sustain . . . students of color" and make faculties of education represent minorities (Holmes Group, n. d.). Goodlad has been more general in his commitment, but has also worked with specific advocacy groups in a few places. In El Paso, Texas, the affiliate with the Goodlad group tried to provide students with experience working with parents in poor communities; they have worked with the affiliate of the Industrial Areas Foundation, which is discussed in Chapter 9 (Pacheco, 1994).

In 1992, the AT&T Foundation, with five teachers unions, launched "Teachers for Tomorrow," one of the more recent programs for inner-city teachers in five cities (*Teacher Magazine*, 1992). Earlier, the American Federation of Teachers had launched its program of professional practice schools in three schools with the support of the Exxon Corporation (Viadero, 1989). Though the union wanted restructured schools, in general, and payment for mentor and lead teachers, in particular, its schools are centered in urban areas with high needs because that is where the membership of the American Federation of Teachers is located.

While the union and some community groups attempted to deal with the needs of urban areas, the Holmes Group changed its name to the Holmes Partnership and decided it must include unions and organizations of educational administrators (Bradley, 1996b). Ann Lieberman, an institutional expert who is codirector of the National Center for Restructuring Education, Schools and Teaching, established a dialogue among all the groups operating partnerships with allied schools. After perhaps a few light years, community organizations, parents, and students will be consulted about the kind of teachers they would like to have.

In the meantime, a major effort to provide teachers for difficult urban areas has been attacked directly by Linda Darling-Hammond, a professor at Columbia University who heads a national commission on professional standards (Richardson, 1996) and indirectly by Frank Murray, executive director of the Holmes Group. The attacks were aimed at Wendy Kopp, founder and president of Teach for America. In 1989, in her undergraduate thesis at Princeton, Kopp proposed to recruit and train the best liberal arts graduates for the positions the school boards could not fill (Stanfield, 1994).

After a series of grants, praise, and emulation by President Clinton for his own volunteer program, and a number of revisions, by 1994, Teach for America had a "9 million dollar budget, 18 offices, a 100-member staff, and two new subsidiaries with some very ambitious ideas" to challenge the monopoly of schools of education for control of accreditation (Stanfield, 1994, p. 227). Kopp also had some major enemies; one wrote a sketch of the future where Kopp was Secretary of Education, which reflected both humor and fear. Immediately afterward, Darling-Hammond attacked Kopp for sending unprofessional people into classrooms. Murray wrote an article for *Education Week* attacking the advocates of "natural teaching:" "well-meaning and well-read persons with good college grades," "untrained and kind persons" and liberal arts graduates who had "met the expectations of the faculty in their field should not be taken as evidence that they were ready to take up work as teachers" (1997). There is no attack on the practice of lower rank university faculty being the ones who often link with such schools in professional development schools (Campoy, 1994).

ADMINISTRATORS PRIME THE PUMP

Those who are wedded to the professional model see change as more of the same—more training, more isolation, and please no challengers to the secrecy and special languages of educational experts. Within education, change is limited by the perceptions of those still in control. For example, teacher success and student motivation are seen as individual power; attempts need to be made to change teachers or students where their behavior occurs, not in the principal's office (Sarason, 1993). Furthermore, school board members and principals have attempted to maintain their organizational influence in spite of drastic changes in some school systems.

Those outside the system primarily act as if their meetings with representatives of the system would change the students' experiences. Power with people at the grassroots level is not typically developed by these outside groups. Coalitions are developed with educators that promote safe changes, and professional development schools are a safe change, otherwise the Carnegie Foundation would never have endorsed them. Group action and effective advocacy are the alternatives for those who want to challenge these new institutionally supported experts. However, passive resistance can always empty the commands of superiors of any meaning (Waller, 1967).

In the long-run, administrative power and authority can be undermined by teachers' passive resistance, but in the short-run administrative push helps break the teachers' habit patterns so that even teacher-initiated programs are more possible. In the example of attendance policy, it was an assistant principal who initiated the study. Generally, administrators must both endorse the new policy and secure the acceptance of some or all teachers, because their willing receptiveness is needed (Huberman & Miles, 1982).

Principals, in particular, are most important to rally the the forces around the innovation plan. They can play a crucial role and provide leadership and encouragement. The principals involved in the "Models of Teaching" program secured the schools involvement in the program, but, more importantly, they brought varying degrees of "pressure and support" on teachers who were constantly encouraged to practice the new strategies (Joyce & Calhoun, 1996, p. 46). To provide leadership, they "borrowed" classes and tried the new strategies themselves, thus modeling for the staff a commitment to the program and also a willingness to show themselves open to change. Other studies reported on a principal who was so confident that he developed teachers by having them critique his teaching (Turnbull, 1985).

There are, of course, many other influences on teachers to adopt innovations. Without realizing it, students teach their teachers through their immediate responses in the classroom; in this way, students influence the spread of an innovation (Huberman & Miles, 1982; Lortie, 1975). Some parents and community activists often oppose any change. Teachers can actively support innovation by the examples they set for their colleagues, their use of team teaching and, of course, their involvement in action research projects (Joyce & Calhoun, 1996; Sussman, 1977; Rosenholtz, 1989).

Though others influence teacher acceptance of change, the most significant cues that teachers receive come from either principals or higher administrators. The symbolic influence of such administrators continues to be very important. As mentioned in Chapter 2, the institutionalization of change in concrete ways, such as the budget, is particularly telling. For the teachers, the inclusion of an innovative program in the continuing life of the school is the opposite of the initiative being labeled an "experiment." If the program is an experiment, teachers are given license to "pick and choose" and few continuing changes are likely to occur (Huberman & Miles, 1982, p. 35).

The appearance of the higher administrators at meetings for teachers is an important indicator to teachers of the significance of a particular innovation. Since teachers are typically involved in over three innovations, sometimes as many as seventeen, they want administrators to show their priorities among innovations, particularly through the signs of support that they give. As discussed in the context of teacher evaluations in Chapter 3, joint training for teachers and administrators also helps them to understand a common language about teaching and change.

Administrators often have to shelter an innovation and keep the initial groups together. For teachers, this protection means that they are a group "set apart" within the schools (Huberman & Miles, 1982, p. 394). A sense of "a part together" can lead students to identify with some of the more innovative teachers. Teachers themselves can find a renewed interest in their work, particularly from the broadened contacts that personnel associated with the innovation bring to the school. The most important influence of this administrative attention is keeping the staff who are working on the change, together. This will influence involvement on the project, and student changes involve more than simple measures.

Teachers must be actively involved over sustained periods because many innovations that come down from experts are underdeveloped (Sussman, 1977). The innovations, such as whole language for French immersion, must be developed for different grade levels or different students in many specific ways. Either teachers must have substantial time to develop general innovations or substantial administrative assistance must be provided. If layers of new authorities are brought in over teachers, then teacher support for the innovation or resistance to the authorities will occur (Sussman, 1977). More independence for teachers is the basis from which greater initiatives can be developed among teachers.

Though not directly influenced by administrators, teacher involvement can lead to the support and recognition of teacher advocates for change (Loucks, et al., 1982). Staff consensus, enriched learning experiences, and teacher advocacy are all related to teacher leadership for change (Rosenholtz, 1989). Teacher advocates can carry the innovations outside the public schools. For teachers, the endorsement by community leaders is even more important than that of educators (Bauchner, et al., 1982). Community leaders help symbolize the support that the innovation has. This is an effective means of obtaining support for change and a way of involving teachers who have remained outside the initiative. As will be discussed in Chapter 8, the initial involvement of parents with reform is likely to be influenced by the mass media. Furthermore, the partnerships of schools with business, higher education, and social services can enhance the entrepreneurial activities of teachers (Mitchell, 1996).

MOMENTUM

The community initially developed a stereotype about teachers as limited people and attempted to keep them subordinated (Waller, 1967). In traditional communities where teachers' lives were so restricted, changes in education were very slow. Before World War II, changes in education, such as the study of Keynesian economics in a high school course, could take fifty years (Baldridge & Deal, 1975; Voege, 1975). In isolated areas and classrooms this slow pace for change can still happen.

However, in change projects it is possible for an innovation to be implemented in an individual school within six months (Huberman & Miles, 1982). More typically, the change occurs in a given school within eighteen months. The shorter period can occur if the innovation is demonstrated by other teachers, supported by them as well as administrators, and the teachers have had positive experiences with previous innovations.

The teachers' experiences with other innovations are influenced by the school district and the larger educational scene. In the 1960s, it took five years for even the simplest innovations, such as language labs, to reach the majority of teachers and classes within a district. In the 1970s, teachers could take five years to reach the mechanical level of adaptation on the level of use and concerns measures (Anderson, 1981). More recently, community involvement and political decisions, such as reconstituting schools, have been shown to accelerate the pace of change, but teacher resistance has been substantial.

If teachers could become active disseminators of innovations, the pace could be more permanently increased, perhaps two years for systems and one term for schools. However, instead of changing the supports for schools, many administrators continue to pretend that change can be instantaneous—the school will adopt team teaching Monday morning! The provinces of Alberta and Ontario claim to change the entire curriculum every five years. Even the paperwork for such magical transformations cannot always occur, and the realities of operating under reduced funding with a mandate for many changes is nearly impossible.

Teachers' own personal views and reactions ultimately influence the interpretation of changes. Using a concept similar to levels of concern, the "Stages of Growth" work on the Models of Teaching has shown how individual orientation influence opportunities for professional development (Joyce & Calhoun, 1996, p. 37). Teachers range from the "Gourmet Omnivore," who seeks out new opportunities and also generates new change and initiatives, to the "Passive Consumer," who tends to conform and be dependent and, finally, to the "Reticent," who actively resists opportunities for professional growth and change and who tends to be highly suspicious of any reform efforts. The stages of growth affect the level of use that an innovation receives. Thus, receptiveness to innovation is a necessary requirement for change; with reticent teachers, only symbolic changes can be expected, but fortunately teachers are not uniform.

CONCERN FOR STUDENTS

Teachers may fear that students will create discipline problems or have other extreme reactions to a proposed change (p. 30). However, major changes are difficult to achieve in schools because students are not involved in the changes and are at the bottom of the organizational hierarchy. For a long time, language has been imported from business into education. Students are to "work, be productive" and their work is "the bottom line" (Kohn, 1997). The language and batch processing leave students with few options (Cusick, 1973). A number of studies have revealed that the caste-like world of students is seldom seriously influenced by innovations. For example, "hall boys" are often similar in their behavior in either a progressive or traditional school; it is still a school that they resist (Whiteside, 1978, pp. 100-102; Novak, 1975).

Alternative schools that do enlist the support of students change both their behavior and the professional lives of teachers (Louis & Kruse, 1995). Students and their parents must be considered together with the professionals so that each group sees how the situation was before, as well as after, the change. The initial match of the program with students' needs and abilities should be followed by a consideration of the opportunities that are provided for students as well as forms of recognition that are available to them. Many programs have actually been based on the administrators' perception of their showroom possibilities, the availability of staff, or the extent to which they will placate unhappy parents or community members (Huberman & Miles, 1982).

In contrast to administrators, teachers, parents, and students need substantial reasons to innovate (House, 1974). For teachers, proof that the innovation changed the reactions of students is more important than being paid to participate in an innovation (Berman & McLaughlin, 1978). The teachers' commitment developed after the innovation affected students, more so than did anything that could be done before the trial (Bauchner, et al., 1982). Experienced teachers have had too many experiences with specific proposals and find it difficult to be enthusiastic about any of them, in contrast to new teachers who tend to have their attentions captured by the aims of a proposal rather than its accomplishments (Levine & Leibert, 1987). For parents, it appears that innovations should improve their children's futures, but they find it difficult to make concrete suggestions for particular school activities (Sussman, 1977). Students have had comparatively few opportunities to be involved with changes and are attracted, if at all, by the individual personalities involved (Fullan, 1982).

In the absence of actual involvement of each of these groups, a symbolic pretense is often maintained. Top administration acts as if a rational organization did exist and a reorganization is undertaken, which is supposed to guide actions but never does. Similarly, teachers act as if their new paper or lesson plan is independent of students and the resistance that they or others may offer.

The delusions of planners and legislatures have reached more astronomical levels. In the case of changes in teacher education, including professional development schools, the major question is the extent to which the traditional socialization of teachers has been changed. The teachers' perspective that they are "martyrs to society, overworked and underpaid" has translated into views by the same groups that academic learning in universities is irrelevant to the serving and sacrificing profession (Mitchell, 1995). The perception of future teachers that they have lower status within the university and they must retreat to teaching tricks; together these limitations translate into lower esteem and a belief that they require a simple, linear approach .

Whether the experts are any better in changing their own university homes, even with the help of partners, is questionable. The record of their work with innovations is likened to an amateur tinsmith who hits the bent place in one part of the metal causing another bend to appear elsewhere. Written plans prevent the interaction of people in different roles and, as a result, realities continue to confound reformers.

Schools need to move away from a stance that sees innovations as intended to solve specific educational problems toward a "fluid, continuous inquiry into how to make education better on a day-to-day basis" (Joyce & Calhoun, 1996, p. 178). The vision should be of schools as centers of inquiry, where "continuous, collegial inquiry" is supported and where teaching and learning are examined continuously as part of a cycle of sustained action (Joyce & Calhoun, 1996, p. 179).

REVISITING EXEMPLARY PROGRAMS

Though many reforms are a reaction to criticisms of schools, the changes may not seriously solve the problem posed by the initial criticism (Sussman, 1977). A study of a series of innovations over a number of years found that innovations introduced by educators seldom result from a search for better alternatives (Daft & Becker, 1978). Computers have been adopted without a consideration of spending options, such as additional teachers rather than technology for the school (Rogers, et al., 1985). It has been argued that many promoters have innovations and are looking for problems to solve with their new toys (Baldridge & Deal, 1983). Once school boards have adopted a change, internal opposition to the change almost never develops (Daft & Becker, 1978).

The more recent cases of politically influenced changes are opposed by those affected within the schools as well as by political opponents outside. In Chicago, principals who lost tenure under the reform act fought the entire measure in the courts, but the act resulted from a program assembled by the dominant pressure group (Mitchell, 1996). In Kentucky, school boards have opposed the governance changes and teachers found some of the educational requirements, such as administering portfolio exams to their students in both mathematics and language in the same year, impossible. In Kentucky, a broad consensus was developed by the Prichard Committee which co-opted most potential leaders, but it has had limited grass-roots support (Mitchell, 1996). In Alberta, political consensus was developed among leading stakeholders and government supporters at roundtable discussions before the act, but there was opposition from Catholic schools and public school boards to their loss of autonomy, particularly for collecting tax support (Mitchell, 1996). Though political consensus is better than arbitrary action, it still represents the trends and fads happening in other places and is not always based upon extensive experience or research about the consequences that are likely to occur.

Individual innovations differ substantially in the consequences that can be expected. Historically, direct classroom innovations have been the most difficult to develop (Cuban, 1984). In this sense, French immersion is a striking achieve-ment, but this language program is very limited; achievement tests are insufficient and considerations of attitude change or social groupings should be considered more just, as they are in either mainstreaming or segregating students who have handicaps or gifts; the art enrichment program supported by Galef involves similar problems for students. However, the DWoK program involves the training of teachers and the effects that such training will have on students; this two-stage sequence is even more noticeable for the other exemplary programs discussed in Chapter 6.

These problems, as well as the polar opposition of teachers to administrators, are involved in the very complicated demands made by school-based management. Interestingly, the best example of transforming teaching, French immersion, has not been able to alter the administration of the school. Conversely, for changes in school decision making to affect the curriculum, it seems likely that procedures like team teaching would have to be developed as a part of an action-research program. The individualistic values of teachers might lead them to prefer a brief period of cooperation, such as the program that was built around a common theme, to continuing team teaching. General team teaching has been the slowest spreading innovation in history because teachers were not receptive. Furthermore, for school-based decision making to affect students, it would have to change student groups, provide support for individual students, and transform the tone and culture of the school.

Other innovations are in between the poles of classroom and managerial change. The NWP has not tried to change the administration or classrooms. It has provided reformers in Chicago with leaders and publications, but it has never taken a political position on change. DWoK has been more concerned than the NWP about involving administrators in its programs since their support for the more marginal art program was viewed as essential. NWP has relied on teachers to carry out their reforms in classrooms with students, and past participants in the program have documented the effects of the program, principally for their advanced degrees. Meanwhile, the Galef Institute has made political connections, particularly in Kentucky, which promoters of other efforts should consider.

To see the possibilities for any program developing, a template is needed to compare them. One of the few empirically supported patterns shows that sites practicing a variety of innovations showed a clear layer sequence (Mitchell, 1992). In a still interesting study, almost all of the sites studied showed that teachers who had changed their daily routines had developed a wider repertoire of teaching approaches. At least half the original sample had gone on to form new or changed relationships; most of those who changed relationships went on, still further, to develop different understandings of the possibilities of change in school. In a continuing sequence, some teachers out of the preceding group developed self-efficacy, an ability to transfer the innovation, and changed attitudes; however, changed attitudes did occur out of sequence (Huberman & Miles, 1982).

This highly correlated pattern should allow one to see precisely how far a specific innovation has developed if it began with the classroom, such as French immersion, or if it includes instructional changes, as does DWoK. For example, French immersion has several times made changes that enlarged the repertoire of teachers and, through the collaboration of artists with teachers, the classroom relationships in a variety of programs have even more dramatically changed. To dock at the wharf of education, the NWP and school-based management would have to proceed in almost the opposite direction from each other. From attitudes toward writing and their own emergent skills, NWP teachers need to develop new repertoires and routines. School decision making has an even more difficult transformation to make, to develop from school-wide policy to any activities that affect classroom behavior.

The entire approach requires that social effects be considered. Social crises have initiated many of the recent innovations. The more complicated and diverse the crisis, the more direct the effect upon the innovation and its splintered consequence, such as in the examples of school-based management. French immersion has a clear and present danger to which it responds, whereas the writing movement developed against a more general malaise. Both programs have navigated around an isolated professional goal that probably needs to be related to the larger community. With regard to art education, the danger arises from the marginality of the field which makes accountability more of a necessity. The accountability movement has itself been influenced by business practices, governance crises related to racial and community change, other managerial theories, institutional experts, and varied individual responses. Changing teacher education may well prove to be as complicated as school-based management. These more recent developments ensure that evaluating this range of innovations is steady work whose complications should not be underestimated.

Evidently it's unwise to restrict our attention, as many evaluators do, to intended, "concrete" first level or direct effects of innovative programs. Nearly all of the non-direct effects can be deemed educationally significant. (Huberman & Miles, 1982, p. 386)

Chapter 8

The Volunteers' Schools

Some volunteers need a lot of support. I once had a full-time volunteer who found the school a place of refuge. She had difficulties and the school was a transition place for her. I wouldn't leave her alone with students but she was a great help. Another full-time volunteer was quite slow and therefore unemployable. She needed a place to go, to feel important where someone was relying on her. She was wonderful with children and a help to me. . . . My job as teacher expanded. I didn't mind. It feels good to help someone and she was helping me. (Brown, 1995, p. 82)

A rapidly growing alternative is "service learning"—community work that is incorporated into the curriculum and typically done on class time. In a science course, for instance, students might test and clean up a local stream; for English, they could teach reading to younger children from poor neighborhoods. . . . In a recently released study, Brandeis University researchers found that students who do community work have higher grades, feel better about school, and are more likely to attend four-year colleges. . . . Phyllis Schlafly, president of the conservative Eagle Forum, has called service learning: "a diversionary tactic" from the real failures of the schools. (Mezzacappa, 1997)

The initiative aimed to recruit 100,000 technology-savvy teachers to serve as volunteer mentors to their peers. . . . But despite heavy press coverage that included a White House unveiling, the initiative has produced almost nothing beyond rhetoric and frustration, key organizers admit. . . . Net Day, which began last year, has also relied on a Web site and received a presidential endorsement, but there have been some notable differences. Net Day has had the full-time services of two corporate executives who have crisscrossed the country plugging the effort. Corporate contributions have poured in . . . tens of thousands of volunteers have taken part in projects to wire thousands of schools. (Trotter, 1997a)

Schools have increasingly come to rely on gifts and volunteers because neither public appropriations nor professionals have been adequate for them to operate as expected. Gifts and volunteer service are often provided by the same benefactors, but they are also related to differences in power of those providing them. A more equal relationship can be associated with volunteering. Furthermore, schools are not only receiving help, volunteers are being provided by schools to the community. For a long time, teachers have provided extra assistance to their students and even to the parents, but, increasingly, students are providing or being expected to provide their services as volunteers to the community. Retirees are believed to be a new source of volunteers for the community and schools and retired teachers are joining this contingent. The joint effect of volunteers for school and community is an integration between school and community institutions that could not have been anticipated in the past. When schools are dominated by other institutions, particularly business, there is reason for alarm, but many different contributors can increase the hopes for meaningful personal involvement for all of those involved.

COMPULSORY VOLUNTEERING

Students have always had their fates mandated by the planners of educational innovations, but now their personal decisions to help are mandated. At one time, writers did not even see students in the expertise hierarchy (Seeley, et al., 1956), but today some authors put them at the center of the stage for developing their own education (Sarason, 1993). An in between group, student-teachers, have had a very different experience when they were contributors to the school rather than guests in the institution (Hannam, et al., 1971). When they become involved in decision making, volunteers in schools become more than guests (Epstein & Dauber, 1991). However, students who put off completing their service requirements to the end of high school do not appear to find more than a very external role experience in fulfilling this requirement (Mezzacappa, 1997).

It is possible to say that in meeting a statutory requirement, students are fulfilling one meaning of community service, performing a duty to society. However, the duty was the view that the elite in society adopted at times, not subordinated students (Brown, 1995, p. 27). Volunteering has also carried the more common meaning of personal realization or choice; college students make such choices more frequently than high school students. High school students find it difficult to fit service of any kind into a life dominated by the selfish pursuit of "jobs, sports, and advanced academic courses" (Mezzacappa, 1997). However, students who have been raised to help others are likely to contribute. Very unexpectedly, students who are both volunteers and rebels against the school's status system help other students with multiple disabilities and, over time, come to bond with them (Murray-Seegert, 1989). Bonding between people and the development of extended networks is the third meaning that is given to volunteering (Brown, 1995, p. 27).

Most new student programs do not visualize students identifying with those they are helping, bonding with them, or pursuing more abstract ideals. Rather, students are seen as needing to be trained in the development of their moral character, which is how duty is still interpreted for students. Character training is the aim of the new program announced by Chicago mayor Richard Daley (Washburn & Martinez, 1997). Sixty hours of community service will be required of all high school students, even though their academic performance has been a constant problem. Blondean Davis, chief of school operations, said that the values of the program were "caring, love, family, giving" (Washburn & Martinez, 1997).

Similar developments have occurred elsewhere. David Hornbeck, the institutional expert who was the primary consultant for Kentucky's reform, headed the Maryland Department of Education in the 1980s, which was responsible for Maryland becoming the first state to require community service (100 hours) during the high school years (Mezzacappa, 1997). As Superintendent of Philadelphia, Hornbeck has announced plans for community service as part of more stringent graduation requirements in that city. Other places, such as Seattle, have publicized plans for requiring volunteer work, whereas many others simply encourage service. In Philadelphia, a high school English teacher, Ellen Weiser, devised a "Community Stewardship program, in which her students take inventory of the open spaces in their neighbourhoods, design and plant tree nurseries and gardens, and remove graffiti" (Mezzacappa, 1997).

For similar reasons, community service has long been supported by a variety of progressive reformers. In 1910, the philosopher William James called for such a program as the "moral equivalent of war;" the 1960s was a period in which advocacy for service reached a high point (Alt & Medrich, 1994). Because Congress considered such service as an alternative to military duty in Vietnam, the Southern Regional Education Board developed a service-learning program in 1967 and the National Center for Service-Learning was founded by the U. S. federal government in 1969. Later, the VISTA, Peace Corps, and National Student Volunteer Program (high school students) were started.

By the end of the 1980s there had again been a revival of such programs; they were increasingly related to experiential learning as a way of making the curriculum more meaningful to students. Over twenty states had adopted some provisions for community service for high schools and two hundred colleges and universities in the United States had formed the Campus Compact for postsecondary student involvement (Alt & Medrich, 1994). The National and Community Service Act of 1990 supported volunteer work by young people, retired adults, and others. Young people's activity was the focus of the National and Community Service Trust Act of 1993, which Bill Clinton had stressed during his campaign. The most controversial program of his administration is the AmeriCorps, which is overseen by the corporation established by the previous acts. AmeriCorps is partially modeled after Teach for America and provides a minimum wage and a college grant for several years of service. Conservatives have attacked it and a related program, Learn and Serve America, because they could displace purely voluntary programs, discourage unpaid volunteers and, consequently, misuse public funds (Portner, 1996).

Though AmeriCorps is directed at college students, student involvement in community service has gradually spread to younger students. In 1988, surveys showed that 18 percent of grade twelve students had done some service work for their courses (Alt & Medrich, 1994). By 1992, service had become a more general expectation, but only one-third of students believed that such service was important and, significantly for the teen world, a minute number of their friends were reported to believe that it was valuable. More recently, experts estimated that 25 percent of the schools in the 130 largest U.S. cities require students to have such service (Portner, 1996).

In 1997, as the Presidents' Summit for America's Future approached a study by the National Center for Educational Statistics, Student Participation in Community Service Activity, found that the most important factor in student service was whether schools arranged or offered such service (National Educational Goals Panel, 1997). From this same study it appeared that close to half of the students had some community service experience and that 93 percent of students who were asked to volunteer did so.

This evidence makes even more questionable the requirement by school systems of service for graduation. Earlier work had shown that the major benefit of service had been personal development, but that bonding and character development occurred when students made actual decisions. When former problem students teach younger students, a striking change was shown to occur in their general demeanour (Alt & Medrich, 1994).

Student testimonials were marshalled at the Presidents' Summit, but critics argued that very few of the people invited to the select group were a part of the group of youths who were being discussed (Archer, 1997b). President Clinton, together with former Presidents Bush and Carter and former Chairman of the Joint Chiefs of Staff Colin Powell, called for a major increase in community involvement at a time of government cutbacks. Sociologists argued that volunteers decrease their efforts during times of cutbacks because the social distance between themselves and those needing help increases; improvements are needed to inspire volunteers to help (McGrory, 1997). Educators attacked Clinton's plan to have volunteers overcome illiteracy because of their limited skills and understanding of the problems that the people would present (Walters, 1997).

During this summit, a number of groups made specific commitments. Big Brothers/Big Sisters pledged to double the number of its mentors to 200,000 (Walters, 1997). The K-12 Compact was organized for school students in imitation of the Campus Compact (Archer, 1997c). The State Superintendents of Education for six states, including California, Kentucky, and Maryland, were on the new group's board. Both compacts are organized by the Educational Commission of the States, a frequent flyer in reform efforts along with the Carnegie Corporation. The National Education Association announced plans to recruit 1,000 retired teachers as volunteers. Finally, many local groups announced their plans for improving education through the use of volunteers.

STUDENT LEADERS

Still, the contributions that students can make are ignored and their expectations for education are underestimated. At no time were students active participants in the research on community service. Significantly, little work has been done on determining whether voluntary or compulsory programs are better. The ability of schools to teach character or civics has been assumed rather than criticized from the students' perspective. Elementary school students have many ideas about the schools they would like (Meighen, 1986, p. 28). When working with land architects, similar students designed their school play areas (Mitchell, 1996). High school students have been contributors to research by academics (Sarason, 1993, p. 190), developers of new products for industry (Rideout, 1997), and providers of accounting services to small companies (Chacon, 1997). However, most writers continue to consult students about innovations as if they were granting a privilege to them (Rudduck, et al., 1997). The work on community service has still not shown respect for students.

Other than community service, several programs have emerged as a way of linking students and schools: peer support systems, peer tutoring, and leadership development. Peer support programs have emerged at times for specific groups such as the sons and daughters of alcoholics, who are notoriously able to cover up their problems. In some communities, support groups operate for both the students and their parents. Student counselors voluntarily act to assist students and refer more serious problems to experts, but there is still some recognition for the unique contribution that they as volunteers can make by relating to other students (Grant, 1987).

Compared to peer support, student tutoring is even more widely used, but usually gives even less recognition to students (Jenkins & Jenkins, 1987). At the elementary level, students are given detailed procedures to follow in order to keep the tutor and tutee on task while trying to prevent any put-downs by competitive students. Particularly in special education, the results are substantial, but there is always an attempt to keep the students in their teams. In high schools, informal recognition is often supplemented by credit for tutoring and the procedures are outlined in even greater detail to maintain control. A review of over fifty studies showed that peer tutoring by students in elementary and secondary schools was overwhelmingly successful in raising examination results (Michael, 1990, p. 33).

The results of peer tutoring can link many special education and at-risk students in ways that teachers could probably never do alone. A common bonding can occur between tutors and disabled students, autistic children, and "inner city minority group children at risk for early special education" (Delquadri, et al., 1986, p. 540). When a special education class is divided into teams, members develop support from the teams and alternate between being the tutor or tutee. As a result, every child in these classes receives ten minutes of direct practice time in a key skill area, such as spelling or oral reading, as well as benefiting from the learning that occurs in preparing to teach another student.

The program is very inexpensive and provides the stimulation that special education students have been shown to need. Aside from limited teacher contact, most of these students are often affected by the "Matthew effect," which means that those who need assistance don't receive it and often become worse students (Chen & Paisley, 1985, p. 54). Gifted students are also neglected, and they require more cross-fertilization of ideas than social stimulation. Such an exchange of ideas occurs in computer labs, which is the opposite of the peer huddle with its specified procedures.

Leadership programs involve broader aims than peer tutoring, but they are only accessible in relatively few schools. Such programs are open to a small number of students, sometimes in courses for credit, but almost always focus the leadership on student activities, rather than academic achievements. Students in peer tutoring, particularly a buddy system between older and younger students, report a sense of leadership empowerment (Goods, 1997). An art education program for at-risk students, DAREarts, attempts to develop leaders from schools by selecting one or two students who will return to the school and contribute to its classes in the arts (DAREarts, 1997). An interesting variation in special education is the peer forum, where the more able students are recognized as expert members of a panel. The peer forum has been found to be very effective in motivating students for learning (Lewandowski, 1989). Such forums involve academics as well as attitudes, self-esteem, and the need for education. All students should be able to focus on the ways in which they can improve.

THE ENTREPRENEURIAL SPIRIT

Unfortunately, students have not been speakers in the extensive discussion of reinventing government, which is the alternative to bureaucracy and rules in education. Students as clients are the reason that a more open, competitive, and risk-taking organization exists (Osborne & Gaebler, 1992), but they aren't seen as active decision makers. The reality is that neither they nor most of the professional staff are entrepreneurs. Likewise, volunteers generally lack this spirit when they enter into these new, uncertain, and changing positions, but, as they become professional volunteers regularly involved in helping other volunteers, this dedicated group develops managerial and policy-making skills with people (Brown, 1995). In the sense of competitors in a market, volunteers would still not be entrepreneurs.

The involvement of volunteers has been shown to connect students to both the school and the adult world. Volunteers often bond with the students; seniors talk about students with whom they work as "my child" or their "little buddies" (Brown, 1995, pp. 34-37). A caring norm is developed for students which they will hopefully practice in the future. Though the volunteer's gifts may not be repaid within a generation, the commitment to these norms has changed the climate of their schools. For example, tolerance for individual and cultural differences has increased as a result of activities such as cooking demonstrations by ethnic minorities in order to learn about their families.

The decision to extensively involve volunteers with the schools was made by the principals; it may be that they want simply to get "people on your side" (Brown, 1995, pp. 38, 64-67). However, the principals can also show their concern and encourage volunteers in many small ways, such as giving up their parking space for these contributors or meeting them in the halls before they reach his office, the official place. The involvement of volunteers can be promoted by creating a room for their use and appointing a coordinator to work with them. Volunteers have themselves created a buddy system to link immigrants with members of the same ethnic group who have been in the country longer or who have been more involved with the schools in the past.

Most changes are brought about by the coordinators of the volunteer projects. Similar coordinators have been involved with family centers, which are the focus of service integration that was introduced in Chapter 5. Though family-support coordinators are responsible for family education and integration of community services, it is when they directly intervene with client problems, such as the electricity being cut off in the winter, or the need for lights so the student can study, that they are most inventive (Olson, 1994a; Mitchell, 1996).

General writing about family centers stresses the charismatic character of center organizers who can find ways to deal with perceived needs (Bowen & Sellers, 1994, p. 29). To support teaching, these centers have introduced conflict resolution training for students who had difficulty working in groups and have developed direct approaches to get tardy students to class. However, new programs often involve the trickery of toy exchanges or baby showers at the centers as a cover for parent education and networking (Susan Schweder, interview, May 8, 1995).

Kentucky has the best developed program of family resource centers, but coordinators are so preoccupied with immediate parental problems and procedures that few volunteers are involved (Susan Schweder, interview, May 8, 1995). The desire to deal with immediate problems has been a goal of those who developed the program as well as those administrators who looked forward to the program as a way of dealing with pressures from parents (Judy Carter, interview, May 1, 1995).

Though the writers and coordinators in Kentucky stress the desirability of involving volunteers in the programs, the elaborate bureaucracy has apparently stymied the effort there. In contrast to Kentucky, in Boston an independent board selects volunteers who effectively integrate social services and the school (Michael, 1990, p. 49). The Kentucky approach has been hampered by procedural specifications, including the criteria for awarding grants to support the centers; the criteria for grants does not mention involving volunteers. Ironically, parents and students constitute the majority of the boards for such Kentucky centers. Furthermore, the national organization that has most influenced the continuing development of the Kentucky program, Cities in Schools, originated as a program for volunteers and has recently given a renewed emphasis to the use of volunteers (Cities in Schools, 1993).

The problems in Kentucky are apparently related to the controls that the state exerts on the program. Center directors have been criticized by a Kentucky state agency for directing an inordinate amount of their time to a few cases, a failure to plan, and undertaking too many field trips for the benefits involved (Office of Educational Accountability, 1994, pp. 156-161). Criticism of centers makes it that much more likely that people in them will take the safe bureaucratic road, rather than a creative one in particular situations.

In specific school situations, volunteer coordinators emerge doing a variety of tasks. One such person arranged for classes in the noon hour. She says:

There are 14 classes this session and these programs involve over one-third of the students. Just about all the classes are full: clay, chess, gymnastics, computer, knitting, beading, Chinese knotting, piano, painting and drawing, drama, and a lunch brunch. . . . It's a big commitment. It takes time and tact and you have to stay cheerful and try to be fair. (Brown, 1995, p. 84)

Another coordinator, with even wider responsibilities for coordinating a district-wide mentor program, brought together parents, teachers, and mentors who were often the age of grandparents; she arranged for twenty pairs and reported a 70 percent success rate in obtaining volunteers for the program (Ibid). Many individual volunteers become involved for up to twenty years, many years after their own children leave the school. It is understandable that those who move toward becoming professional volunteers would link volunteering to decision making. However, the increasing focus of volunteering toward learning, with less emphasis on serving as a teacher's helper, has combined with a more assertive role for parents, resulting in an increasing number of volunteers who are interested in changing school policy.

The parents, volunteers, and coordinators must work together with principals, who have repeatedly been shown to introduce a variety of changes (Fullan, 1982). Most principals who initiated the volunteer programs believed that they were "community orientated" rather than "entrepreneurial" (Fullan, 1982, p. 64). However, in contrast to the bureaucratic pattern, everyone involved in the volunteers' school is different and all are capable of promoting the cause that they believe in within education. Businesspeople who complain about school executives whom they have met as being rule-bound and cautious should recognize this set of principals as risk-takers whom they should prefer (Mitchell, 1996). It is such principals who have also initiated partnerships with businesses (Michael, 1990).

Those business and community representatives who would help educators in promotions such as Net Day are a resource for future campaigns in the educational war. The aim of partnerships as well as individual ties must be related to a greater sense of purpose than the "bottom line." Several school boards have become entrepreneurial, but they could be more effective as part of a social movement. The Peel Board of Education's Community Education Department reportedly received two-thirds of its annual revenue of $30 million from corporate clients for services from driver education to assessing, evaluating, and training staff (Tymko, 1996, p. 16).

Though educators may get some respect for also being businesspeople, they cannot claim that such business is their reason for existence. The difference between such a businesslike approach and community positions involves an understanding of how money and resources can be used together with people; the combination of the expanding relationships and knowledge of change is sometimes referred to as "social capital" (Brown, 1995). A striking example of such a program is Project Think/Write in San Francisco, where teachers and business volunteers were trained in a joint program by the National Writing Program (Michael, 1990, pp. 81, 123). As preparation for employment, the businesspeople taught effective writing, critical thinking, and creativity. The students worked with letters, memos, press releases, and job applications as well as short stories and movie reviews.

The volunteer programs have often been introduced at the same time as business partnerships, particulary adopt-a-school projects. Such partnerships have been mainly public relations exercises that have not improved academic achievement among students or changed the climate of schools (Mitchell, 1996, p. 100). The Parent Teachers' Association attempted to develop guidelines whereby all such partnerships would be geared to the needs of education rather than business opportunities and that the curriculum would remain the responsibility of educators. However, most groups were too hungry for business dollars and declined to support a common program (Weisman, 1991). Giving students equipment or treating students paternalistically does not empower them. In fact, the only ones who have been empowered in many such programs are the coordinators.

In contrast to business efforts, volunteer efforts break the mold and establish continuing patterns in the school. A program in Washington, D.C., involved mathematicians, physicists, and engineers who were recruited by a local service group (Michael, 1990). The consternation among teachers on how to relate to experts in their classrooms was intense. This program worked only when teachers were encouraged to write job descriptions of all such volunteers, developed an effective match between themselves and the volunteer experts, and form an overview committee of community representatives. However, these are the tasks that are required for all volunteer programs.

PARENTS AND OTHER PARTNERS

Until recently, parents, particularly mothers, have been the dominant source of volunteers. Parents as partners is a way those in formal organizations have of viewing families as members of an organization. Families and communities are more primary and adaptable structures than are organizations or reform campaigns; they have endured and will continue to do so long after the reformers have disappeared. However, single issues or events are needed to ignite the reaction of parents.

Religion and sex are likely to touch a nerve among parents and their reactions may seem quite comical. Parents in Sacramento demonstrated against the teaching of classical myths as the practice of witchcraft (Sanchez, E., 1997). Community members in Michigan became agitated about the removal of references to God and morality in a mission statement. Parents in St. Louis organized a pressure group,

Parents for Math Choice, to oppose the "new, new mathematics," which is based on the report of the National Council of Teachers of Mathematics (Walters, 1997). Parents react against these issues but cannot develop much enthusiasm for school reorganization or councils; they react with emotion to broad issues.

Parents can be connected with school issues first by linking such issues to benefits for their children and, later, to how other students can be improved. Parents must be asked to help, and the way they are asked is important; visits to their homes by both a parent and school staff members are particularly helpful (North Central Regional Educational Laboratory, 1994). Parents can be engaged in social and recreational activities including a toy exchange. Those involved with early childhood education are particularly likely to increase their own learning, including going on to become teachers.

Once caught in the educator's web, parents can develop specific skills for themselves and their children. For pre-school children, learning readiness skills is important. For elementary school groups, reading programs that involve parents and improve reading scores of students are effective; parents can learn instructional strategies to supplement school work at home in reading and mathematics. For the high school level, parents can limit television viewing, encourage homework, and learn to conduct discussions with teenagers. At all levels they can be confronted with the findings that parents who attend school events, help with homework, or support learning are likely to have children who graduate rather than drop out (North Central Regional Educational Laboratory, 1994).

Active volunteers in schools make the transition to broader concerns about children and learning (Brown, 1995). Most parents are satisfied with schools and do not realize how much they are misled by teacher grading as compared to standardized examination results (Office of Educational Research and Improvement, U.S. Department of Education, 1992). Parents who are involved as volunteers over a long period are likely to develop influence at the school (Epstein & Dauber, 1991). Don Davies, founder of the Institute for Responsive Education, which is a major organization supporting parental involvement, claims that by encouraging parental decision making, reformers are building support for their efforts; conversely, parents are in a position to undermine all efforts by withdrawing their children or withholding their votes (Baldauf, 1997). An institutional expert, Linda Darling-Hammond, has discovered that teachers need to be taught how to communicate with parents.

Parents are an increasingly organized force in education and are being joined by a variety of volunteers, all of whom are focused on the learning of students. In Rochester and Anchorage, parents are evaluating teachers (Lawton, 1997b). In Palo Alto, California, Wilmette, Illinois, and many other communities, parents have organized their own Internet sites as a basis for circulating information about their schools (Trotter, 1997b). Parents on the net are a part of a movement of critical consumers who often want and read the published results of standardized exams.

A variety of other groups are joining the consumer movement in education at the same time as they are volunteering to help with schools. The groups include college students, retirees, and, of course, business executives (Michael, 1990, p. 2).

College students have been discussed in relation to the volunteer summit, and their contribution is similar to peer supports, tutoring, and leadership developments. Training and direction is as essential for college students as it is for retirees, but retirees have been shown to bring a personal perspective to the history that they lived (Goods, 1997). One such retiree said:

Following four periods of energetic bombardment, we 60-plus "interviewees" should have been drained and exhausted. No way. The inquisitiveness and spirit left us elated. The rapport was such that Helen, my wife, said that she wished time had allowed her to ask them about their lives in today's America. The adjective "rewarding" best expresses why we do this work. (Friedman, 1997, p. 2)

An exemplary program in Salt Lake City, Utah, Senior Motivators in Learning and Education Services (SMILES), has developed dramatically since it started in 1977 (Goods, 1997). It has gone from seventeen volunteers to four hundred. SMILES gives recognition to the senior as an asset and provides students with individual attention; the improvement in students' attendance and work habits is particularly notable.

The potential of retirees for education is discussed widely, particularly as a replacement in schools for mothers who are increasingly working outside the home. Retirees as mentors are able to increase the attendance and achievements of youth while improving their own ability to communicate and retain their memories (Strom & Strom, 1995, p. 329-331). The ability to communicate across generations is important, since grandparents are raising an increasing percentage of children whose parents are not able to do so. Therefore, a curriculum for grandparents has been developed.

However, most retirees devote less than an hour per week to volunteering and few organizations have developed programs with the American Association of Retired Persons in spite of the availability of federal U.S. grants for this purpose (Strom and Strom, 1995). A national survey found that 14 million Americans over 65 would be willing to volunteer while the 4 million current volunteers would be willing to contribute more time (Freedman, 1994, p. ii). Even with these projections, only a minority of seniors would be involved in community services and a community mass of participants, particularly men, has not been built.

In the United States, only 100,000 older people are engaged with the three largest government programs for which they are partially paid: Foster Grandparent, Senior Companion, and Senior Community Service Employment (Freedman, 1994). Foster Grandparents work with young people with special needs. Senior Companions serve homebound seniors and others who are at risk for institutionalization. The largest of these programs, Senior Community Service Employment, provides services similar to the other two, but it is also designed to provide income maintenance. Two thirds of these services are provided to the community—15 percent to education—and the remainder for other elders (Freedman, 1994).

Among private programs, Linking Lifetimes is most significant for education, because it provides mentors for at-risk students in nine cities who are either in trouble with the schools or the law. Similar services are provided by Boys and Girls Clubs. In Springfield, Massachusetts, a Linking Lifetimes program is particularly notable because it matches older adults with blue-collar elders who have experienced many problems with youths in trouble with the justice system; these elders are described as "like walking-life-skills curricula" (Freedman, 1994, p. 32). In Chicago, retired executives with the Executive Service Corps have been critical in supporting educational reform and in providing related social services in some areas (Mitchell, 1996).

A wide host of community members have been involved in other programs, particularly in encouraging at-risk students, and have linked them to the community to the same extent as retirees have established links across generations. In Louis Armstrong Elementary School in Queens, New York, a variety of male readers are invited into the schools to serve as readers of books and as models for those who lack male parents. In Calgary, more prominent readers, including the mayor, police chief, and top fireman come into G. W. Skene Elementary School (Goods, 1997).

Though many of these efforts have not developed into continuous programs, they are grist for the mill of journalism and the source of issues for advocacy groups. Increasingly, civic journalism has attempted to focus on the gaps between educational achievement and needs for such diverse problems as art education or racial differences (Archer, 1997a). Advocacy groups are working together with parent and community groups who are their shock troops for demonstrating and raising legal issues: the advocates are, of course, providing training for volunteers and attempting to augment their influence (Mitchell, 1996).

The power of all these groups is being both increased and directed by foundations (McKersie, 1993). In Chicago, though foundations were not important in organizing community groups before passage of the Reform Act, they were crucial in implementing the reforms, particularly in training the new school councils (Mitchell, 1996). To keep reform groups going, more money was required than fund-raising could provide, and the continuation of reform is widely acknowledged as needing continuing foundation support (Coretta McFerren, interview, October 26, 1993). Kentucky has been an active seeker of all foundation and government funds. In Canada, government funds have been provided for advocacy groups since World War II, but with budget restraints, foundations are becoming a more important source of funding. Reform efforts have become dependent upon foundations, government grants, or a combination of the two sources.

A striking example of such dependency was revealed when the fifth largest American foundation, the Pew Charitable Trust, announced a major commitment to integration of social services of as much as $60 million for ten years, but then abandoned this position after only two years with allocations of $4 million a year (Sommerfeld, 1994). The Pew grants were originally intended to initiate a network of family centers, and the state of Kentucky had spent an estimated $1 million of staff time in planning for the grants. But the prospect evaporated and Kentucky, as well as other states, had to turn to the Annie B. Casey Foundation and the Foundation for Child Development for continued support for integration of services.

In Kentucky's case, as well as other states, government has to provide for integrated services and would have been better off without the false promise of large foundation assistance.

CATALYSTS FOR VOLUNTEERS

Generally, the efforts to support the volunteer movement for schools would begin with local advocacy groups and later on would involve governments and foundations (Michael, 1990, pp. 6-11). Organized efforts to promote volunteers in schools began in 1956 with a well-known citizens advocacy group in New York City, the Public Education Association (PEA). The PEA offered its services to a local elementary school to provide trained tutors for reading. In 1959, the Ford Foundation gave PEA a grant to expand the program in New York City and, in 1964, the same foundation gave them another grant to expand the program nationally. Though seventeen cities received grants from this expanded effort, the independent national program, the National School Volunteer Program, barely survived until 1975 when the Edna McConnell Clark Foundation provided a sustaining grant. In 1988, the National School Volunteer Program merged with a similar organization to form the National Association of Partners in Education. This latter organization continues to be dominant today and is an important source of training materials for volunteers.

While training programs would expand to all American states and Canadian provinces and, by 1987-1988, over 60 percent of schools would report that they used volunteers, government and foundation efforts would come and go (Michael, 1990). For two years, between 1970 and 1972, the U.S. federal government maintained an Office of Volunteers in Education. In 1972, an affiliate of the Charles F. Kettering Foundation, the Institute for Development of Education, which also supported the work of John Goodlad, convened a national conference on school volunteers. This conference showed how widespread the support for volunteers had become, but it revealed a continuing deference to educators when it asserted that volunteers would be "reinforcing" rather than ever teaching students (Michael, 1990, p. 8). However, by the 1980s, racial and educational crises in education brought forth greater numbers of volunteers who would be very critical of the system. So called "Ninja parents" are demanding more and more support for education; they have even tried to hire additional teachers themselves (Chaddock, 1997).

The traditional suppliers of volunteers, the National Parent Teacher Association and the Junior League, are showing signs of wanting changes in the educational systems (Chaddock, 1997, p. 10). The PTA was founded in 1897 as the National Congress of Mothers; with almost 7 million members, it calls itself the largest volunteer organization in the United States. In many schools, the PTA, similar to Home and School Associations in Canada, is the largest supplier of volunteers for schools. Over the years, PTA supported a variety of progressive programs in schools; mothers and volunteers were expected to become "professional." The PTA has consistently stressed programs for juvenile delinquency, including separate courts (National Congress of Parents and Teachers, 1947). The PTA has been a member of an association of organizations fighting for educational reforms and opposing budget cuts in education; as previously mentioned, they have opposed the commercialization of education (Weisman, 1991).

Since its founding in 1901, the Junior League has tried to promote social, artistic, and attitudinal changes in education. This work was prompted by Jane Adams and directed by Mary Harriman, the sister of railway magnate and statesman, Averell Harriman. This organization was originally called the Junior League for the Promotion of Settlement Programs (Caputo, 1983). There are some 238 affiliates in North America; the eight Canadian junior leagues form one national organization with Mexican and American affiliates. Many different programs are promoted by the League, which typically attempts to develop a project and find others who will carry it on more permanently. For example, beginning in 1973, the Junior League in Calgary started Music Alive, a program of bringing musicians to students so that even the deaf students could hear the vibrations of the instruments. But in the 1980s, the program was turned over to a local radio station that, unfortunately, discontinued it after a change in administration at the station (Goods, 1996).

All of the programs seem similar to the original vision of Jane Adams and Mary Harriman. Aside from the music activities, current programs in Calgary range from those about child abuse, teen sexuality, family violence, and disabled students, to children's theatre. A puppet program to teach elementary kids about disabled students, Kids on the Block, is a typical League effort. In 1979, after the school system began integrating handicapped students, the Junior League in Calgary, together with the Calgary Association for the Mentally Handicapped, began a puppet program with life-sized characters:

There was Renaldo, a blind puppet with a real Braille watch, sunglasses, and a cane. Mark is the puppet with cerebral palsy and a real, miniature wheelchair. Ellen Jane is mentally handicapped, Mandy is deaf, and Jennifer has a learning disability, Brenda is the puppet who thinks she is fat and Melody is the puppet who wears glasses. Each puppet discusses the way in which they are affected by other people's reactions to them. (Goods, 1996, p. 7)

This effort, like others by the Junior League, is a supplement to a government program, but the reduction of government efforts for the handicapped has made the continuation of the program difficult. However, the variety of programs that the Junior League supports is always a part of its continuing attempt to develop the different interests of its volunteer members.

MORE RECENT ORGANIZATIONS

Among the newer organizations that have emerged in the last thirty years, two of them, the Atlanta Project and Cities in Schools have brought about alliances among business, education, and social services that have particularly relied upon volunteers. Beginning in 1991, former President Jimmy Carter turned his attention from international problems to Atlanta problems of health, education, and welfare.

The Atlanta Project attempts to organize clusters of community resources around individual schools so that the entire city is covered by them. The Atlanta Project has mobilized 12,000 volunteers to identify 17,000 children who need their immunization shots as part of their urban revitalization effort (Kaplan, 1995).

Similar to the Junior League, the Carter Center attempted to develop drama around a number of social themes such as guns and violence or growing up Black in Atlanta in the 1920s and 1930s; partners for this project have included the Alliance Theater, the Atlanta School System, and the Turner Broadcasting System. Many other businesses have joined their social efforts, such as BellSouth, which leads a major literacy effort (Tapline, 1994a). The Carter Center is attempting to mobilize volunteers as part of a national effort (Tapline, 1994b), but it seems to be dependent upon strong or united leadership. An attempt to follow its example in Chicago failed to work when the leadership core changed (Mitchell, 1996).

In contrast, Communities in Schools (CIS) tries to develop local leadership through the use of volunteers and is not dependent upon central leadership, though it certainly has a charismatic leader in Bill Millikin. This program began with the work of volunteers in education and continues to emphasize their importance today. In Chicago, Kentucky and in Canada, Communities in Schools, which until 1996 was generally called Cities in Schools, was a crucial organization involved with social agencies, in general, and family resource centers, in particular. It has become the focus of a complex set of activities for dropout prevention among adolescents in poverty. CIS was a major partner with a number of projects in Chicago (Janet Hudolin, interview, May 15, 1995). It has always been an informal partner with Kentucky in developing family and youth centers (Marsha Morganti, interview, May, 5, 1995). The Georgia CIS is also a partner with the Atlanta Project.

Mentoring is often a central activity of CIS, and a one-on-one relationship for every child is one of its four aims along with safety, a marketable skill upon graduation, and a chance to give back to community and peers. CIS works with One to One: The National Mentoring Partnership, which acts as a catalyst between children and mentors (Communities in Schools, 1996, p. 14). In Chicago, CIS works together with TOUGHLOVE, which trains parents to run their own support group (Chicago Communities in Schools, 1996, p. 6).

In 1994, to make students an important part of the health initiative and the fight against AIDS in particular, CIS, with the U.S. Department of Health and Human Services, organized the Teen Health Corps; leaders were to provide information, develop career possibilities, and perform a service for communities (Network News, 1997b). Altogether, there are 121 CIS local programs that serve 262,000 young people. Extensive evaluations of the program have been made and CIS now attempts to ensure program standards by granting "charter" status to those local activities that meet specified criteria (Ibid, p. 1).

By 1994, an international program had developed in England and Canada (Communities in Schools, 1996). The British program, "CIS Bridge Course," is an independent organization based on the American model. The British course concentrates on no more than ten students who are attending a Further Education

College or Adult Education Centre. Recently, groups in Ireland and Northern Ireland have been organizing with assistance from the American organization and as well as the Canadian leader.

The Canadian group has been more directly linked to the American parent. In 1995, CIS formed a national organization building upon several projects in the Toronto area and Yorkton, Saskatchewan, and had a National Coordinator for Canada, Janet Longmore (Cities in Schools, 1995). During 1996, CIS expanded its program to six sites in Atlantic Canada. This program focuses on entrepreneur training and includes counseling, peer networking, personal development, transition from school to work, community direction, private sector investment, and business start ups. The Atlantic project is supported by a grant of $138,000 from the Atlantic Canada Opportunities Agency. In Ontario, the Trillum Foundation made a substantial grant for evaluation of the local CIS from 1997 to 1998. On September 15, 1997, the Canadian Director, Janet Longmore, became the Executive Director of the American CIS; she had developed a pilot Internet program for youth for the wider CIS world (Network News, 1997b).

Since 1977, CIS has constantly developed a variety of organizations that are in tune with publicized demands for change. The dynamic director for its entire history has been Bill Milliken, who came out of street life himself in Pittsburgh and began his efforts with a street ministry in Harlem (*Business Week*, 1989). This former dropout then started street academies by working with students who had dropped out of regular schools, using both tutoring programs and alternative schools. Later, social and health services were provided through postal academies with the sponsorship of the U.S. Postal Service. Academies currently exist mostly within schools and are sponsored by the U.S. Department of Justice, Burger King, and an investment banking firm, Goldman Sachs (Cities in Schools, 1994). The academies are an alternative for the most-difficult-to-reach students, although, in over seventy communities, CIS attempts to integrate social services within typical schools without academies. Milliken has sought and obtained corporate support for these integrated services from General Foods, BellSouth, GTE, Amoco, Coca-Cola, and Federated Department Stores (*Business Week*, 1989). As President, Milliken says he has the "best working relationship ever" with his new Executive Director, Janet Longmore (Network News, 1997b).

CIS has support on the highest levels with both former Presidents Carter and Bush. The organization continues to be influential through the support of President Bill Clinton and leading entertainers. Each year, leading music artists come together to record a song or music on video, while other entertainers have added 25 cents to the price of concert tickets to support CIS. The entertainment industry supports CIS through a separate foundation, which has, in turn, supported scholarship programs, national music competitions, and special concerts. Entertainers involved include Garth Brooks, Barbara Mandrell, and Charlie Daniels for the 1992 video, and those providing support through their concert prices include Madonna, Janet Jackson, and Prince. After each Super Bowl, the National Football League establishes a new academy that is run by CIS, and two teams individually sponsor academies.

With its high profile, CIS stresses local programs that are not controlled by any outside group including CIS. Milliken is particularly concerned about overcoming reliance on government. He wants to avoid "paternalistic helping" and "parachuting in the experts" (Lewis, 1991). Thus, a part of community initiatives, volunteers are frequently used as mentors, tutors, and facilitators within schools, such as in Chicago. There, under the leadership of a local businessperson, a local board composed of educators, religious leaders, health and social service representatives, and businesspeople, community activities were established; the board members are expected to be "stakeholders and have a vested interest in seeing the effort succeed" (Lewis, 1991). Milliken sees these organizations as mediating structures that can replace the community that has been lost by the decline of religious institutions and the extended family.

In Kentucky, CIS was supposed to become an official partner for integrated services, but to date has not done so. It has been an informal partner in developing the family centers from the beginning (Marsha Morganti, interview, May 5, 1995). CIS has trained the coordinators for the family centers in Kentucky and operated a national training program for any interested group. Bill Milliken has stressed that, aside from bringing resources to the schools, student interns and volunteer mentors and tutors are primary groups for the integration effort.

There are a number of specifics in the CIS approach, including the training of teachers in the case method of social work when these other professionals are not available in schools. The ability to deal with the immediate problems of families has probably been part of the learning experiences of CIS leaders over the last thirty years; CIS has brought knowledge based on these experiences to Kentucky, as well as other states (Marsha Morganti, interview, May 5, 1995). CIS is also currently in tune with the appeal for volunteer efforts that has been related to the aspirations of university graduates who cannot find jobs. In general, CIS always seems to make an impact on any program in which it is involved as well as to relate to the people involved.

MENTORING

Though CIS, like many of the other programs, includes mentoring and tutoring, it does not focus on establishing an effective program to carry out these tasks. To encourage talent, gifted programs have particularly tried to provide support to students. For example, in the Enrichment Triad Model, such students are provided with a "real" audience for the products they create (Renzulli, 1977). Mentoring is a critical component of many gifted programs, such as the Javits program in Kentucky where it was developed with the Kiwanis Club and the Chamber of Commerce (Taradash, 1994). Local businesses have been involved in providing many programs, developing marketing, and providing resource people (Linnemeyer & Shelton, 1991).

In Canada, a new program by the combined Big Sisters and Big Brothers shows how a local service organization can provide mentoring in schools. Students are supported right in the schools and mentors gain an inside view of schools (Jim Campbell, interview, September 25, 1997). This approach is designed to deal with the reduced availability of volunteers due to mothers working. Employers can donate an hour each week of employee's time and can see that employees who devote time to volunteer work are more productive. A research study in the first site for the program provides powerful support for this approach (Opinion Research Centre, 1995).

This program for elementary schools will be evaluated in new sites just as it was in the Hamilton area; it will also be a partnership between the school board and the Big Brothers organization. The mentors who participate in any of the programs are screened and a police check is made to determine if they have a criminal record. The current concern about sexual abuse is reflected in this approach as is the use of the school setting. Such security is necessary because the program attempts to develop a close friendship between mentors and students. For example, a promotional video depicts a mentor and a student playing a board game together; tutoring in school subjects is not the objective of this approach. For older students, career identity may be stressed in future programs. For the current program, mentors learn to focus on program outcomes.

In the research in the Hamilton area, separate evaluations were made by principals, social workers, teachers, students, and mentors. Principals generally were positive about the program and saw increases in self-confidence, but a few were concerned about the loss of class time and the disruption that mentoring caused (Opinion Research Centre, 1995). Social workers who generally referred the students to mentoring were also positive about the program, but they suggested that mentors and students should also have an opportunity to meet in a larger group and that the mentors should be recruited from ethnic communities since the students were not homogeneous. Teachers emphasized gains in personal development, particularly self-esteem; they report that students often look forward to visits by mentors. In some cases, mentors were invited to contribute to the class, but, if the class is a problem for students, they need their mentors alone with them.

The students' self-esteem improved with this program and the results were statistically significant (Opinion Research Centre, 1995). The students and the mentors believed that mentoring enriched their lives. Many mentors mentioned that clear improvement in the student was the source of their satisfaction. Mentors as well as others evaluate the program in terms of how good the human relationships were.

Complementing the Big Sisters' and Big Brothers' program for elementary students, in Calgary, the Alberta Mentoring Foundation for Youth (AMFY) provides mentoring for secondary students (Deidre Halferty, interview, October 10, 1997). This program is also a copy of a program developed in another city, the Prometheus Project, which was organized by Jeunes Associes en Education in Montreal; again there is research evidence to justify borrowing a program. As with Big Sisters and Big Brothers, security is a major concern; mentors are required to undergo a security and child welfare check as well as psychological testing. The legitimacy of this program is carried further in that there is a contract between

AMFY and the Calgary Board of Education.

School counselors and teachers identify the students to be involved in the program and AMFY is responsible for selecting and training the mentors. To avoid labeling, the students are not identified as at-risk students. AMFY provides positive "role modeling" for students; it does not want to "fix" them.

The training sessions include material on adolescent development, self-esteem, and boundary setting as well as the history of AMFY. Intensive training attempts to develop a vision of mentoring, which research has shown to be important. In Montreal, students felt that mentors should be reliable, motivated, understanding, friendly, honest, and have a good sense of humor. The students felt the relationship should be based on equality, acceptance and, most importantly, honest feedback. Mentors themselves receive feedback from a network of other mentors. The support network allows for debriefing and problem solving on a regular basis and a monthly wine and cheese party among mentors helps to create a common interest among them.

Beyond the information sharing of the networks, a research study in Calgary has shown the need to recruit mentors who are more ethnically diverse than the present group (Halferty & Fouts, 1996-1997). More generally, the evidence shows that students improved their attitude and gained self-esteem; they were also happier with their families.

Over 87 percent of the students improved in at least one of these ways. One student commented: "The program allows students to have a good adult role model plus someone who pays attention to that person only" (Halferty & Fouts, 1996-1997, p. 26). Other students believed the program helped them understand their feelings as well as their school work by providing them with critical help. A mutual relationship that benefited both mentor and protégé developed. A high proportion of mentors planned to return in the following years.

BRIDGING THE GAP

The challenge is to link volunteers with protégés or other people within organizations so that the students are encouraged and not smothered in a one-sided relationship. Volunteers can be an effective link between students and educators as well as other professionals; they are, at least, as valuable as foundation grants. Furthermore, it has increasingly been recognized that professionals need to jointly organize their services for high-risk clients and that they need the support of volunteers, including other students, to do so. This effort can bring together social agencies, businesses, the higher professions, and artists into a variety of partnerships (Mitchell, 1996).

In spite of the potential for involving volunteers and developing a greater sense of community, those who plan such integrated services seem to think more like businesspeople than as members of a family (Mitchell, 1996). In Kentucky, the form required to receive a grant for family resource centers is like the business bottom line. In Alberta, the emphasis on reinventing government as a basis for integrated services involves the application to government practices of business guidelines. In Chicago, only exceptional individuals have been able to transcend the boundaries of professionals and organizations; for example, the lawyers refused to accept paralegals in assisting parent councils and other reform actions, which could have provided jobs as paralegals for people in the communities that the councils serve. Protection of professional spheres acts as a barrier to integrated services and the development of aids as well as volunteers as a component of larger plans.

Although parents have often found access to schools to be controlled by educators, the family resource centers have particularly welcomed parents where they have not been accepted before (Kay & Roberts, 1994). Parents have been viewed as individual constituents of the schools, rather than members of organizations, such as Big Sisters and Big Brothers, which, together with schools, are a part of a community (Ibid). Parents' involvement has been shown to evolve from obtaining information on raising their own child to participation in decision making (Epstein & Dauber, 1991). A further extension has been proposed to include collaborating with community groups for services not available from the school. However, the work of an organization that proposes changing the governance of schools is only recognized as having a different way of including parents on committees.

The longstanding work of organizations, such as the Junior League, or the more recent work of autonomous groups within leagues, such as CIS, needs clearer recognition. Chart 8.1 shows the transition from concerns about the evolution of parenting to the broader view of developing diverse volunteers. Support for children and understanding of their development is augmented by the work of mentors who provide more immediate support for them. The view that primary groups with their associated religious ties in a particular setting has been lost and needs to be replaced (gemeinschaft) long ago led to the characterization of such progressive positions as suffering from the gemeinschaft goose (Cremin, 1961). CIS currently acts on the basis of this lost world.

The largest difference between a focus on parents and on volunteers is the second stage. Communication between the school and parents, no matter how varied, is less creative than the many ways in which facilitators act. The principal who encouraged volunteers by giving them his parking place is modeling one of the many ways in which such entrepreneurs have attempted to empower people. Even if the coordinator is providing emergency service, the actions provide immediate social support while changing the practices of what schools have done in the past. Continuous communication is like the difference at the first step between a workshop that merely provides information and mentoring that is organized around regular interaction.

Chart 8.1
Stages of Parent Participation and Volunteer Action

Parents	Volunteers
1. Positive home conditions	Mentoring
2. Communications by school	Facilitating
3. Volunteers for the school	Volunteer commitment
4. Learning activities at home	Tutoring
5. Decision making	Decision making
6. Community and support services	Integrating services

The third stage requires a recognition of the variety of volunteers. Unlike retirees, businesspeople, or students, parents are initially alone in focusing on their individual children. Parents have to develop a link with a broader issue and their initial concerns in order to have any substantial effect upon schools (Mitchell, 1992). In contrast, business executives frequently view students as future employees (Mitchell, 1996). Such executives, as well as other new kinds of volunteers, must come to see students as individuals. In Canada, volunteers generally participate to help others, act on the basis of a cause, seek something that is personally satisfying, or look for a sense of accomplishment (Duchesne, 1989). Students who are required to participate in order to graduate are a further exception.

For parents, a focus upon learning activities at home, the fourth level, has the highest relationship to promoting volunteering in school and becoming active in decision making within schools (Epstein & Dauber, 1991). The established pattern of families reading together has been augmented by both parents and children enrolling in writing programs. New books have been designed to assist parents to work with their children in mathematics. Parent work at home is being linked with school requirements by having parents sign contracts to ensure that homework gets done, particularly in Philadelphia.

However, volunteering within the school, the fifth alternative, is a parallel opportunity to home teaching. As previously stressed, such volunteering can reach the point where parents influence decision making within the school. When volunteers continue to help long after their own children have graduated, they are very likely to be accepted and consulted about the school's plans. The creation of parent rooms within schools equipped with telephones are essential, and using either volunteer or paid facilitators to promote work with parents creates a link between volunteers and the school's formal structure.

The parent coordinators often help relate the school's program to the increasing likelihood of social services being offered in schools, particularly for those with high-risk students. From combining formal programs with a concern for individual students, parents can probably help resolve the conflicts concerning the effectiveness of volunteers' tutoring. There is as yet no clear evidence that the large-scale tutoring program for literacy by AmeriCorps or the Carter Center results in an improvement. Training teachers to work with parents prevents discrimination against poorer families or single-parent mothers (Mitchell, 1992). Training of both parents and volunteers might help them to overcome the barrier that separates teachers from their world; it would also ease the transition for them to become instructional assistants. The transition from volunteer to professional status, which is involved in the Teach for America program, may also be critical for the evolution of tutoring programs.

Neither parent nor volunteer involvement in decision making appears to be very well developed. Chicago is probably the only site where parent involvement has been meaningfully carried out on a large scale; the training programs for school councils were the reason why parents have done as well as they have as council members (Mitchell, 1996). When a particular approach, such as the Algebra Project, shows poor people what their children need to be successful in high school, the results can be dramatic; instead of needing to sell a program, over 150 schools tried for 7 slots for the new program (O'Neill & Valenzuela, 1992, p. 10). However, generally the decision makers are still trying to convince parents and community members of the promise that new innovations hold. One school out of a group of schools had over half of its students experiencing some tutoring because its principal, unlike others, believed in the approach, and the other principals and faculties had to be advised by a consultant to renew the program (Joyce & Calhoun, 1996, p. 129). The proposition that elites make most of the organizational decisions in voluntary organizations as well as unions is still widely supported (Michels, 1949)

Stage 6, participation by either parents or volunteers in community service, appears as a double dream. Integrated services have been defined to include integration of services for clients, integration of programs, and policy integrations. Policy integrations reflect a philosophy of government and organizational change (Kagan, 1993). Most of the efforts at integration have focused on the more indirect forms of integration. Group casework and a common location of services for people have been among the few efforts directed at clients. Parental decision making, about any of the different kinds of integration to be undertaken, has been minimal (Dryfoos, 1994; Kagan, 1993).

In places that have had the most dramatic changes, there are some signs of increased involvement of parents and volunteers in school governance. Kentucky requires an advisory board for each of the family centers with two students, parents, and community members parcipating, whereas Chicago has active parent coordinators who are representative of the community. However, almost everywhere key decisions are made by professionals. For example, the decision to require police checks on the background of possible volunteers may represent the concerns of community members about sexual abuse, but the decision to introduce the checks and the location of the programs in schools was made by the Big Brothers Association.

Parents and volunteers view organizations as supplements to their own views and resources. Parents welcome the opportunity to discuss the disciplining of their own children with one another though not in formal parenting programs designed by experts (Kay & Roberts, 1994, p. 8). Similarly, community members do not accept the experts' view that education should be geared to growth through the study of science and mathematics. They prefer education for the basics that provide ordinary jobs (Immerwahr, et al., 1991). Indeed, for ordinary people, moral development of students is viewed as more important than expertise!

The mutual learning and respect that appears to be a crucial part of mentoring programs suggests that organizations can bring people together. Though the security measures may be more important than the imitation of an existing program or the reliance on research for legitimacy, the matching between mentors and students is crucial. The support that each receives from the school and the sponsoring agency or school board also contributes to a meaningful relationship; the case of AMFY is particularly revealing. Such supports for mutual learning can give direction to broader attempts at integrating services about which teachers, at least, still have serious doubts (Jones, 1991). The politics of education issues require a vision that focuses on the meaning of innovations for people.

Chapter 9

Very Special Interest Groups

The thirteenth rule: Pick the target, freeze it, personalize it, and polarize it. Go outside the experience of the enemy, stay inside the experience of your people. . . . There is just so much more than can be squeezed out of the Have-Not so the Haves must take it from each other. (Alinsky, 1971, pp. 130, 139, 149)

In addition to the Greater Baltimore Committee, Pinderhughes was also able to secure the support of BUILD (Baltimoreans United in Leadership Development), a church-based group that could have easily become an antagonist of the Superintendent. . . .BUILD began in Baltimore in 1977 under the leadership of Arnie Graf, a protégée of the late Chicago community organizer Saul Alinsky . . . Finally, the Greater Baltimore Committee needed support from BUILD and the rest of Baltimore's African-American community for its education initiatives. BUILD, for its part, saw the chance to gain a powerful and prestigious ally. (DiConti, 1996, pp. 131-133)

A special education resource student who started out with serious reading and emotional problems, Gerald now wears a proud smile and can be heard constantly saying, "I am a super reader! If you don't believe me I'll show you. Listen, I'll read for you. Do you have the time?" (Slavin, et al., 1993, p. 106)

The latent rage of poor people is articulated by specific interest groups such as those founded by Saul Alinsky, whereas the more general interest with which privileged parents are identified is represented in wide-ranging national programs to improve education, such as those which a former Dean of Education at Harvard, Ted Sizer, has led. At times, model programs and foundations have tried to bring the different types of programs together as a part of a gigantic effort to combine elements in the search for a way to turn them into innovative gold.

However, a more fundamental consideration is needed before unifying these disparate groups and their approaches. All of these groups are part of a broad social movement that reacts to perceived problems in education. Commissions and reports, beginning with *A Nation at Risk* (National Commission on Excellence in Education, 1983), alerted the public to the need for change. At the surface of the movement, specific programs work to improve the quality of education. At a deeper level, community action programs with their diverse interests, have coalesced in marathon activities to promote educational reform. Concerns for equality, discipline, and basic education, as much as excellence, are at the core of the effort and the vision of the future as much as they reflect the tradition of the past.

Many of these groups developed specific programs as a result of the call for excellence in education. The Coalition for Essential Schools offers a core curriculum where teachers are coaches and students are workers. The Accelerated School Projects offers all the enrichment activities that have been available for gifted students, to at-risk children. Success for All provides tutoring and active learning that has expanded from reading for at-risk students to a progressive approach to mathematics, science, and social studies for a greater variety of students. The Comer program has developed a program of social services and governance changes primarily for poor students, which is related to other programs including Schools of the 21st Century, both of which are based at Yale University. Each of these programs has been inspired by individual experts, but institutional or superexperts are superseding them, and the individual programs are being combined into gigantic reform efforts, such as the ATLAS project, which are supported by New American Schools.

Aside from these promotional programs and their increasing permutations, specific communities have developed movements of many indigenous organizations around one kind of innovation. Choice and charter schools have been the basis for modest reform efforts in Minnesota and Alberta (Mitchell, 1996); in such places, prosperity and reputations for established schools have led active parents and businesspeople to seek increased options in education. The conditions for a social movement built around site-based management have occurred in both Chicago and Baltimore (DiConti, 1996). Only in such cities did experts lament how bad the schools were; in poverty-ridden areas that are common in such cities, experts and reports were less important than grass-roots organizations (O'Connell, 1991).

The values of equality and endurance, which are part of the common tradition, need to be considered as much as the new development. Attention is given to at-risk students and gender equality, racial respect, and multicultural aims are equally important, and will be considered in another book. Innovations must be weighted against these more enduring aims; only then will it be possible to know when to undertake an innovation and when to abandon one.

LOCAL ADVOCACY GROUPS

Depressed cities and rural areas were among the places where Saul Alinsky originally developed a large number of community organizations and trained their leaders (Kyle & Kantowicz, 1992). Alinsky was a criminologist who initially developed community organizations near the packing houses of Chicago. He believed that getting people organized was even more important than promoting literacy, since they would have to learn how to read in order to run the organization.

In Baltimore, Alinsky laid the foundations for BUILD as he did for community activism among Natives in Canada, evident years later! Alinsky went to Native reserves himself, and his ideas were carried to other reserves by adult educators with Frontier College (Joy Nielsen, personal communication, November 26, 1994). The tactics of Natives in creating extreme positions, using humor against the authorities, and barricades to prevent business as usual in the community, are all borrowed from the Chicago organizer. Alinsky left his ideas somewhat like Johnny Appleseed; they have sprouted and grown.

The importance of this approach and others similar to it are not recognized because such community activists make links with politicians and religious leaders, rather than with educational experts. The original development of social organizations in Chicago by Alinsky was linked with the Catholic Church. Currently, Catholic Latinos, with related advocacy organizations inspired by this founder, are the most stable supporters of educational reform in Chicago. After Alinsky's death, the organization, the Industrial Areas Foundation (IAF), moved to New York under the leadership of Edward Chambers, but the links to local groups in Chicago were broken (Ken Rolling, interview, October 23, 1993). Local groups exist with only a one year agreement with the national organization, since they, like individuals, are to follow the iron law of never becoming dependent upon anyone when you can do something yourself.

It has been the Texas organization under the leadership of Ernesto Cortes that has developed the largest alliance with churches (Rogers, 1990). As it expanded from its original Catholic base in San Antonio and the predominantly Catholic area of West Texas to the more Protestant cities of East Texas, IAF has obtained support from these conservative religious groups, including the Church of Christ. IAF also has local organizations in California, Arizona, Maryland, Tennessee, and the United Kingdom as part of its quest for social justice, a quest that corresponds to Jewish and Christian ideals. The IAF is helping organizations in over a dozen other areas and claims to provide leadership training for over thirty organizations, which represent nearly one thousand institutions and over one million families (Texas Interfaith Education Fund, 1990; Cortes, n.d.).

In Texas, a growing number of schools in twelve cities are organized by IAF as part of the Alliance School Initiative in order to teach parents and community leaders how better to make decisions to improve the education of poor children. The training sessions cover everything from reading school budgets to how one should negotiate with educational experts to make them accountable (Cortes,

1995). Cortes argues that once parents become empowered as parents with teachers they have a common interest in educational innovations. Parents learn to be powerful by organizing to get exemptions from the state for Alliance Schools and by working together with educators to make experts accountable. Like politicians whom the IAF endorses, Howard Gardiner signs a contract to return to the Alliance after a year to show how his ideas are improving schools. However, it is important to realize that Cortes is very much a part of the educational establishment, serving on three different national commissions involving education and answering the call when other experts want to know how to reach parents.

In spite of its many achievements, the IAF became isolated from the organizations inspired by it in Chicago, a city that is always a cauldron for reform and change. In 1993, meetings were held between IAF organizers and religious leaders to consider IAF's return to Chicago. Two community organizers reported that these meetings were occurring, but both added that the Catholic church in Chicago has promised IAF over $1 million and that the organization was seeking $.25 million from Jewish organizations and Protestant churches (Ken Rolling, interview, October 19, 1993; Peter Martinez, interview, October 29, 1993). The IAF reportedly received $2.3 million from churches; the Moslems joined other religious groups and provided the IAF with moral support, though no funds. As in Texas, the IAF in Chicago wanted support from all religious groups in order to present a combined moral front for social justice. Finally, the IAF has established a local organization for the northern Illinois area that includes Chicago (Ken Rolling, interview, May 11, 1995).

In Baltimore as well as other cities, where they have acted on behalf of poor people, the IAF has had a much more continuous presence. However, until 1984, BUILD was perceived as creating confrontations, particularly with the very powerful Mayor Schaefer. The Superintendent of Schools, Alice Pinderhughes, made it clear that, unlike the Mayor, she wanted BUILD's help in improving the schools (DiConti, 1996). During his seventeen years as Mayor, William Schaefer concentrated on building up the city's physical facilities while spending less on the city's escalating number of poverty-racked children who were needy, compared to those in any other part of Maryland. By 1983, Baltimore's students showed some of the lowest education achievement scores in the United States, and the state had a higher percentage of students classified as learning disabled than anywhere else.

Beginning in 1984, BUILD started working with Superintendent Pinderhughes on a number of problems designed to improve education without increasing educational spending. Additional support for schools was to be obtained from business through partnerships. A group of businesspeople, the Greater Baltimore Committee, agreed to work with BUILD and the school system on a plan similar to the Boston Compact because it allowed businesspeople to provide jobs in exchange for student achievements without getting unduly involved in battles with the school system (DiConti, 1996). By 1988, only a small number of students met the criteria, an 80 percent average grade and 95 percent attendance, for work assistance. Employers then began offering counseling in the schools and assistance for college bound students.

All of these programs encountered resistance from the educational bureaucracy, which resented the invasion of its turf. Specifically, employer counseling for scholarship assistance encountered the opposition of school counselors. Perhaps one of the most striking examples was the bureaucrats' diversion of tickets for baseball games. The tickets were provided by employers and intended for students, but were used by school officials. In 1988, the system's opposition, combined with changes in superintendents, undermined the combined attempt of BUILD and employers to develop school-based management in the Baltimore system (Ibid).

In the same year that school-based management was being sabotaged by the system's managers, businesspeople in Chicago discovered that they held a common position on schools with a whole series of community organizations that had been initiated by Alinsky and his followers. The Chicago effort was far more successful than the one in Baltimore and led to reform legislation and a substantial reduction in the size of the bureaucracy (Mitchell, 1996). An organizer who had worked for the Alinsky groups states that four elements contributed to the local reform movement: a history of militancy among a number of organizations, the development of collaborative efforts among these and other organizations including those run by business, the dissatisfaction of the business community with the school system because of the low skills of students, and the presence of several professional educators who also worked with advocacy organizations to reform education as the local efforts developed (Peter Martinez, interview, October 29, 1993).

However, as they go about the business of trying to change education, organizations, even those in Chicago most influenced by Saul Alinsky, have stopped dealing with the school system and businesses as polar opposites. The two most influential advocacy organizations in Chicago, Designs for Change and the Chicago Panel on School Policy, have differed in the extent to which they represent specific constituencies who are trying to change educational policies. Designs for Change is more likely to represent interest groups, such as the families of special education students, whereas the Chicago Panel on School Policy is prone to speak for a variety of liberal organizations with different concerns. Neither of these two organizations are church related; they both confront the school system, though Designs is clearly the stronger alternative, a sort of school board in exile, particularly since the Mayor took over direct appointment of his own administrators for the schools.

The original basis for these two organizations, as well as others that employed Alinsky-trained organizers, was the Civil Rights Movement. The civil rights effort led to the development of groups that acted to develop fairer policies for racial minorities in American cities in the 1960s (Moore et al., 1983, pp. 47–48). The civil rights campaign led, in turn, to movements to improve the rights of women, homosexuals, and the disabled. The Children's Defense Fund at a national level and Designs for Change in Chicago, had attempted to improve the status of the handicapped. The racial crises in this one city led to the formation of a biracial group of businesspeople, Chicago United, so that Blacks would feel there were opportunities for them. In 1979, the financial collapse of the schools led the organizations for education to combine into the Chicago Panel on School Policy, in order to monitor school finances and student achievement. Designs for Change emerged at the same time when its leader, Don Moore, transformed a national study into a local advocacy group with Latino and Black organizers, trained according to Alinsky's principles. These advocacy organizations, which were directly or indirectly inspired by the demand for racial equality, were hardly sheer pressure groups. Their leaders have been so personally dedicated and knowledgable that they might be said to resemble Ralph Nader.

The more specific the constituents, the more likely is the group to maintain its opposition to the educational establishment. Designs for Change works with local groups who have a specific grievance, providing them with resources and counsel as a way of remaining close to the source of resistance (Mitchell, 1996). Designs for Change and the Chicago Panel have formed many alliances, including one with their former opponent, the principals' association. However, some of the middle-level and local community groups maintain an idealistic stance. For example, the husband and wife team of Bernie and Joy Noven and their successor are very independent; they operate under the revealing acronym, PURE, which stands for Parents United for Responsible Education (Diana Lauber, interview, April 28, 1994). National organizations are more likely to represent general interests and promote leadership in the larger community than are parochial organizations. That is probably why Alinsky and his followers always stayed with local conflict groups.

BROADER PROMOTIONAL EFFORTS FOR AT-RISK STUDENTS

Many of the promotional efforts have never been seriously related to specific community reforms and have moved to the national arena as rapidly as possible. For example, in Baltimore, though becoming involved at the same time with the same superintendent for the same type of students, Alinsky's BUILD and Robert Slavin's group have never cooperated (DiConti, 1996; Slavin, et al., 1993). These groups have coexisted in a number of other cities, apparently without recognizing each other's efforts for the poor. Just before starting Success for All (SFA), Slavin worked with a local school that was trying a so-called Calvert program of school-based management and, though BUILD was beginning a campaign to support school-based management, the two have never joined their efforts.

Success for All is one of a series of efforts to improve the education of at-risk students. From its founding in 1987, when the Baltimore school system asked Professor Robert Slavin to put his ideas about assisting high-risk students into practice, the program has emphasized reading improvement (Slavin, et al., 1993, pp. 83-86). It has stressed a daily structured ninety minute program of instruction in small groups, which is supplemented by individual tutoring for twenty minutes a day for all those students who, in the early grades, showed poor performance.

Professor Slavin had previously established himself as an expert on cooperative learning so this approach is, of course, incorporated into the reading program together with a family support team.

The cost of SFA is no greater than that of the usual program. In terms of per pupil expenditure, Baltimore consistently spent less than any other part of the state on education (Slavin, et al., 1993); in other sites, the program has been adopted with a very modest budget by the use of volunteer tutors. Slavin has been convinced that tutoring is the most effective form of instruction known and he attempts to relate classroom instruction to tutoring. Always using control schools, SFA shows impressive results in improving the reading of students. In grade one, the effects are a third of a grade level greater than the matched school and are greater as they progress to grade four; the effects are even larger for the lowest 25 percent of classes (Slavin, et al., 1994). The program has been extended to Canada, with a training center at Concordia University, to Israel, Mexico, and, most of all, to Australia, where it is being combined with Reading Recovery, which will be discussed later (Slavin, 1995).

Of the over 457 schools in 31 states that had been evaluated in 1994, it is claimed that in only one case were the control group results higher than those of the SFA school. The exception was a school in Idaho that had a remarkable faculty, although matching procedures normally reduces the chance for such variability. By making choices among students for tutoring, the younger ones are selected for the preventative approach and, by involving parents as substitutes for certified teachers when necessary because of budgetary restraints, SFA is able to achieve remarkable results.

In contrast, there is an appealing program, Reading Recovery, which "may cost as much as $8,333 for one successful 4th grader" (Viadero, 1994b). Reading Recovery has been shown to be most effective in preventing students from being transferred to special education. It relies exclusively on teachers who have been extensively trained to diagnose individual student problems through the use of one-way mirrors. The program does not seem to adjust to changing circumstances, but like SFA it uses phonetics in context. In the 1970s, Reading Recovery was developed by Marie Clay, a teacher of Native children in New Zealand. The program came to the United States from New Zealand in 1984 and has been widely used with at-risk students ever since.

In spite of some critical research, this program has some impressive credentials, including an endorsement by the National Diffusion Network. In successive years, Marie Clay and Robert Slavin were each given the same award for outstanding educational accomplishments. In 1996, Hillary Clinton visited a school in Florida that used the program and endorsed it. According to the central office at Ohio State, there are currently 35,000 students in this program.

Success for All (SFA) has itself spread to more students, more schools, and the entire elementary school curriculum (Olson, 1998a). The program is now being heralded as a success and is growing so rapidly that its founder is worried about the rapid rate of increase. In early 1998, SFA has grown to 750 schools and another 400 schools were expected to join the program by Fall as a results of funds from the Comprehensive School Reform Demonstration Program which passed the U. S. congress in 1997. Robert Slavin played a key role in advising the sponsors of this act, Edward Porter and David Obey, and has reaped his reward; SFA's revenue is expected to double from $15 million to over $30 million (Hoff, 1998). The program has been endorsed by the American Federation of Teachers and adopted by a number of urban cities that have joined the pursuit for comprehensive school reform.

Earlier, Slavin had widened his curriculum; as a result of a grant from the American School Development Corporation, Slavin has created Roots and Wings, which was designed to break the mold of education (Slavin, et al., 1994). Roots and Wings combines constructivist mathematics with a world laboratory that covers both science and social studies. The mathematics program tries to match the standards set by the National Council for Teachers of Mathematics, whereas the lab attempts to use the most advanced ideas about simulating real problems in schools. This represents an enormous expansion of the original focus as it attempts to incorporate many of the inventors' previous ideas, just as the reading program tried to include the cooperative learning approach.

THE ACCELERATED PROCESS

Unlike Success for All, the Accelerated Schools Project, from the very start, has emphasized a wide ranging philosophical focus. In 1987, the radical economist, Henry Levin, developed the program as a way of reversing the usual approach whereby the poorer students are given more repetitive and structured material, while gifted students are given more enriched and varied projects. In treating at-risk students as exceptional, the program stresses purposes or visions, empowerment, often through school-based management, and building upon the strengths of students, parents, and communities, rather than their deficiencies. There is no significant difference between this program and SFA with respect to empowerment; both programs stress the support of 75 percent to 80 percent of teachers before the program is begun, the involvement of teachers through task forces as the program develops, and the desirability of school-based management as a formal plan (McCarthy & Still, 1993, pp. 69, 71).

However, Levin's theory is richly developed with respect to his vision, one which attempts to enhance the poor's perception of their strengths (Levin, 1993). The program combines the traditional emphasis on ceremonies, which is typical of primitive societies, with a modern stress on individual reflection. The latter is encouraged to prevent simple copying among schools or between students. Celebrations and parades are encouraged to mark the creation of a new Accelerated School site. In one site, teachers dressed up in historical costumes borrowed from a local theatre group. However, reflection and selection is encouraged rather than the wholesale adoption of a whole language program, and teachers are encouraged to run their own staff development program for each other based on research studies (Accelerated Schools Project, 1993).

Attempts to honor individuals, such as a particular volunteer, combine festival and individual approaches. Teachers are encouraged to recognize the worth and importance of individuals in the community so that they, in turn, can get more help from the community that they are otherwise inclined to depreciate. Afternoon sessions can, on occasion, be turned over to community and university volunteers as teachers meet and plan future sessions. The love and support of parents for their children is one of the unused assets that the program attempts to tap. The transformation of a school yard occurred; it was a visual symbol of the changed relationship between the school and its community.

A small rectangle of ground [that] was previously an eyesore was cleared by students, staff, and parents and replaced with a multitude of petunias, begonias, and other flowers and plants. Picnic tables were donated by the local community. . . . [T]he garden produced and supported dozens of monarch, sulphur swallowtail and painted lady butterflies last spring (Accelerated Schools Project, 1993, p. 8).

The renewal of a sense of purpose is important for new members of the school community, particularly students, and art is seen as an essential part of the process. It may be recalled from Chapter 6 that Levin had become involved with the Galef Institute's art program. In a variety of settings, the students revealed their renewed visions. An accelerated school pledge is followed by a special song that a music teacher has written. In another setting, students display what the words mean and then act them out. In still other places, students develop collages and drawings; participate by attaching a hand to a giving tree; place Accelerated symbols on t-shirts, folders, or mugs; or dress up and act out parts of the vision as "guiding hands, touching hearts, and unlocking minds" (Accelerated Schools Project, 1993, p. 16).

The visionary activities by students became more varied as the program spread into middle schools. For example, after everyone developed student cards to be displayed on the wall, students did one of a variety of activities as "creations:" songs, essays, poems, crests, and raps. The students display both their independence and the meaning of the project. A grade seven student, Candace Meloyer, wrote this Accelerated Rap song:

Pay attention 'cus we won't repeat:
No more dittos, no more sheets!
We're tired of being second best,
If you give us a chance, we could be the best.
Stop calling us names, stop saying we're slow,
we could be smarter than you know!
So stop focusing so much on our badness and start paying
more attention to our "radness" (Accelerated Schools Project, 1993, p. 12).

This extensive development of creations to represent the vision statements are necessary to help overcome the pervasive pessimism regarding poor inner-city schools. Both the Accelerated School Project and SFA try to overcome an environment of failure, with consequent disempowerment, mutual antagonism, and low expectations. Both of these programs involve tutoring, which has repeatedly been shown to be effective, but neither has added the use of a computer, particularly as a part of a "take-home" program (Joyce & Calhoun, 1996).

However, the computer would be just one more activity for the Accelerated School Project or Process to include, together with its other activities. The research process and social interaction are combined in many ways, as they were for John Dewey. Initially, the teachers do a survey and conduct an inquiry about their purposes, but the troops then go out in the streets to meet the parents at their homes; a herald announces, "The teachers are here!" (McCarthy & Still, 1993, pp. 70-79). The school community learns how to do research and even draws on a comparison with a control school. Parents are taught how to be effective volunteers, college students and businesspeople become "Friday Faculty" to teach a variety of sessions that combine doing and learning, while older students often escort their "little buddies" to their classrooms for the day (Ibid, p. 74). Some of the local Accelerated projects, particularly in Missouri, appear to follow more of a fixed pattern.

Another action research program shows how effective programs such as these can be, when combined with other elements. When added together with take-home computers, a reading and writing program, administrative support, and staff development, a whole innovation, despite initial skepticism, proved to be viable and "parents literally stood in line for the opportunity to participate" (Joyce & Calhoun, 1996, p. 130). Particularly striking in this case was how well the equipment was looked after, negating another fear of those who were pessimistic about innovations with poor communities. SFA has particulary noted the increased reading of public library books and the care that they are given (Slavin, et al., 1993, p. 99). The tools of education are employed when the attitudes toward education change.

PASSING BEYOND PSYCHIATRY: THE COMER SCHOOLS

At-risk students and communities require a diagnostic effort to overcome the perception of continuing failure. Systematic change requires the combination of curriculum and training and social organization. The social organization to support a revitalized school approach has been suggested by the work of James Comer. In 1968, Comer began work in New Haven, Connecticut, the home of his university, Yale. After 1980, the approach was generalized for other communities. Though calling for university programs to be related to school settings, the leaders who expanded the program to other sites were still brought to the Yale campus for "immersion" (Comer, 1980, p. 275).

Employing a governance system that allows the community to be represented and a task structure that encourages partially paid employment in the school for parents, Comer was been able to develop a sense of ownership of their school by the community (O'Neill & Butts, 1991). Besides the governance and management team, parent involvement and a mental health/support team are the other "mechanisms" used. Comer believes that the omission of paid parent volunteers and planning times led to some of the inconsistencies in results (Comer, 1980).

The Comer program pioneered the use of family support services, though both SFA and the Accelerated School Project have been just as successful in offering integrated services to schools. Problems of health, behavior, attendance, or academic performance are followed up by a team that often involves a nurse or a social worker as well as parents or parent facilitators; however, teachers have to learn to work with these new supporters. The guiding principles of the Comer approach, the School Development Program (SDP), are a no-fault approach, consensus decision making, and collaboration, while the operations required are a comprehensive school plan, staff development, and regular assessment.

Unfortunately, SDP has been less successful when Comer is not personally involved (William McKersie, interview, November 2, 1993). The problems may result from a paternalistic approach to the program. For instance, specialists on the Mental Health Team cannot be replaced by volunteers—after all, Comer is a psychiatrist! Though Comer can relate to poor families—he comes from such a background in the Steeltown of East Chicago, Indiana—some of his followers cannot do so. Like other efforts that attempt to make caring a basis for instruction, the program has not shown a way to develop the technical core of instruction. In an epilogue to his earlier book, Comer admitted that a curriculum program is needed to supplement his project (Comer, 1980, p. 297). In contrast, the Algebra Project can motivate poor people to study algebra rather than general mathematics, as their children enter junior high school (Moses, et al., 1989).

Apparently, to overcome the curriculum limitations, Comer has combined his project with a variety of curriculum efforts, including the Coalition of Essential Schools that will be discussed shortly. As discussed in Chapter 6, Henry Levin was willing to work together with the Galef Institute Foundation. SFA has expanded its curriculum to gain support from the New American Schools Development Corporation, which is supported by major corporations and foundations to break the mold of American education. These three programs continue to evolve and their developments are related to available funding.

Many of these programs try to develop new roles. SFA employs or arranges for school systems to appoint facilitators on a part-time or full-time basis in each of its schools; the facilitator had often been the Title 1 master teacher; if not, these two relatively new roles needed to be coordinated. Facilitators help make arrangements among all the institutions involved, including business partners, integrated services, and special education as well as teachers and tutors (Slavin, et al., 1993, p. 89-90). All of the programs involve paid or volunteer tutors who often initiate the diagnosis or testing of all at-risk students in order to develop different intensive approaches with them. However, particularly when arrangements were disrupted by politicians changing administrators, as in Baltimore, tutoring only some of the students would be abandoned in favor of the more traditional practice of teaching small groups of students in order, hopefully, to remediate their deficit (Slavin, et al., 1993, p. 110).

Places and names are used to create a different set of symbols for education even if the buildings remain the same, particularly in depressed areas. Parents are in evidence where Parent Centers are created, Newcomers Centers are for immigrant children, Task Forces exist for particular needs, and Facilitators bring things together for all the parties (McCarthy & Still, 1993). This symbolism, such as Roots and Wings introduced by SFA, seems to make proposals attractive to foundations. SDP has its discovery room, where disillusioned students can be re-interested in learning, and a crisis room, where out-of-control students can overcome traumatic home experiences, and the COZI projects, which combine the names of Comer and Edward Zigler, the co-founder of Headstart, in a program for pre-school children (Comer, 1980). These names may, of course, create the illusion that change will occur.

MORE GENERAL ENTREPRENEURS

Unlike the efforts by Alinsky organizers, the various efforts to improve their lot have not generally been related to political power in our society. Promotional efforts are more likely to be related to community organizing and political action when these expert designed programs are supported by state government. The largest American effort to relate education to the political system is the Coalition of Essential Schools (CES) initiated by Ted Sizer in 1984 (McQuillan & Muncey, 1995); the most significant Canadian effort has involved federal government support for French immersion for which the late H. H. ("David") Stern was the most significant force (Yvonne Hebert, interview, November 5, 1997).

The Canadian Parents for French (CPF) is the organization that represents parents and provides a meeting place for experts and their supporters (Poyen, 1989). The organization has been funded since its founding by the Canadian federal government; it maintains provincial branches that parallel the organization of government. In contrast, CES is a broadly based organization that has been highly publicized and supported by a variety of foundations. Most recently, it has received directly more than $100 million, and it has been involved indirectly, through Ted Sizer, in the administration of $500 million for reform. These huge gifts have been from the Annenberg Foundation. Both organizations stress that they are an avenue for civic leadership and are performing on the basis of a broader vision, not a narrow concern (Poyen, 1989; Sizer, 1992).

Organizations that have wanted to influence schools have often had fairly limited aims; however, both CPF and CES have larger visions than those with more local concerns. Advocates from outside the schools have usually sought favors through selling goods or obtaining access to children in order to change their attitudes. Advocates within the system, including teachers or trustees, have usually wanted to influence salaries, tax rates, or employment practices (Gross, 1958). Pressure groups in this sense thought of themselves as disadvantaged; they tried to correct their situation by acquiring advantages for themselves. On this basis, the Alinsky-style organizations are more limited than CPF or CES. Having already obtained substantial financial support, these organizations are not as caught up in the chase for foundation grants as are many of the local advocacy groups.

RE-LEARNING

Since 1988, the most direct link between governments and interest organizations has occurred between CES and ten state governments, which have formally united as Re-Learning States to support CES schools. This large-scale American effort appears to relate national and local efforts on a continuing basis. CES is the most important effort to engineer support from state governments (Charles Kyle, interview, November 10, 1993). The CES program, centered at Brown University, leads local schools to a humanistic common core of education through the cooperation of some ten state governments (Educational Commission of the States and Coalition of Essential Schools, 1990).   State governments are connected through the Educational Commission of the States, a voluntary cooperative effort of forty-nine states, which was first suggested by an earlier reformer, J. B. Conant.

Re-Learning and CES were both initiated by Ted Sizer, who personally persuaded many school people and government leaders to join these efforts. Sizer had previously been associated with a call for great books in education, the Paideia proposal. The new effort by Sizer was designed to have a wider appeal and to focus on doing the essentials well. Foreign languages, physical education, and most electives have been omitted so that there is a focus on mathematics and science together with English and social studies (Sizer, 1984). Essential schools often have four teachers from each area forming a team around which students are grouped.

The project began as a study project by Sizer and other scholars on the crisis in American education described in the report *A Nation At Risk* (1983). The Sizer effort began slowly but progressed rapidly after 1993 when CES received a large grant from the Annenberg Foundation and, simultaneously, Sizer became responsible for the larger Annenberg Foundation. School enrollment had risen to some 800 schools by 1995 (North Central Regional Educational Laboratory, 1996). During the same year that it received the Annenberg grant, Sizer was also instrumental in obtaining the grant from the New American Schools for the ATLAS projects together with some of the most dominant experts in education: Howard Gardiner of Project Zero in the arts at Harvard, James Comer, and Janet Whitla of the Education Development Centre. Though now retiring from some of his duties, Sizer has clearly made CES the most dominant reform effort in America, a position reflected in the recent issue of *Time* magazine (October 27, 1997).

However, Sizer's program has not attempted to alter the distribution of power in society or even between education and other institutions. Sizer is conservative; he claims CES does not want much more money—10 percent—just money spent more wisely (Sizer, 1992). Furthermore, he has described his program as "old chestnuts" and, concerning his key principles for schools, he said:

They go back into the mists of time. There's nothing there which hasn't been successfully used. It's a very familiar list. Just because it's old-fashioned and familiar doesn't mean it's easy. (quoted in Muncey & McQuillan, 1990, p.5)

Though Sizer's program has come to be more like a stew to which many other approaches, such as school-based management and self-initiated professional development, have been added, it did not involve parents or volunteers until it joined with Comer's efforts.

The CES philosophy has primarily attempted to empower teachers and students in familiar schools. Teachers are to be empowered by focusing on learning rather than trivia and students are expected to "learn more while being taught less" (Sizer, 1992, p. 34). With the teachers as coaches rather than instructors, students will "teach themselves more" and class time will be "used better" (Sizer, 1992, p. 197). Sizer looks for changes that can be accomplished within our existing framework of what schools can be like. Furthermore, by working with state governments, the leader has committed CES to a position that can boomerang so that politics controls CES.

No other national program in the United States has become involved with state governments. The state governments typically provide about $30,000, ideally $50,000, for a summer session for each individual school to plan its program. Additional funds for planning and provision for critic teachers and substitute teachers are sought from foundations and businesses, so that the teachers involved in the program can learn and travel to other sites (Coalition of Essential Schools, 1992, November, p. 5). Even before the more recent large grants, over fifteen corporations and thirty foundations had contributed over $30 million to CES (McQuillan & Muncey, 1995). In Chicago, over $1 million was obtained to get such schools started (Lourdes Monteagudo, interview, April 14, 1994).

In each state, Re-Learning is governed by a steering committee that usually includes the governor, state legislators, representatives of governors from higher education, and teacher unions. In Illinois, the group is chaired by the state superintendent of education and Re-Learning is housed at the Illinois State Board of Education (Illinois Alliance of Essential Schools, 1991–1992). In Chicago, the deputy mayor for education, Lourdes Monteagudo, saw the program as a way of clustering schools and relating the usually separate city and state policies. In every state, the steering committee is supplemented by working members, a "cadre" from professional organizations that is involved at the top level and provides more specific technical and program support than their superiors.

Re-Learning attempts to capture evaluation studies, competing interest groups, and potential opposition. For example, in Illinois, only the University of Illinois does research on the Re-Learning project (Warren Chapman, interview, November 22, 1992). In the same state, affiliates of both the American Federation of Teachers and the National Educational Association were both persuaded to join with CES so that each could watch the other. Extreme right-wing groups have frequently objected to the CES emphasis on progressive education. In Alton, Illinois, one such right-wing religious and political leader was outsmarted; the local CES leaders successfully labeled her before she could stereotype them in the media and in group meetings (Warren Chapman, interview, November 22, 1993).

However, there are costs to CES for its political involvement. The CES affiliate, Illinois Alliance, has been limited to twenty schools because of a standoff between areas in the state. The Illinois State Board of Education, which administers the program, is dominated by rural areas that want to keep the current division between ten city and ten rural schools intact. Suburban schools have particularly wanted more designated schools, and while the education crisis in Chicago calls for them to be given every advantage, the representatives of rural schools protect their interests and, as a result, no more schools were added to the program (Warren Chapman, interview, November 22, 1993).

There are substantial divisions within CES that also prevent decisive action. Sizer specifically rejects any attempt to specify any one way to implement his general theory; he is, in this respect, unlike salvation movements (Muncey & McQuillan, 1990). The central staff are ambivalent about the autonomy of affiliates; the evaluation procedures, even self-evaluations, have resulted in schools being led to "rethink their membership" (Ibid, 1990, p. 14). In joining CES, most schools have often only adopted changes related to teaching, such as the student as a worker and the teacher as a coach, which have been widely accepted by schools in the confederacy. Changes in the curriculum and in the school structure appear more imaginary than the concrete changes teachers can initiate.

For many teachers, joining CES was an ambiguous decision. For most teachers, it was the wider society (single-parent families, drugs, and student disrespect for authority) rather than schools that most needed to change. Even the teachers' vote to join the coalition is frequently not very meaningful for those involved. In spite of the policy that the majority of teachers should endorse participation in CES, the decision was made by the principals in four of the six original schools, and it has often resulted from an interpretation of ambiguous results ever since. Furthermore, when only one part of a school joins CES, intense divisions can develop between the part of the school that takes up some of the program's ideas and that which does not.

The local teachers are provided with training sessions, a national faculty, and outsiders who serve as critics, as well as a large number of other teachers who are supposedly further along in understanding CES rules. The support of other teachers can be part of a year-long "trek" process between neighboring schools (Holly Bartunek, interview, April 27, 1994). However, the treks are organized by staff, as are various forms of evaluations and professional development. The staff is divided by various functions, such as research or new forms of evaluations, which means that the staff is concerned about the interpretation of CES's mission. For a time, Sizer had a staff member oversee the continuing development of CES's philosophy, because he was so busy promoting the enterprise. After Sizer's retirement, who will speak for the philosophy of autonomous schools and how will their interests be represented? The growth and increasing specialization of the central office staff of CES, when combined with Sizer's reduced commitment, makes the centrality of support for local teachers questionable.

All of the developments in CES may make teacher and school isolation greater, the twin problems that CES was supposed to solve. CES has not suggested what specific changes need to be made in education or how commitment to those changes needs to be nourished. The CES calls for testing ideas through exhibitions and an integration of knowledge (Sizer, 1984, p. 135). The lack of specialization is the largest difficulty for CES. The emphasis on integrating specialists means that the oracle, Sizer, does not want generalist teachers (Sizer, 1984, p. 191). However, a state, such as New Mexico, is defined by CES as making progress when it reduces the number of recognized specialties from 134 to 25 (Coalition of Essential Schools, 1993b, p. 7). It seems strange that specialization among teachers should be discouraged at the very time that CES's staff is becoming more segmented.

There are some positive appeals involved in the CES approach. For example, students liked interdisciplinary connections, but they objected to any additional work being imposed upon them as a result of adopting CES; it seems doubtful that they had become more intellectual as envisioned in Sizer's first principle. The essential school concept is more attractive to the less specialized middle schools than it is to high schools because of their departmental specializations. However, because the program has been directed at high schools, individual middle schools are not usually connected to it.

For all schools, more than an integrated curriculum is needed to complement the teaching approaches and schedules. Cross-disciplinary integration should mean more than being "unbounded by disciplines," it should be framed by concerns and claims to know (Coalition of Essential Schools, 1992, p. 4). Unlike CPF, CES has not focused on a particular kind of knowledge, nor has it caught the research interest of scholars who care about the same problems as do teachers and parents. CES also seems to reinforce the division between educational and related fields of research.

The CES program seems ethnocentric as well as politically naive. According to John McCarthy, who was the separate school superintendent at the time, CES sought to establish one of its initial schools in Calgary; no other school in Canada joined subsequently. Nor has the program been copied in other English-speaking countries. In contrast, the National Writing Project, which spread to Canada within a year of its start in Oakland, has been widely adopted in Australia as well as other countries. Within the United States, there seems little sense in ignoring vocational education, as CES does, because vocational education has the most tightly organized lobby of any teacher group (Toch, 1991, pp. 107–110). Vocational educators could also be helpful in the practical assessments of general ideas that Sizer wants.

This coalition needs to go beyond connecting with everything that is going on in terms of politics and education; learning when not to innovate should be a primary principle for all reformers. The Educational Commission of the States (ECS), CES's partner, also needs a greater sense of direction. For Kentucky's major reform initiative, ECS provided general advice, helped select a consultant, and then disappeared (Harp, 1994, p. 11). At times, ECS has talked about becoming an advocacy organization and becoming more politically active, particularly in California, but they have done neither consistently (Mitchell, 1996).

The culture of educational change in the United States has perhaps been accepted too much by Sizer and his organization. They assume the problem is one of how to do it, not why it should be done. CES has probably opened itself up to even more problems by becoming a sponsor of charter schools (Celis, 1994). The Annenberg Foundation, with its enormous gift, has provided Sizer with a great opportunity to develop the coalition, but the National Writing Project (see Chapter 6) has had more effect with less money.

Without solving its current curriculum and organizational problems, CES has raised the stakes by entering into even more demanding projects, such as (ATLAS). Connections are made between the different levels of education from preschool to high school so that one academic community works together with other pathways to set standards and policies (ATLAS Communities, 1997). For example, high school students mentor younger students in a middle school while a kindergarten opened a family resource center for the entire community, including another school that sends its staff there as a part of their professional development. Similarly, community agencies cooperate with schools to build and support facilities that they may both use.

ATLAS is supported by the New American Schools which, it might be recalled from Chapter 3, supported the program in Illinois that became known as the New American Fools. The results from the pathways seem to be more encouraging. Students' reading scores have improved, their motivation to learn has climbed, and the involvement of parents and teachers has greatly increased. The curriculum seems to be based on integrated themes and Sizer's slogans, such as the student as a worker. Particularly in Norfolk, Virginia, student participation in community service increased dramatically, which more than matched parent and community involvement with schools (New American Schools, 1996).

CANADIAN PARENTS FOR FRENCH

As previously mentioned, the largest Canadian effort to support education that is in any way similar to Sizer's programs, is French immersion, for which the advocacy organization is the Canadian Parents for French. The founding conference and first newsletter of CPF were supported by the federal Office of the Commissioner of Official Languages (Poyen, 1989). Federal financial support has continued through the office of the secretary of state. At no time between its founding in 1977 and 1989, did the federal support fall below 64 percent of the organization's total financing (Ibid). In 1982, the secretary of state also began funding provincial branches of the organization (p. 106). By 1990 there were 200 chapters and 18,000 members (Manzer, 1990).

The organization has always tried to influence the federal government rather than be influenced by it. CPF has also been able to lobby broader political bodies representing all the provinces, such as the Council of Ministers. CPF has targeted key federal departments such as the Treasury Board, where budget decisions affecting bilingual education were made (Poyen, 1989). Because its mission is already accepted by the federal government, CPF has been an advocate through lobbying the bureaucrats, rather than the legislators. Official bilingualism has also made CPF more successful because doubts are not constantly raised about programs, as is often the case with American efforts for Latinos or Blacks. It has received a government grant of $1,230,380 for the next four years (Canadian Heritage, 1997).

CPF has also been effective because it has consistently had excellent advice and counseling. It was in navigating the official world that David Stern, a professor at the University of Toronto, was particularly effective as a guide (Yvonne Hebert, interview, November 7, 1997). Dr. Stern also traveled to different parts of the country together with executives of CPF, to promote both French immersion and the French core program in the language (Janet Poyen, personal communication, 1989). Though less important, the writing and presentations of other linguists have been a continuing contribution to this program.

Though drawing upon experts for knowledge concerning the curriculum, parents have been an active group within CPF. Parents in CPF tell bilingual researchers what they think and go well beyond asking the experts questions (Poyen, 1989). As parents advance to the provincial or national organization, they become caught up in the causes that the organization supports, and not just their own children. Furthermore, federal support for the provincial and national organization means that new leaders can arise. As a result, parent members show less resentment against a single isolated elite who is running the organization, as often happens in Canada.

Because of the wide-scale involvement of experts with parents in CPF, the organization provides a critical focus for the development of research and not just for disseminating results. CPF has repeatedly been seen as the clearinghouse for research on bilingual education (Poyen, 1989). However, it is important to realize what a key role Dr. Stern, a very disciplined academic, played until his death, in directing the program and setting the agenda for the future. In establishing such directives, CPF had far more specific points in its program than CES has had under the leadership of Ted Sizer.

It is clear that a separate kind of education, one that is based on knowledge of linguists, became the focus in the French program for parents, teachers, and researchers; however, this type of focus is rare. The major political battles of Canada in the 1960s involved the acceptance of French as an official language and the promotion of immersion programs in French for English-speaking children. Budget cuts in the 1980s, as well as today, have made the maintenance of these programs a continuing controversy.

As governments have cut their budgets, they, as well as some right-wing groups, have questioned the necessity for French immersion. Ironically, those who have questioned the French program have also wanted choice among programs and have advocated charter schools and vouchers (Dan Levson and Colin Penman, interviews, May 26, 1994). French immersion is the most successful large-scale innovation that has affected classroom instruction rather than fringe areas, and it has provided a meaningful option for Canadian families. The position of CPF has been so substantial that the Alberta government has backed off from suggesting it be eliminated, and groups such as Albertans for Quality Education have not attacked it in various public forums, roundtables, and conferences.

CPF has long been able to influence political leaders at both provincial and national levels; it has provided leadership for the educational debate as well as maintaining support for French immersion. The CPF suggests how important an advocacy group can be. Unlike some of the American groups, it is relevant to local situations and helps provide national support for particular school and community efforts; aspects of reform that have been a concern for an increasing number of foundations (Warren Chapman, interview, November 22, 1993).

AN INTERNAL PRESSURE GROUP

Both the community and broader interest groups act from outside the school system, but some groups work for change from inside schools. Internal groups can organize on various equity issues, though the pull toward assimilation into the administrative hierarchy with its many rewards, can be powerful. Administrators usually insulate themselves against instruction from outsiders, and from community issues, by a variety of tactics: preparing reports before considering any complaints, delaying action if the administrative barricade is not in place, arranging material to arrive at a "stacked deck solution," or pretending to influence a decision when they must give in to an outside group (McGivney & Haught, 1972).

For many years, the Calgary Board of Education used similar tactics to avoid dealing with complaints and avoided any admission of discriminating against women in terms of promotion (Steele & Boyle, 1997). Between 1973 and 1989, a series of reports repeatedly showed discriminatory promotion practices with regard to women for promotion; the report in 1989 showed little change, if any, since 1973. In fact, a senior administrator responded by proposing an Inquiry on Opportunities for Women, to monitor the problem for the next five years.

After conducting a survey, publishing statistics on administrative positions by gender, and inviting in an expert to give her views, the Inquiry realized, part way through its mandate, that no progress was being made. In 1992, it recommended that a Special Advisor on Women's Issues be appointed and that all superintendents submit reports on past accomplishments and plans for the year (Steele & Boyle, 1997). The Special Advisor was made responsible to the Chief Superintendent and a continuing Gender Equity Committee, which replaced the Inquiry, was appointed, with representatives from all employee groups. The permanent plan ensured that the equity demands were seen as a continuing requirement that must be met rather than a faddish issue that would disappear. The broad representation widened the constituency that would expect corrective action.

In fact, the wide coverage led to many issues, besides advancement, being discussed. Gay rights, the isolation of small groups, whether support staff, or male teachers in elementary schools, and security against sexual attacks, were all discussed. The openness of the individuals who served as the Special Advisor also contributed to this changing scope; stories, analogies, and metaphors were used to convey the message and the commitment of those who served as Advisors. In 1995, the title of the Advisor was changed to Special Advisor on Gender Issues to reflect these many varied questions.

In the meantime, substantial progress was made on the original issue, promotion. By 1997, the percentage of women in leadership positions was equal, though not proportional, to their numbers in teaching. Furthermore, the application process and the procedures used in making decisions were far better understood by all groups. However, the diverse representation and wide-ranging discussion led to the Special Advisor becoming an ombudsperson for people's concerns. Gender discrimination was linked to racial issues and prejudice against immigrants, gays and lesbians, and people with disabilities. Contacts were made with representatives of these groups as well as others.

The focus on the classroom ensured that teachers and students continued to be involved in the process of change. The advisors raised issues that people had not discussed before, such as the prejudice against women by female administrators who assume a male role model. Students were reached by approaches including the conference, "Enabling Visions," which brought out the concerns and anxieties of junior high girls for those involved. Unlike other school districts, where support for programs for promotional equality has declined, support for this exceptional and wide-ranging program has grown.

However, the Calgary program needs additional external supports. On the one hand, this school system is currently under review by the Conservative politicians, some of whom are concerned about the liberal positions that the board has adopted, particularly with respect to gay rights for students. On the other hand, many liberals who might support the program are unaware of its existence, because of the lack of publicity about its evolution. To develop the program without community support is commendable and interesting, but to sustain it without mobilizing the concerns and commitment of those in the community is unlikely. The program needs to evolve together with the Calgary community.

Many reforms in other situations, such as Chicago, are carried out by a very large number of talented women who run the related business, civic, community, and educational organizations (Diana Lauber, interview, October 26, 1993). Often, teams of women, or occasionally men and women, act to complement each other in community efforts. Dedicated women are even more crucial in many program areas, particularly art education (Mitchell, 1997). However, the current educational reform movement is so widely separated from earlier feminist efforts that gender is not usually a conscious basis for reform decisions.

Reform efforts often involve women who are providing the ideas and energy to complement the political dominance of men. Women generally work in teams to achieve their aims (Mitchell, 1996, pp. 27-28). For example, in lobbying against changes in the Illinois legislation of 1993, Joan Slay was the director who coordinated the lobbying like a chess game, while Coretta McFerren articulated supporters' feelings and kept them involved in the game, as it were. Both women reflected a relationship to male experts to whom they were responsible, and both had been trained by Alinsky and a follower, respectively (Coretta McFerren, interview, October 26, 1993).

However, the relationships in educational reform between female leaders and male executives has been broken up without developing any consciousness of discrimination. In late 1993, the distrust between the reformers and business increased when the Civic Committee President, Lawrence Howe, decided to absorb its advocacy group, Leadership for Quality Education (LQE). The president of LQE, Diana Nelson, resigned in protest. Among the six women who worked at LQE, there was clear discrimination; all of the staff were denied severance pay if they rejected alternative positions with the Civic Committee (Diana Lauber, interview, November 23, 1993). Strangely, the reorganization of LQE was not resisted on gender or racial grounds, even though two white men were making the decisions about the futures of six white women on staff and the one black woman assistant (Mitchell, 1996, pp. 137-138).

Though the reform movement in education has given little attention to gender differences, there are explicit efforts to deal with the problems of female students, particularly in encouraging them to enter science and mathematics. Since these fields tend to be dominated by males and male values, individual mentoring has been shown to be effective in providing support and guidance for aspiring females (Subotnik & Arnold, 1995). For progress to occur in a given field, mentors were needed in order to have a realistic picture of possible relationships and career options, so that life dilemmas could be more effectively confronted. Mentors are important, particularly early on in the career; role models can provide insight about the thought processes in a research field. However, the female students also learn that personal issues remain in flux, as even their professional advisors struggle with these issues.

Aside from individual mentoring, there are a number of programs that encourage nontraditional career choices by women in these same fields, that report attitude changes toward mathematics and science, and that attempt to relate changing self-confidence to program participation (McCormick & Wolf, 1993). Almost all of the programs are aimed at gifted girls but none has been made a centerpiece of reform by local or national organizations.

The first project, REACH, is an intervention program to develop awareness of the "sexist language and message in the media, textbook, tests and society" (Erikson, 1997). The program deals with the dilemmas that gifted girls face, and it attempts to make personal problems external, though not political. The girls learn to see themselves in a situation that can be slowly changed. Anecdotal evidence suggests REACH has changed the attitudes of the girls who have participated.

A second program, Expanding Your Horizons, attempts to develop direct interaction between students and women already working in the sciences and mathematics (McCormick & Wolf, 1993). Since its inception in 1976, this conference has been successful in emphasizing early intervention, combating sex typing of career choices and encouraging students to advance in these fields. A series of studies has found the conference helpful in providing information and clarifying interests, particularly regarding occupational plans. Concurrently, more actual options are being created by schools as the number of single sex schools increases in spite of legal opposition on the grounds that girls' schools discriminate against boys! Professional women are themselves starting private schools for girls in the sciences (Lehmann-Haupt, 1997). However, neither REACH nor Expanding Your Horizons has related their efforts to the development of single sex schools.

A third program, Multiplying Options Subtracting Biases (MOSB) has attempted to mobilize all the people around female students, male peers, mathematics teachers, parents, and counselors, in order to increase the students election of high school mathematics courses (McCormick & Wolf, 1993). For each group that can be expected to influence girls, a facilitator's guide is developed, which is the basis of a two-hour workshop. Thirty-minute videotapes try to increase student attitudes and plans for mathematics but the results for others is mixed. In contrast, the Algebra Project has mobilized many parents because they experienced the program themselves and were concerned about the consequences of their children being placed in general mathematics, rather than algebra; the program also paralleled major political efforts in the civil rights movement (Moses, et al. 1989).

Another partial program that does not relate to a broader social movement or political action is EQUALS, which focuses on changing the attitudes of teachers (McCormick & Wolf, 1993). For over sixteen years, this program has reached a large number of teachers and students. It has attempted to develop girls' confidence in mathematics and an awareness of career possibilities. The goal of this program is to increase the enrollment of girls in calculus in order to enhance their career choices. There are related programs for parents. Though this program has been effective, the consequences of simply requiring more higher mathematics courses, including calculus, such as is the Japanese practice, does not seem to be have been considered. Rather, changing individuals is again preferred to changing requirements or quotas.

A final effort to enhance the choices of individuals is the Minerva project, which takes the Roman goddess as the symbol of support for girls in the practical areas of science and technology (Erikson, 1997). The conference, originated in Calgary, was designed to meet the needs of grade eight students and has been adapted to the needs of rural areas. Though the program has pinpointed the crucial age group, it has not provided them with wider social support or with links to significant business or political groups that can be perceived as allies in their individual quests.

Though Minerva has been overwhelmingly successful in providing career counseling and support, it has been unable to obtain continuing funding.

Ironically, the program that attempts to provide support for grade eight students through job-shadowing, is now dependent upon professional women to not only contribute their time, but to make all other arrangements as well. Though all these programs need to be developed and continually reinforced, this one was more adaptable to changing circumstances than the others that were discussed (Erikson, 1997, pp. 32-38). Nevertheless, these five programs have stimulated a substantial literature and they could become very significant if educational reform ever combines with the feminist movement.

THE IRON LAW FOR AVOIDING DEPENDENCY

Individual attitudes should be the concern both of organizations representing specific interests, and of broader groups within society, but these organizations should also create options for individuals by decisive political actions. Individuals should neither be isolated in small groups nor made dependent upon organized powers for changes that they believe are essential for their lives. Advocacy for successful programs, such as SFA, can lead to the belief that innovation is dependent on outside change agents (Slavin, et al., 1993).

Educational reform has become so dependent on grants that even the grass-roots organizations founded by Alinsky in Chicago now believe that they could not exist without foundation support (Mitchell, 1996). It appears that they, as well as the national promotional efforts, could benefit from Alinsky's iron law. Never do for anyone something they can do themselves. The money chase, the pursuit of foundation support, has led the promoters to take very strange positions in their campaigns. There never seems to be any limit as to how far a position can be carried, as shown by the spread of Success for All to almost the entire elementary curriculum or the other developments into compounds of previously separate efforts.

The programs, and even the research on them, become self-fulfilling prophecies. The proposition formulated for Chicago, namely that the "fix" is in for reform, is probably true for all the promotional efforts discussed (Mitchell, 1996, p. 18). Even French immersion has been preoccupied with evidence that would support its effectiveness, rather than let one understand the effect of administrative limits on the program. Other efforts seem to make failure impossible by constantly changing their positions, as is particularly the case with the Coalition of Essential Schools. Each of these programs is more of an ideological truth than one possible answer to a problem.

The higher truth to which these programs should be accountable are the values of the American people, which can be achieved in a variety of ways. Reversing the usual status order, the Accelerated schools can allow one to see social equality in action. However, internal action groups, such as the gender program in Calgary, can help people achieve equality if those within bureaucracies will just act as if they are not in iron cages. Basic education can be achieved by teachers and administrators working together with students; they can be open to outside groups, including foundations, without becoming dependent upon them.   Ultimately, programs to reduce gender differences are as important as those for at-risk students, but neither advocacy groups nor foundations seem to think so.

"When the elephants fight, only the grass suffers." Avoiding this result requires an explicit recognition of the limits of policy as an implement of reform. Policies, as we have seen, are useful, but blunt, instruments. Under the best of circumstances, they can influence the allocation of resources, the structure of schooling, and the content of practice; but those changes take time and often have unexpected effects. Under the worst circumstances, they communicate hostility or indifference to the very people whose commitment is required to make them work, they fragment organizations in ways that make them more responsive but less effective, and they initiate demands at a faster rate than the system can carry them out. (Elmore & McLaughlin, 1988, p. 60)

Chapter 10

Conflict and Consensus

Even though individual teachers create more variety within schools than exists among schools, the school is to be the unit where achievements are measured and rewarded. Parents have more effect than any other formal group on the learning of students, but parents are themselves not rewarded. (Mitchell, 1998, p. 4)

In aiming to change the scientific community so that it is inclusive, it is important to recognize the variety of people's experiences that can be as validly used for innovation as abstractions by experts. (Ibid, p. 38)

Administrators and teachers have contributed to the cycle whereby greater distrust leads to more evaluation and more evaluation leads to still higher levels of suspicion. (p. 55)

Paralleling these general findings, a former administrator with a state department of education that has undergone massive changes, speaks of the war between the bureau responsible for evaluation and agencies supporting innovations. (p. 85)

Creation can, however, be thought about as an action of a dominant power which so contains itself as to allow the development of a new independent agent, say, the student. (p. 88)

This partial review of our most surprising observations and conclusions show that, with respect to change, the conflicts are more striking than the consistencies. The conflict perspective allows for scanning for missed opportunities, such as the variety among families or classrooms (Mitchell, 1995). The limitations of the experts as a source of reforms suggests the need for reform in the community from which they take their bearings. Conflicts, of course, contain explicit contradictions, such as that between evaluation, which innovators need for legitimacy, and innovation to resolve crisis or provide opportunities for creative contributions. Continuing conflicts are suggested by the cycle between evaluation and the trust that people place in schools. The seesaw between progressive and traditional proposals for change is a further case of such repetitive patterns.

Currently under the guise of vision statements, educators are discovering how important myths about creation can be (Hopfenberg, et al., 1993). The perception of alternatives and the resolutions of conflicts are both a part of developing vision statements; visions can also involve problem solving, which reveals creative possibilities. People living today can create culture; it does not have to be solely a product of previous generations. In both the present and the past, the recurring pattern of cultural differences involves the differences between city and country; the experts and their individualism are based on variety in the urban world and are at the opposite end of the pole from members of stable rural communities.

The original model of subordination, which compounds cultural differences, occured through the family (gender and generational differences). Racial difference, when compounded with poverty, is the dominant example of past cultural and social divisions. However, people do overcome even racial subordination and relate different traditions in new ways, particularly in the arts (Mitchell, 1997). Though innovations should be based on cultural and social differences, when they are not, cultural and social variations should still be considered when implementing the new programs designed by experts.

Direct awareness of these differences requires political programs or media blitzes before they become a part of educational restructuring. Only at-risk students and unemployment among youth have as yet been a focus for the promoters in education, and even these efforts tend to be isolated from community organizations. The school knowledge of teachers and the more general understanding of community members are needed to supplement the ideas of scholars and the plans of educational reformers. Some organizing of these groups and their contributions has occurred, but this is only the tip of the iceberg.

The problem of the separation between layperson and expert can be partially overcome by developing links in the education process. To further increase these links there must be imaginative reversals of the usual ways of doing things. Organizational interventions as well as individual efforts are now required for such reversals. The separation of the national scene from the local one as well as the distance between superexperts and ordinary people have meant that community organizations must battle against the national establishment on behalf of ordinary people. The example of the Texas Industrial Areas Foundation under Cortes, who had Howard Gardner sign a contract to ensure his accountability for their support, is a good beginning.

The two sides can be bridged when innovations are considered as a whole program, rather than as isolated proposals. After relating innovations to each other, systemic reform needs to allow for competition of ideas as well as competition of policies between local advocacy groups and national coalitions. A consensus can emerge after this debate, not before it. Governmental controls and measures to ensure accountability can coexist with school autonomy and teacher independence.

The political process between schools and among policy setters needs to be set toward the vision of individual development and creativity. Students, parents, teachers, and administrators must progress toward the broader goal of a learning society. A narrow focus on training or educational outcomes will not contribute to this end. Education should be judged by the extent to which it provides meaningful experiences. However, the organized groups that affect educational policy are more interested in their own aims than they are in an educated community. These groups and, indeed, government itself, must be made responsible to the people; the people should judge, not the experts; the experts should act for the people.

MODEST ACHIEVEMENTS AND GREAT EXPECTATIONS

Change can be both a community project that links schools to a larger purpose and a personal experience that reverses the usual ways of seeing things. Chart 10.1 suggests how links among schools and between schools and other organizations can change the way people in schools see their work. A number of organizations provide social occasions in which individuals in the most remote areas or working with the most subordinated groups can learn about innovations and choose appropriate ones. The National Diffusion Network (NDN) became the largest effort at demonstrating innovations in the United States. NDN fairs with innovative materials, and teachers in attendance to discuss their experience with these materials, have stimulated the interest of other teachers in these same innovations or in creating combinations of them.

The NDN has also shown that the role played by experts can be redefined. Experts can judge the innovations and establish an approval list from them. While the innovations are developed by those closer to the local scene, experts could use their more abstract abilities to evaluate these innovations. They may also obtain outside resources for schools from foundations and governments. However, this redefinition of the expert's role is threatened by both the emergence of superexperts, with their octopus-like tentacles among organizations, and the attacks on the NDN. The argument has increasingly been made that the NDN has limited itself to small innovations and is very inappropriate for the areas of systemic change or restructuring (Viadero, 1995a). Supporters of NDN have rallied to prevent its elimination, but they have had their own doubts about its viability in the area of mammoth change. How can the NDN evaluate philosophical programs such as the Coalition of Essential Schools?

Chart 10.1
Combining Experts and People

A.   **Links in the Diffusion Process**

1.   Innovation fairs, such as the National Diffusion Network
2.   Creating occasions for role changes and reversals
3.   Developing networks among schools and within communities

B.   **Changing Positions**

1.   Expert acts as more of a judge who sees the local context
2.   Local alternative schools and community advocates
3.   Alternatives that relate similar ideas or processes in both schools and community organizations

C.   **Blending of Interests**

1.   Relating the variety of individual motivations to decision making
2.   Expanding the "in-group"
3.   Developing innovations for people and their political awareness of innovation
4.   Finding overlap between divergent positions

Perhaps the question should be: What is wrong with CES that it cannot be evaluated by NDN? CES and all of the other promotional programs seem incapable of providing a realistic assessment of the increased financial and time costs involved in their programs (Olson, 1994a). Ted Sizer once claimed that the cost of reducing class size and restructuring schools for CES would be no more than 10 percent, but because of expenses for planning and retraining, he does not know what the total costs are. None of the promoters are clear about the total time requirements.

Furthermore, the problem with these approaches is that they do not consider education as a contributor to the major social and cultural differences in our society. Professionalism is not improved by becoming more gargantuan, but it is limited by its narrow vision. For example, external consultants only link with internal consultants from within the schools; facilitators within schools, on behalf of parents and volunteers, can go further and link the school to volunteer and advocacy organizations in the community. For example, for all its current glory, Success for Schools and its founder do not link with community organizations or community changes.

However, various experts can come to understand local conditions. Cooperating leagues of schools and the requirement for cooperation between universities and schools have established common tasks where experts can represent opposite positions and become diplomats. Role reversals by experts is suggested by a conference on creativity so that special educators would become more dedicated to gifted students. Special educators who were otherwise more interested in education for the developmentally delayed, would make statements at the conference about their own commitments for educating creative students (House, 1974). Reversals of interests, even if limited to a public stance, are important in forcing biases into the open.

The success of experts with their growing promotional efforts makes an examination of biases unlikely because their work with these programs is so apparently successful; failures are more likely to lead to an examination of the people responsible (Sproull, et al., 1978). A recent American legislative proposal specifically mentions the big four programs: CES, Accelerated Schools, Comer Schools, and Success for All (Hoff, 1997c); more ominously, the same legislation stressed "proven models" of reform rather than encouraging new efforts. The piling up of a few programs suggests that the lessons of the Rand Study on the value of small programs will have to be learned all over again (Mitchell, 1992). Perhaps antimonopoly legislation needs to be extended to education!

Programs developed at the local level tend to be eclipsed by national efforts. Debbie Meier's program was a local innovation that attached itself to a national approach, but it definitely overshadowed other schools-within-schools. The program started many years earlier in Chicago by the local Alinsky organization at Hyde Park High School, is only one more addition to a list of schools-within-schools (Weissmann, 1992). Conversely, local programs can lead to significant new ideas and role reversals for both teachers and administrators brave enough to take the risk. For example, a small program was shown to create a sense of common purpose with an initial project and a reversal of teacher perceptions by having every high school teacher act as a generalist who follows up on the work of another teacher when he or she acted as a specialist (Louis & Kruse, 1995).

Large-scale programs are engaged in a search for legitimacy by showing their effectiveness, not new insights. Several efforts have been made to suggest that the well-advertised programs are the solutions to our problems. Kentucky has assemblied a survey of all programs whose effectiveness can be documented (Lawton, 1997d). A supplement to a large-scale survey of Title 1 programs, which are themselves inadequate, has stated that Success for All and the Comer project were capable of overcoming social class differences (Hoff, 1997b). However, if the school administrators were not committed to these special buys, they were not effective. The problem has always been to get commitment; the evidence in support of these programs does not help in this respect.

The separation of the promoters and advocates from ordinary people makes it likely that cynicism rather than commitment will be the result of these efforts. The example of the New American Fools should not be forgotten. Organizations that represent subordinated people, such as the Industrial Areas Foundation, may themselves become very suspect when their leaders are co-opted by the educational establishment. The Association of Community Organizations for Reform Now (ACORN), which organizes in the poorest and most crime-ridden areas, is an alternative that has also become active in educational reform (Madeline Talbot, interview, April 5, 1994). Still other local organizations exist or can emerge to represent poor local groups as long as they have not given up hope.

Volunteers from local communities can replace the experts, particularly during emergencies. When experts and administrators failed to resolve a desegregation problem, a volunteer task force produced an acceptable, if not perfect, plan (Weiner, 1983). Such task forces are one example of role reversal that can result from educational conflict. By accident, this conflict led to a greater sense of common purpose.

SYNCHRONIZING POLITICAL POSITIONS

The California Learning Assessment System (CLAS) was enacted because of a rare consensus among the three centers of education power in California—the governor, Governor Pete Wilson; the legislature, in the person of State Senator Gary Hart, chair of the Senate Education Committee; and the state's department of education in the person of former State Superintendent of Public Instruction. . . . Governor Wilson wanted CLAS for one major reason—it will include individual-level student scores. . . . Governor Wilson would eventually like to move to a system of merit pay. . . . Hart sees a more valid form of assessments as the quid pro quo for allowing schools to move to site-based management. For him, the school site is the unit of accountability . . . . Honig's motivation . . . he was interested in assessments that are more congruent with a particular kind of curriculum, that measure real-world performance, and that influence teaching. (McDonnell, 1994, pp. 403-404)

Similarly, the direct stakeholders in education can be expected to change their positions overnight. Principals are not going to relinquish all their keys, and teachers are not going to surrender their grade books. Middle-class teachers are not going to adopt the survival tactics of the working classes. Rather, each of these groups can learn how its position overlaps with others, the third major area of future changes suggested in Chart 10.1. Teachers can, for example, allow the tough boys to play the gentleman role. One group can see the other as a mutual stimulus. Working-class language can force a simplicity into the written expressions of teachers, while students learn a greater range of ideas. Whether in terms of class or other divisions, administrators who play an intermediate role have been urged to discover common ground through negotiations (Hewton, 1982).

The blending of players' perspectives can be shown to begin by relating the personal interests of individuals. Teachers can be approached in ways that are more concrete than the general literature, such as the levels of concerns, suggests. Teachers' frustration with a lack of resources and boredom with their existing programs can be used as grounds for gaining their support of an innovation in spite of the increased efforts involved (Huberman & Miles, 1982). Complicated innovations are particularly likely to produce diverse student responses. Teachers for whom the National Writing Program was a success have been shown to interpret success as pursuing an individual path in a fixed way, developing a dialogue with a few others, or relating to many other people without finding oneself (Sunstein, 1994). Student response to a successful program serves as a sign to teachers and, together with the teachers' own development of a more general ability to undertake change, can further attach teachers to innovations.

The effect of expanding motives is also clear for the more diverse parent and student groups. Initially, parents are united only by their concern for their own children, while students are linked most of the time only by their preoccupation with their peers. Parents have become active in the governance of the school their child attends (Comer, 1980). Where social movements have developed in places like Chicago or Minnesota, parents and even students have become more broadly involved in the alternative programs. Parents and students have only begun to make the hard choices that education planning involves; they are forced to see that one cannot have everything. The concerns of any group can be built into a career or a life as suggested by one million parents who have reportedly pursued their own education as a result of their involvement in their child's early childhood program (Joffe, 1977).

Getting beyond a single-minded motivation and developing a diversity of interests is needed in order to develop innovations among all the stakeholders. Most innovations are underdeveloped even when proclaimed by expert planners so that those affected must take up the plan and expand on it in order to succeed. When teachers become polarized in opposition and try to destroy an innovation, they see the promoters as selfish individuals concerned about their own careers or wondering who will get a doctorate out of the effort (Wolcott, 1977). Yet administrators reported that career advancement was only a minor motivation for them; they were far more concerned with the development of their staff (Huberman & Miles, 1982). Furthermore, innovations that are undertaken for opportunistic reasons do not succeed. Ties between the stakeholders, a common purpose or vision, is needed together with diverse, rather than single-track, concerns. For the North Carolina Center for the Advancement of Teaching, discussed in Chapter 3, common purpose, promoting teaching excellence, was perceived by Jean Powell, the legislature, and the governor.

When singular motives do develop and diverse groups exist in a hierarchy, then close "in-groups" of those who are in the dominant position are likely to appear (Sproull, et al., 1978). The in-group can be affected by a religious-like conviction of the importance of the chosen innovation for "saving" others. The sectarian quality can probably be diminished only by widening the circle of those most heavily involved with the innovation and diminishing the stratification associated with such groupings. Student advocacy at the classroom level would help diminish the exclusive preoccupation of those in the upper strata. As the group involved becomes less of a closed church, resource exchange with other organizations and professions might become more possible. Certainly, service integration that has proceeded to involve such joint activities as budgeting or staff training has represented the development of a strong "we-feeling" (Melaville & Blank, 1993, p. 20).

Teachers have been reported to be frustrated with divisions operating within their own profession that prevent coordination and the development of any sense of a professional community. For example, elementary teachers labor long and seriously over individual student reports that are often ignored by junior high school teachers. Similarly, the junior high school reports are frequently ignored at the high school level (Sarason, 1971, p. 114). Each segment assumes the lower level's assessment is not relevant to their work! Each segment is also a part of a hierarchy, as revealed by teachers' talk of "moving up" from one grade level to another.

Just as teachers need to relate the segments of their own profession, they must develop their relations to other adults in the community. These relationships have to be strengthened while making tough decisions. Special education and mainstreaming are particularly complicated, as was discussed in Chapter 3. There is a sharp division between regular and special teachers, which integration must overcome. Among parents, there is the divisive question of whether integration provides better service to their children. And, among governments, the increasing question is one of costs for special education versus the comparative benefits of expenditures for other children (Associated Press, 1997; Gubernick & Conlin, 1997). The involvement of the community might answer some of these criticisms, perhaps through more varied programs for special education students including mentoring by volunteers, contributions by business and professionals, and focused effort by community schools.

For all programs, the simultaneous involvement of specialists, parents, and students is a challenge to administrators, and is far more than just a question of general priorities regarding schools. In a time of limited resources, administrators have to develop new innovations to meet many pressing problems. Furthermore, calls are increasingly being made for systemic reforms, such as those in Kentucky, that transform an entire educational system (Mitchell, 1996).

The more drastic the reforms, the greater the demands that are made upon administrators to lead teachers, parents, and communities. In the radical reforms of Chicago, administrators who could not or would not lead have been replaced by those who will. Even in smaller crisis situations, racial and social divisions can be overcome and these same groups can be involved with schools and innovations (Metz, 1979). Changes in the governance of schools has meant a huge increase in the number of people involved in setting policy for schools; many more people have become board members in individual schools.

Schools have reached more stakeholders who, because of their perception of a crisis, want to become involved in education. In a number of diverse communities, parents became involved when they felt they must change the system. Inequities of financing have led to advocates arguing on behalf of rural areas. Working-class parents became involved when they felt they must change the schools or when they came to see that slotting their kids for general mathematics rather than algebra was determining their futures (Moses, et al., 1989). In the racial and community crisis in Chicago, the educational crisis in Kentucky, or the financial crisis in Alberta and Ontario, these demands become so intense that they could not be ignored by the governments concerned.

Crises and deadlocks can reveal the ways that diverse groups can find common ground. In Chicago, for example, businesspeople and leaders of mothers on welfare discovered that their positions for reform were increasingly similar, particularly as the bureaucrats in the school system resisted both their efforts (Kyle & Kantowicz, 1992). Often, generally opposite positions are seen as coinciding with particular actions. Liberals could support an increase in social insurance as a basis for further increasing private pensions through collective bargaining, whereas conservatives could support the same increases as a means of preventing the further spread of private pensions through collective bargaining. Education groups in suburbs can see financial support by the state as meeting their needs without focusing on the help it would give inner cities, which they still see as a "black hole" (Lauber, interview, May 3, 1996). Tactics involve bringing opposite positions into a common focus, as illustrated by the quotation about California politics at the beginning of this section.

More generally, synchronizing positions concerning innovations requires more than just relating positions about a particular innovation. It is important to relate people to the innovations. It has been argued that schools, similar to universities, exist as much for the development of the faculty as for the education of students (Sarason, 1990). Creative work, such as art integration, has been shown to increase the attendance and morale of teachers as much as students (Mahlmann, 1978). Expanding the meaning of innovations into the lives of parents and students together with greater teacher professionalism requires a great deal of coordination.

Expanding the innovation to more people can overcome the problem of an overworked inner core of advocates for innovations. All the stakeholders, not just administrators, are increasingly dealing with the enormous number of innovations. School-based management and other changes in governance approaches to education have involved the broader constituency of those involved with schools. Chicago is a striking example. Increasing community and school involvement from the high school to higher education can mean that there is no longer a polarity between the few who are too involved with innovation projects and the many who are not involved enough (Sproull, et al., 1978). In the past, it has seemed that the most creative efforts are made in spite of the blinders that different policymakers bring to education.

THE EVOLUTION OF PLAYERS IN THE REFORM REVOLUTION

However, French immersion and NWP are both caught up in their professional limitations. Together with school councils, school-based management and DWOK are more open to society and changes happening within it. (Mitchell, 1998, p. 135)

Teacher advocates can carry the innovations outside the public schools. Community leaders help symbolize the support that the innovation has and this is an effective means of obtaining support for change and a way of involving teachers who have remained outside the initiative. (Ibid, p. 153)

The mutual learning and respect that appears to be a crucial part of mentoring programs suggests that organizations can bring people together. . . . The politics of education issues requires a vision that focuses on the meaning of innovations for people. (p. 181)

However, internal action groups, as with the gender program in Calgary, can help people achieve equality if those within bureaucracies will just act as if they are not in iron cages. (p. 205)

Increasingly, common purposes and processes are emerging between those who are inside the school system and those who are on the outside trying to influence education. People working with older programs are still caught in the grip of institutional interim, but those connected with newer ones reflect social influences and changes. Mentoring among teachers and students is not perfectly parallel, but these similarities are brought about by community organizations working together with schools.

Mentoring as well as many other programs lead to an increasing degree of networking. Networks among teachers for innovations are parallel to the networks that emerged in Impact II, a program that was originally developed to provide small grants to teachers. The attempts to protect a government program, the National Diffusion Network, led to a network of those who wanted to protect it from budget cuts. Networks that were originally intended to promote research have, in the case of the one initiated by John Goodlad, led to a network for professional development schools. The variety of sources for networking seems endless.

Similar principles seem to guide the efforts of community groups and those of educational bureaucracies. Superintendents and administrators can focus concern for innovations by their sheer presence. Similarly, community leaders can show how crucial a change is and increase the commitment of those involved by the support they provide. Unexpectedly, efforts to advocate for gender rights, which are neglected by reform groups within schools, was shown to occur within the Calgary School Board. Teachers and special educators have been urged to become advocates for minority students (Grant & Sleeter, 1986). Art educators with the Calgary Separate Board are attempting to form a joint advocacy group with parents and community members.

The movement away from experts and direct instruction to networking and mentoring is a part of the increasing involvement of diverse groups with education (Chart 10.2). This change began simply enough with the inclusion of parents in most of the reforms after 1970. However, in many cases, French immersion, integration of the handicapped, or head start, parent involvement was related to governmental support for the innovation. In some cases, such as early childhood education, parent involvement was required in order to get government support, and in others it was required by legislation. In either case, government was no more a stranger to the school door than were parents.

Chart 10.2
Major Influences on Educational Reform

1. Parents
2. Businesses
3. Local advocacy groups
4. Foundations
5. Integrated services
6. Promotional organizations
7. Governments
8. Media
9. Reform publications
10. Student activists

Parents were followed by business in linking with education. However, until 1980, business was not a consistent supporter of innovation reforms. Indeed, in the late 1970s, a comparative educator could contrast the Russians with their planned connections between factories and schools and the isolation of American schools from business (Cowan, 1978). In 1978, Boston began the first of many business partnerships (Barbour & Barbour, 1997, p. 228). Thousands of partnerships have developed and only occasionally is the instrumental basis of this reform challenged by politicians or moralists.

Though generally successful, business has, in a variety of ways, attempted to transform education while viewing partnerships with schools as a means toward other ends. Education has been seen as an investment opportunity that may even surpass the opportunities provided by health. Businesses, such as the Edison Project, have opened schools to make a profit. Through small grants projects, such as in Minnesota, businesses have tried to encourage teachers to become entrepreneurs. Students have also been sponsored to run businesses on school property or with school cooperation. However, it is with its bottom-line thinking that business has most affected education. School-based management is similar to decentralization efforts made by some companies, while the focus upon educational standards and indicators is an attempt to find the equivalent of profit to guide educational decision making. Even if the intentions are humane or paternalistic, business looks at students more as potential employees or customers than as people who live for their own purposes.

The partnership idea has been extended to many other groups: health agencies, hospitals, social service organizations, and even universities. Artists, sports activists, and the police are drawn into cooperation with the schools, although their cooperative relationships are less publicized. Surprisingly, the original institution with which schools were integrated, religion, is largely ignored. Religion is looked to as a support in times of emergencies for integrated services, but ministers are not ones to which organizers of social services will refer their clients (Mitchell, 1996). The literature of integrated services is striking in the way in which it omits ties to religion while considering relationships between schools and almost every other kind of organization.

However, the extent to which social institutions are involved with education is suggested by civic journalism. This form of reporting has emerged as an alternative to traditional reporting, which, because of its emphasis on sensational exposure, may reinforce cynicism. Civic journalism tries to provoke a common dialogue through town meetings and focus groups, leading to improvements, particularly in education (Archer, 1997a). Civic journalism is itself a joint effort between separate media organizations; typically, a television station and a newspaper promote a joint survey. The people are provided with an opportunity to say how they want the news reported. Major foundations, including the Pew Charitable Trust, have made grants to support public journalism and to further its development.

The media and the heavily promoted changes are the most direct influence on the innovations that students experience. Foundations are often the indirect sponsors of these efforts by the media and the promoters. However, the foundations are indirectly influenced by the major determinants of educational change: business and government. Foundations may be doing nothing more than responding to government's withdrawal from support efforts, as in Canada, but usually the ties are closer. In Kentucky, the Knight Foundation supported Galef as did the newspaper which the same family owns. Foundations may support integrated services as a supplement to government or because of the omission by business. However, both business and government directly support innovations. Particularly through its support of model programs, business is becoming more important than government. As discussed in connection with Success for All, the recent comprehensive school reform has provided additional funds for the model school efforts supported by business (Hoff, 1998).

However, a strange turn occurred as many of these groups became involved with educational change; they became preoccupied with manipulation, rather than problem solving. For example, the large-scale collaboration attempted by Galef in its search for the Annenberg prize may have been spoilt as much by the career changes among the foundation people involved as by disagreement among the partners (Steve Prighohzy, interview, March 6, 1998). Because of his national links, David O'Fallon with the Minnesota Center for Arts Education emerged as the winner of the Annenberg lottery with two grants of over $30 million (George Sand, interview, February 16, 1998). Such experts are often involved with groups; however, the complicated political positions changes reform into a chess game in which the positions of many groups have to be calculated. Navigating between many diverse positions has become a new task for the expert.

The media has been the stage on which these games were played. At one point, the educational television station in Chicago, WTTW, devoted over fourteen hours of viewing during one week to an educational summit. The media changed education reform when it discovered it, just as it transformed war and the management of war news at an earlier time. Educators and classroom teachers have learned that they have to join the media circus if they are to have a voice in education (McDonald, 1987). Indeed, the major publication about new developments, *Education Week*, emerged in relation to wide-scale and highly advertised reforms beginning with *A Nation at Risk*. Chicago, Philadelphia, Denver, and New York are among the many cities that have newspapers devoted entirely to educational reform; Milwaukee is perhaps most interesting, since several individual teachers are the source of that publication (Diegmueller, 1996a). In general, the media tends to enhance national or international experts.

For all publications, educational reform news has the support of foundations which has not usually supported organic leaders as an alternative to experts. The influence of the media on reform is perhaps most revealingly shown by the Pew Charitable Trust, which supports the Pew Forum. Ignoring publicity has become a reflection of its importance for this elite group who do not hesitate to make judgments on educational revolutions (Mitchell, 1996, p. 202). The Pew Forum brings together top experts, who, unlike the individual entrepreneurs of the past, shun the media publicity and act like a secret society!

Whatever the new Masons may think they are doing, there is still little evidence that reform is working until it reaches the object of all the collective excitement, students. Sizer and CES have attempted to chart a course for increasing involvement, which would move students from asking to be involved with reform to demanding their right to participate in decisions. Students have formed national organizations, developed publications, and attempted to meet with reformers so that voices will be heard (Mitchell, 1996, p. 196). For over ten years, an independent student newspaper has existed in Chicago. Similar papers have been established in four other cities with the help of foundations and businesses. Several leaders of teacher networks that are a part of the National Writing Project have encouraged students to write and develop these publications (Steve Zemelman, interview, October 9, 1993).

The active involvement of students with their own publications and organizations appears to be the result of the media's attention to education as well as specific programs for education. The most powerful organizations, business and government, have not been able to bring about interest by students. Nor have the organizations that represent or organize adults, parents, or advocacy groups been able to reach into the world of students. Advocacy groups and parents are affected by the improvement efforts that foundations make. Advocacy groups, such as in Chicago, cannot sustain themselves without the support of foundations. Parents are influenced by the organization of family resource centers, such as those in Kentucky, which provide parent education as well as direction to students; recently, model parents there have been selected for training in a special institute (Blackford, 1997).

Chart 10.3
A Flow Chart of Change

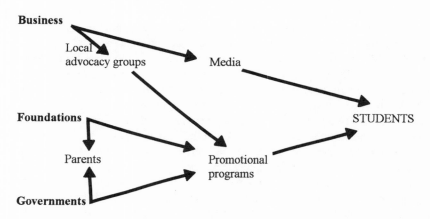

Reform itself was a different game from the simpler world of singular innovation. Indeed, "systemic" became a label that was the silver bullet for change. Any systemic reform involved coordinating a whole range of innovations to either totally rebuild a system of education or to make sense out of the varied changes that particular groups were introducing. The emergence of advocacy groups has meant that new players would be empowered to introduce school changes. When a large number of parents become involved in community organization, even a subject like mathematics can become a political issue (Chicago Panel on Public School Policy and Finance, 1992). In Kentucky, it is assumed that parents will be obedient followers to the new educational empire, but in Chicago a resistance movement to external rule is expected.

This example reveals the incredible degree to which parents and their advocacy groups can become involved in education. Indeed, the grass-roots support of diverse constituencies for reform has also meant that every group interested in reform has been transformed into a highly organized army for political change. In Chicago, businesspeople have formed such an organization, Leadership for Quality Education (LQE). LQE lobbied for particular policies, criticized the Board of Education, and organized opposition to the Board together with advocates for the poor. Chicago reform gelled when the leader of welfare mothers, Corretta McFerren, crossed the aisle and shook hands with Ken West, CEO of the Harris Bank; they agreed that the bureaucratic school system stonewalled them both, almost equally (Kyle & Kantowicz, 1992). Educational reform has emerged from combinations of constituencies in other places, for example, the religious right wing and businesspeople at roundtables in Alberta.

CIRCLE OF RESISTANCE

However, these coalitions can come apart. In Chicago, the withdrawal of business from radical reform was symptomatic of the discovery of the limits of the new consensus about education. Currently in that case, government, with the support of business, is locked in a major confrontation with local advocacy groups. Mayor Daley's appointees to run the school are on one side and Designs for Change and their allies on the other, arguing about who claims most credit for improvements in the educational performance of students in this very depressed city (Lawton, 1997c).

Perhaps parents in Chicago, who are organized into militant organizations, such as Parents United for Responsible Education, are most representative of the interests of individual families. Though businesspeople may say that they are only parents and governments may act as if they can speak for parents or, at least, organize the issues that are involved in parent education (Mitchell, 1996), the organizations that are closest to parents and volunteers tend to differ greatly. Most of these organizations, even if they have tried to professionalize the family or compensate for it, such as the PTA or Communities in Schools, are very different from the promotional organizations, such as Success for All.

The PTA has recently very strongly raised most of the issues involved with business support. The PTA particularly attacked the use of students as a captive audience, such as with the importation of television with commercials or advertisements in schools, while affirming that "curriculum and instruction are within the purview of educators" (Weisman, 1991). And they promoted the view that teachers should decide on the use, if any, of sponsored materials. Organizations that were concerned with promoting business partnerships, such as the Association for Supervision and Curriculum Development, refused to support the PTA.

The PTA has been pushed into taking strong positions by the emergence of other, even more radical, groups representing parents and community members. In 1993, Parents for Public Schools, which is a local Mississippi organization begun in 1989 to prevent the flight of white parents, attempted to organize an army of parents to support education reform (Sommerfeld, 1993). Parents for Public Schools is part of the National Coalition of Advocates for Students of which Designs for Change in Chicago is also a member. The National President of the PTA characterized the campaign as divisive.

The PTA has supported all of the types of parent involvement discussed in Chapter 8 (Jacobson, 1997). It was particularly interested in teachers designing assignments that require interaction between parents and students. It has formed alliances with most educational organizations to prevent cuts in the federal budget for education and to promote educational reform. However, the 1992 conference, the Parental Involvement Summit, called for greater commitment to parents by educators, and twenty-three organizations attending signed on (Sommerfeld, 1992). The PTA reported a large survey showed that between 25 percent and 35 percent of parents felt "inferior" or "intimated." There were also problems in understanding the school system or how to change it and there was a failure to provide for childcare by schools. In adddition, schools of education were criticized for failing to prepare teachers for working with parents. The PTA distributed 75,000 copies of a report on the conference.

Compared to the PTA, a stronger concern for the rights of students has been offered by a whole series of advocacy groups. For example, since 1974, the Coleman Advocates for Children and Youth in San Francisco has campaigned on behalf of high-risk children, including a requirement that the city give priority to such children in its budget. The San Francisco group has had the support of the national association representing children's groups, the Child Welfare League of America (Gross, 1991). In Illinois, the Voice of Illinois Children has often been a supporter of the coalition for Chicago reform, which nationally has linked with pre-school groups and the Children's Defense Fund. In spite of the growing problem of child poverty that has resulted from cuts in public welfare, the PTA has not adopted so strong a position as these associations.

GUARDIANS AND MARKETERS

The problems of children and communities have been matched by the difficulties confronting schools. Schools developed strategies for additional support or allies in their battles for government funding. The financial restraints alone have pushed schools to obtain gifts and advertising from businesses. Accountability measures mean that the days when a school system could keep its failures secret are limited. The reality of failing innovations can no longer be denied as inspectors increasingly include former FBI agents (Mitchell, 1996).

Barricades against the invasion of foreigners with their new gods requires at least diversionary actions. Local innovations are unlikely to be born fully developed as mature innovations. They need to be protected in their early years and supported during their adolescence. There are now two major policies that attempt to advance the cause of change programs: grass-roots democracy and business-inspired initiatives. There are those who would maintain the democratic tradition of public education and try to develop local people for higher tasks (Jacobs, 1992; Barlow & Robertson, 1994). Parent and child advocacy groups with a moral or religious basis, such as those influenced by radicals, wave the guardian banner above schools even more fiercely (Rogers, 1990).

Professionals can become part of the guardian tradition if, like the lawyers, accountants, and public relations experts in Chicago, they provide services to support local reforms (Mitchell, 1996). Professionals can realize themselves as democratic members of local communities rather than as monopolies with only specialized functions (Strike, 1993). In this guise, other professionals could provide a meaningful model for teachers who could become the first among equals in democratic communities.

The first profession, religion and its supporters, can become sponsors of social action to improve the position of high-risk groups in an area. The action programs for Natives in Canada or the Industrial Areas Foundation, particularly in Texas, are examples of this approach (Texas Interfaith Education Fund, 1990; Mitchell, 1996). There are groups still acting to create greater equality and social justice in our society. The PTA and child welfare organizations are even more dedicated to protecting and educating children, the guardians' function. When the guardians do more than take a defensive position, they can encounter the risks of criticism in attempting to radically change the system (Whiteside, 1978). However, the case of gender advocates with the Calgary Board shows that educators do not always follow the safe course.

Education has pursued more conservative reforms and linked with the growing power of business and instrumental approaches to education. Though the moral guides for resisting the influence of business suggested by the PTA have been essentially followed by the Calgary Roman Catholic Separate District, there are many other groups outside the educational establishment that can be expected to continue to uphold these concerns. The public guardian inspiration continues to diverge from commercial aims.

A whole series of reforms is inspired by instrumental business thinking including charters, vouchers, and, most of all, schools operated as private businesses (Chubb & Moe, 1990). Schools with a commercial contract to offer parents and students promise to provide competition for local communities. Voucher plans for parents to use state money for private choice remain in limbo in the United States because of the costs and constitutional questions. However, charter schools and private for-profit schools continue to expand in Canada and the United States (Mitchell, 1996). The marketers' emphasis on results and competition means that schools must satisfy consumers rather than serve the political purposes of the community (Barlow & Robertson, 1994).

To a certain extent, the distinction between moral and commercial purposes has changed the axis of development among educational alternatives. When educators developed innovations primarily for themselves, changes within the educational establishment alternated between progressive education and discipline-based pedagogy. On the one hand, progressive education attempted to develop a philosophy regarding the relationship between the individual and community; it focused on process and usually stressed social interaction (Mitchell, 1995). Particularly as a support for democracy, progressive education has been close to the guardian ideology.

On the other hand, the commercial nexus for education provides an emphasis on results, which is more like traditional or discipline-based alternatives. After Sputnik, the initial explosion of innovations included the new math, new science, and even new social studies. Unlike cooperation or team teaching, the discipline emphasis in reform provided direction to schools, perhaps too much so when it called for "teacher proof" devices (Sarason, 1982). The commercial-based links for alternatives may adopt diverse approaches from cooperative teaming to great books, but those who seek profits expect measurable results of students' learning. To overcome a soft education that progressivism promotes, those who want schools for profit or other conservative aims have placed an emphasis on discipline as well as exam results. There is a call for prime attention to the customer and to changes in the culture of the school.

A further reaction developed against attitude education, which led religious and political conservatives to reject outcome-based education (Cibulka, 1996). Individual rights and character development are seen as being endangered by these conservatives. On the other side, education professors continue to represent the most extreme position among more liberal supporters (Public Agenda, 1997). For these professors, the concern for process makes any endorsement of standards empty. Extreme positions mean that a more moderate position must be considered to avoid total absurdity. Reforming schools has become dependent on changing the professional education of teachers and containing extreme community groups. Guardians and marketers must find common ground as has been suggested for progressive educators and more traditional ones; the experts can play a strategic role in the development of a more common ideology.

The Associated Scientists, a group headed by three Nobel Prize winners, filed a formal appeal with the state this month after another group, dominated by educators, was chosen to write the science standards. . . . "The 'dumbing down' of science in school curricula has prevented most productive dialogue between scientists and K-12 teachers, and is a continuing source of frustration and disappointment," the group wrote in its proposal. (Manzo, 1997)

Bibliography

Accelerated Schools Project (1993). *Accelerated schools*, 2(3), 1, 4-18.

Alberta Education (1995). *Accountability in education discussion paper*. Edmonton, Alberta: Alberta Education.

Alinsky, S. (1971). *Rules for radicals*. New York: Random House.

Allington, R., & Cunningham, P. (1996). *Schools that work-where children read and write*. New York: Harper Collins.

Alt, M., & Medrich, E. (1994). Student outcomes from participation in community service. Paper prepared for the U.S. Department of Education by MPR Associates [On-line], 55 paragraphs. Available URL:http://www. quest.edu/slarticle13.html.

Alberta Teachers' Association (1993). *Trying to teach*. Edmonton, Alberta: Alberta Teachers' Association.

American Association of Colleges for Teacher Education. (1997). Professional development schools at a glance [On-line], 5 paragraphs. Available URL:http://www. aacte.org/glance.html.

Anderson, B. (1978). Teacher in-service training and implementation of change. Unpublished class paper, University of Calgary.

Anderson, B. (1981). The relationship between training and the adoption of an innovation. Unpublished master's thesis. University of Calgary.

Anderson, J. (1994). Who's in Charge? Teachers views on Control Over School Policy and Classroom Practice. *Research Reports*. Washington, D.C.: Office of Research, Office of Educational Research and Improvement, U. S. Department of Education.

Anderson, J. (1997, June 18). Getting better by design. *Education Week* [On-line]. Available URL: http://www. EdWeek.com.html (Archives).

Ansam, P. (1988). French immersion: Whose opportunities? Unpublished class paper, The Univesity of Calgary.

Appalachia Educational Laboratory (1996). Five years of education reform in Rural Kentucky. *Notes From the Field*, 5(1), 1-4, S1-S4.

Apple, M. (1982; 2nd ed., 1995). *Education and power*. New York: Routledge.

Archer, J. (1997a, April 9). Civic journalism. *Education Week*. [On-line], 42 paragraphs. Available URL: http://www. EdWeek.org/ew/com/htbin (Archives).

Archer, J. (1997b, April 23). Summit to issue call for service in name of youth. *Education Week* [On-line], 42 paragraphs. Available URL: http://www.EdWeek.com/htbin (Archives).

Archer, J. (1997c, May 7). Seeking to turn summit promises into service. *Education Week* [On-line], 23 paragraphs. Available URL: http://www.EdWeek.org/ew/current/32sum mit.h16.

Artsconcept. (1997). *The power of learning in art: Four stories*. Calgary: Artsconcept, Inc.

Ashton, P., & Webb, R. (1986). *Making a difference: Teachers' sense of efficacy and student achievement*. New York: Longman.

Askins, B., Mezack, B., Sorley, M., & Newton, N. (1994). Collegial support teams replace teacher evaluations in a partnership school. Paper presented at the Annual Meeting of the Association of Teacher Educators (ED367654).

Associated Press. (1997, March 3). Are too many kids in special ed? Experts divided. *Boston Globe* [On-line]. Available URL: http://www.boston.com/globe/met.html.

ATLAS Communities. (1997). *ATLAS-learning communities* [On-line], 21 paragraphs. Available URL: http://www.naschools.org/ greatsch/atlas.htm.

Baldauf, S. (1997, June 25). Reinvolving families in children's schooling. *Christian Science Monitor* [On-line], 9 paragraphs. Available URL: http://www.csmonitor. com.2html.

Baldridge, J. (1975). Organizational innovation: Individual, structural and environmental impacts. In Baldridge, J. & Deal, T. (Eds.), *Managing change in educational organizations* (pp. 151-175). Berkeley, CA: McCutchan.

Baldridge, J., & Deal, T. (Eds.). (1975). *Managing change in educational organizations*. Berkeley, CA: McCutchan.

Barbo, S. (1987). French immersion: An educative innovation. Unpublished class paper, University of Calgary.

Barbour, C., & Barbour, N. (1997). *Families, schools and communities*. Columbus, OH: Merrill/Prentice-Hall.

Barlow, M., & Robertson, H. (1994). *Class warfare*. Toronto: Key Porter.

Barnes, D., & Shemilt, D. (1974). Transmission and interpretation. *Educational Review*, 26, 3.

Batiuk, M. (1993). The National Writing Project. Unpublished course paper, University of Calgary.

Bauchner, J., Eiseman, J., Cox, P., & Sachmidtr, W. (1982). *Models of change*. Andover, MA: The Network.

Becker, H. (1985). How schools use microcomputers: Results from a national survey. In Chen, M., & Paisley, W. (Eds.), *Children and microcomputers*. Beverly Hills, CA: Sage.

Becker, H., Greer, B., Hughes, E., & Strauss, A. (1961). *Boys in white*. Chicago: University of Chicago Press.

Belton, L. (1996). What our teachers should know and be able to do: A student's view. *Educational Leadership*, 54(1), 66-68.

Berlak, A., & Berlak, H. (1981). *Dilemmas of schooling*. London: Methuen.

Berman, E. (1984). State hegemony and the schooling process. *Journal of Education*, 166, 239-253.

Berman, E. (1986). The improbability of meaningful education reform. *Issues in Education*, 3, 99-112.

Berman, P., & McLaughlin, M. (1978). *Federal programs supporting educational change*. Volume VII. Santa Monica, CA: The Rand Corporation.

Bienvenue, R. (1986). French immersion programs: A comparison of immersion and non-immersion parents. *Canadian Modern Language Review*, 42, 806-813.

Blackford, L. (1997, November). Parents learning to be leaders. *Herald Leader*. [On-line], 35 paragraphs. Available URL:http://www.kentuckyconnect.com/heraldleader/news. html.

Blumberg, A. (1985). *The school superintendent*. New York: Teachers College Press.

Bornstein, T. (1996). On being a facilitator and a learner. *Teacher-To-Teacher*, 4(2), 4-5.

Bowen, L., & Sellers, S. (1994). *Family support & socially vulnerable communities.* Chicago: Family Resource Coalition.

Boyd, W. (Trans. & Ed.). (1956). *The Emile of Jean Jacques Rousseau Selections.* New York: Teachers College.

Bradley, A. (1990). M.S.U. education school is on a mission: 'Teaching for understanding'. *Education Week* [On-line], 72 paragraphs. Available URL: http://www.EdWeek.com/ htbin (Archives).

Bradley, A. (1991, May 15). Teacher educators signing on to 'movement' to implement Goodlad's proposals for reform. *Education Week* [On-line], 38 paragraphs. Available URL: http://www.EdWeek.com/htbin (Archives).

Bradley, A. (1993, May 12). Professional-development schools flourish despite some doubts. *Education Week* [On-line], 37 paragraphs. Available URL: http://www. EdWeek.com/htbin (Archives).

Bradley, A. (1995a, March 22). Thinking small. *Education Week* [On-line], 69 paragraphs. Available URL: http://www. EdWeek.com/htbin (Archives).

Bradley, A. (1995b, October). Tennessee Waltz. *Teacher Magazine* [On-line]. Available URL: http://www.EdWeek.com/htbin (Archives).

Bradley, A. (1996a). Test Pilots. In Editorial Projects in Education (Eds.), *Thoughtful teachers, thoughtful schools* (pp. 202-209). Boston: Allyn & Bacon.

Bradley, A. (1996b, February 7). Holmes Group expands scope to link colleges, schools. *Education Week* [On-line], 33 paragraphs. Available URL: http://www. Edweek.com/htbin (Archives).

Bradley, A. (1997, June 25). Schools take fresh look at bolstering teachers. *Education Week* [On-line]. Available URL: http://www.Edweek.com/htbin.

Bratcher, A., & Stroble, E. (1994). Determining the progression from comfort to confidence: A longitudinal evaluation of a National Writing Project site based on multiple data sources. *Research in the Teaching of English,* 28(1), 66-68.

Brim, O., & Wheeler S. (1966). *Socialization after childhood.* New York: Wiley.

Britian, G. (1981). *Bureaucracy and innovation.* Beverly Hills, CA: Sage.

Brown, D. (1995). *School with heart: Voluntarism and public education.* Vancouver: Faculty of Education, University of British Columbia.

Bucher, R., & Stelling, J. (1977). *Becoming a professional.* Beverly Hills, CA: Sage.

Burk. S. (1989). Social impact on immersion programs in schools. Unpublished class paper, University of Calgary.

Edwards, J. (1984). The social and political context of bilingual education. In Samulda, R., Berry, J., & Laferriere, M. (Eds.), *Multiculturalism in Canada*. Toronto: Allyn & Bacon.

Efland, A. (1995). Change in the conceptions of art teaching. In Neperud, R. (Ed.), *Context content and community in art education*, (pp. 25-40). New York: Teachers College Press.

Eisner, E. (1995, June). Standards for American schools-Help or hindrance? *Phi Delta Kappan*, pp. 758-764.

Elliot, P. (1972). *The making of a television series*. London: Constable.

Elmore, R. (1993). The role of local school districts in instructional improvement. In Fuhrman, S.(Ed.), *Designing coherent education policy* (pp. 96-124). San Francisco: Jossey-Bass.

Elmore, R. (1996). Getting to scale with good educational practice. In Harvard Education Review (Eds.), *Working together toward reform*. Cambridge, MA: Harvard Educational Review.

Elmore, R., & McLaughlin, M. (1988). *Steady work*. Santa Monica, CA: Rand Corporation.

Epstein, J., & Dauber, S. (1991). School programs and teacher practices of parent involvement in inner-city elementary and middle school. *Elementary School Journal*, 91(3), 289-305.

Erikson, J. (1997). The effect of education on the choice of science careers. Unpublished M.Ed. critical essay, University of Calgary.

Erskine-Cullen, E. (1992, July). *The Learning Consortium annual report*. Toronto: The Learning Consortium.

Everhart, R. (1983). *Reading, writing and resistance*. London: Routledge & Kegan Paul.

Faculty of Education. (1996-1998). *Prototype for a proposed master of teaching program 1996-1998*. Calgary: Faculty of Education, University of Calgary.

Feldman, M. (1985). The workplace as educator. In M. Fantini, & R. Sinclair (Eds.), *Education in school and nonschool settings*. Chicago: National Society for the Study of Education.

Ferrell, B., & Compton, D. (1986). Use of ethnographic techniques for evaluation in a large school district: The Vanguard Case. In Fetterman, D., & Pitman, M. (Eds.), *Educational Evaluation*. Beverly Hills, CA: Sage.

Follett, M. (1924). *Creative experience*. New York: Longmans, Green & Co.

Fourth grade students at Mildred B. Janson Elementary School in Rosemead, California. (1996). An interview with Sir Francis Drake. *Teacher-To-Teacher*, 5(1), 3.

Freedman, M. (1994). *Seniors in national and community service.* Philadelphia: Public/Private Ventures.

Friedman, J. (1997). *Volunteers make history come alive.* [On-line]. Available URL: http://nisus.stusd.K12.caus/sfsv/meet.html.

Fuchs, E. (1969). *Teachers talk.* New York: Doubleday.

Fullan, M. (1982). *The meaning of educational change.* Toronto: The Ontario Institute for Studies in Education.

Fullan, M., & Stiegelbauer, S. (1991). *The new meaning of educational change.* New York: Teachers College.

Gadoury, G. (1991). Administrative concerns in French immersion schools: Response to Dagenais. *The Canadian School Executive*, 10(8), 3-11.

Galef Institute. (n.d.a). *Different ways of knowing.* Louisville, KY: Galef Institute.

Galef Institute (n.d.b). What work requires of schools: A Scans report for America 2000. Louisville, KY: Galef Institute.

Galef Institute (1996a). Annenberg Challenge Grant for the arts, culture, and technology. *Teacher-To-Teacher*, 4(2), 1.

Galef Institute. (1996b). Egyptian connections. *Teacher-To-Teacher*, 4(2), 7.

Galef Institute. (1996c). Philip Morris Companies Inc. helps support future Kentucky educators. *Teacher-To-Teacher*, 5(1), 8.

Galton, M., & Willcocks, J. (Eds.). (1983). *Moving from the primary classroom.* London: Routledge & Kegan Paul.

Galtung, J. (1971). A structural theory of imperialism. *Journal of Peace Research*, 8(2), 81-117.

Gamble, C. (1996, October 16). Meier submits proposal to run Boston pilot school. *Education Week*. [On-line], 15 paragraphs. Available URL: http://www.EdWeek.com/htbin (Archives).

Gaskell, J. (1995). *Secondary schools in Canada.* Toronto: Canadian Education Association.

Gaskell, J., & Lazerson, M. (1980-1981). Between school and work: Perspectives on working class youth. *Interchange*, 11(3), 80-96.

Genessee, F. (1983). Bilingual education of majority language children: The immersion experiments in review. *Applied Psycholinguistics*, 4, 1-46.

Gerstner, L., Semerad, R., Doyle, D., & Johnston, W. (1994). *Reinventing education*. New York: Dutton.

Getty, K. (1987). Bilingual education. Unpublished class presentation, University of Calgary.

Getzels, J., & Jackson, P. (1962). *Creativity and intelligence*. New York: John Wiley.

Gibson, J. (n.d.). So, you're worried about becoming an immersion parent. Ottawa: Canadian Parents for French.

Gibson, T. (1973). *Teachers talking*. London: Allen Lane.

Goldberg, M. (1989). Portrait of James Gray. *Educational Leadership*, 47(3), 65-68.

Gomez, M. (1988). The National Writing Project: Creating community, validating experiences, and expanding opportunities. *Issue Paper 88-2*. East Lansing: National Center for Research on Teacher Education.

Gomez, M. (1990). The National Writing Project: Staff development in the teaching of composition. In Hawisher, G., & Soter, A. *On literacy and its teaching*. Albany, NY: State University of New York Press.

Goodlad, J. (1994). The National Network for Educational Renewal. *Phi Delta Kappan*, 632-637.

Goodman, J. (1995). Change without difference: School restructuring in historical perspective. *Harvard Education Review*, 65(1), 1-29.

Goods, K. (1996). The Junior League and their contributions to education. Unpublished class paper, University of Calgary.

Goods, K. (1997). Volunteers—making a difference in education. Unpublished class paper, University of Calgary.

Goodson, I. (1983). Subjects for study: Aspects of a social history of curriculum. *Journal of Curriculum Studies*, 15(4), 391-408.

Gorham, J. (1987). Sixth grade students' perceptions of good teachers. Unpublished paper (ED359164).

Gracey, H. (1972). *Curriculum or craftsmanship*. Chicago: The University of Chicago.

Grant, D., & Sleeter, C. (1986). *After the school bell rings*. London: Falmer Press.

Grant, T. (1987). Peer Assistance and Leadership (PAL) Program. Unpublished paper

(ED 292 047).

Graves, D., & Coffey, S. (1996). Welcome to Coffeville, Carolina! *Teacher-To-Teacher*, 4(2), 11.

Gray, J. (1985, December). Joining a national network: The National Writing Project. *New Directions for Teaching and Learning*, 24, 61–68.

Gray, J., & Sterling, R. (n.d.). *The National Writing Project a university-based, teacher center partnership program*. Berkeley, CA: National Writing Project.

Gross, J. (1991, September 23). San Franciscans to vote for the sake of children. *New York Times*, A10.

Gross, N. (1958). *Who runs the schools?*. New York: John Wiley.

Gubernick, L., & Conlin, M. (1997, February 10). The special education scandal. *Forbes* [http://www.forbes.com].

Gulbrandsen, C. (1997). Correlates of mediator competence: The moral development and perspective taking abilities of fourth grade, peer nominated mediators. Bachelor's thesis, Department of Psychology, University of Calgary.

Haertel, G. (1993). *A primer on teacher self-evaluation*. Livermore, CA: EREAPA Associates.

Halferty, D., & Fouts, G. (1996-1997). *Evaluation report on mentoring activities for the Alberta Mentoring Foundation for Youth*. Calgary: Alberta Mentoring Foundation for Youth.

Hall, G., & Hord, S. (1987). *Change in schools*. Albany, N.Y.: State University of New York.

Hall, O., & Carlton, R. (1977). *Basic skills at school and work*. Toronto: Ontario Economic Council.

Hannam, C., Smyth, P., & Stephenson, N. (1971). *Young teacher and reluctant learners*. Harmondsworth, Middlesex, England: Penguin Books.

Hargan, L. (1995). Dear DwoK Teachers. *Teacher-to-teacher*, 3(2), 1.

Hargreaves, A. (Ed.) (1997). *International handbook of educational change*. Norwell, MA: Kluwer.

Harp, L. (1994, January 26). New challenges seen as key tests of E.C.S.'s political muscle skills. *Education Week*, 13(18), 11.

Harp, L. (1996, March 20). Getting down to business at next week's summit. *Education Week*, 15(26), 1, 22.

Harp, L. (1997, July 17). Teachers may lose state rewards. *Herald Leader* [On-line]. Available URL: http://www.kentuckyconnect. com/heraldleader.html.

Harvard Graduate School of Education. (n.d.). Project Zero Development Group. Cambridge, MA: Harvard Graduate School of Education.

Hecht, B. (1997, February 17). Net loss. *New Republic* [On-line]. Available URL: http://www.enews.com/magazines.html.

Heck, S., Stiegelbauer, S., Hall, G., & Loucks, S. (1981). *Measuring innovation configurations: Procedures and applications.* Austin, TX: University of Texas.

Heller, P. (1995). *Drama as a way knowing.* Los Angeles: Galef Institute.

Hendrie, C. (1997, March 26). Politics of jobs in city schools hinder reform. *Education Week* [On-line], 65 paragraphs. Available URL: http//www.EdWeek.com/htbin (Archives).

Hering, W. (1983). Teacher centers. In Paisley, W., & Butler, M. (Eds.), *Knowledge utilization systems in education.* Beverly Hills, CA: Sage.

Hewton, E. (1982). *Rethinking educational change.* Guildford, Sussex: Society for Research into Higher Education.

Hodge, R., Siegel, P., & Rossi, P. (1966). Occupation prestige in the United States, 1925-1963. In Bendix, R., & Lipset, S. (Eds.), *Class, status and power* (pp. 218-302). New York: Free Press.

Hoff, D. (1997a, February 26). The National Writing Project is the little federal program that could. *Education Week* [On-line], 11 paragraphs. Available URL: http://www. EdWeek.com/htbin (Archives).

Hoff, D. (1997b, April 23). Title holder. *Education Week* [On-line]. Available URL: http://www.EdWeek.com/htbin (Archives).

Hoff, D. (1997c, September 10). Proposal would link school collars, proven models. *Education Week* [On-line], 18 paragraphs. Available URL: http://www. EdWeek. com/htbin (Archives).

Hoff, D. (1998, April 22). Reform effort expects wave of new takers. *Education Week* [On-line], 35 paragraphs. Available URL: http://www.EdWeek. com/htbin (Archives).

Holmes Group (n.d.). *The Holmes Group.* East Lansing, MI: Holmes Group.

Hopfenberg, W., Levin, H., & associates (1993). *The accelerated schools.* San Francisco: Jossey-Bass.

House, E. (1974). *The politics of educational innovation.* Berkeley, CA: McCutchan.

House, E. (1979). Technology versus craft: A ten year perspective on innovation. *Journal of Curriculum Studies*, 11, 1-15.

House, E. & Lapan, S. (1978). *Survival in the classroom*. Boston: Allyn & Bacon.

Huberman, A. & Miles, M. (1982). *Innovation up close*. Andover, MA: Network.

Huffstutter, N. (1996). *KERA Connections*. Louisville, KY: Galef Institute.

Hurn, C. (1993). *The limits and possibilities of schooling*. Boston: Allyn & Bacon.

Iannacone, L. (1967). *Politics in education*. New York: Center for Applied Research in Education.

Illinois Alliance of Essential Schools. (1991–1992). *The Illinois Alliance of Essential Schools*. Chicago: Illinois Alliance of Essential Schools.

Immerwahr, J., Johnson, J., & Kernan-Schloss, A. (1991). *Cross talk*. Washington, D. C.: Business-Higher Education Forum.

Ingersoll, R. (1994). Organizational controls in secondary schools. *Harvard Education Review*, 64(2), 150-172.

International Association of Students in Economics and Business, Carleton. (1993). *Excellence in education: A student perspective*. Ottawa: Carleton University.

Jacobs, Jane. (1992). *Systems of survival: A dialogue on the moral foundations of commerce and politics*. New York: Vintage Books.

Jacobson, L. (1997, January 29). PTA issues parent-involvement standards for schools. *Education Week*. [On-line], 17 paragraphs. Available URL: http://www.EdWeek. com/htbin (Archives).

James, M. (1992, April). I came, I saw, I was conquered. *BPI Newsletter*, 1-7.

Jamous, H., & Peloille, B. (1970). Change in the French University hospital system. In Jackson, J. (Ed.), *Professions and professionalization*. London: Cambridge University Press.

Jenkins, J., & Jenkins, L. (1987). Making peer tutoring work. *Educational Leadership*, 44, 64-68.

Jobs for the Future (1991). *Voices from school and home*. Summerville, MA: Jobs for the Future.

Joffe, D. (1977). *Friendly intruders*. Berkely, CA: University of California Press.

Johnson, B. (1978). Educational trends and teacher evaluation: Tyler, Stufflebeam and Popham, the erosion of trust in public education. Presentation at Institute on the

Professions, University of Calgary.

Johnson, D., Proctor, W., & Corey, S. (1994/1995). Not a way out: A way in. *Education Leadership*, 52(4), 46-49.

Johnson, J., & Immerwahr, J. (1994). *First things first: What Americans expect from the public schools*. New York: Public Agenda.

Johnson, S. M. (1983). Performance-based staff layoffs in the public schools: Implementation and the outcomes. In Baldridge, J., & Deal, T. (Eds.), *The dynamics of organizational change in education*. Berkeley, CA: McCutchan.

Jones, D. (1991, June 19). One school, many services. *USA Today*, 7A.

Jones, R. (1997, July 1). City teacher transfer thrown out. *The Philadelphia Inquirer*, p. 1.

Joyce, B., & Calhoun, E. (1996). *Learning experiences in school renewal*. Eugene, OR: Clearinghouse on Educational Management, University of Oregon.

Joyce, B., & Showers, B. (1980). Improving inservice training: The message of research. *Educational Leadership*, 37(5), 379-385.

Junior League of New York. (1991). *Leading the way: Partners in volunteerism*. Conference Report #6. New York: Junior League.

Kagan, S. (1993). *Integrating services for children and families*. New Haven, CT: Yale University Press.

Kallick, J., & Jobs for the Future. (1990). *Voices from school and home*. Sommerville, MA: Jobs for the Future.

Kaplan, P. (1995, April 19). *Because there is hope*. [On-Line], 12 pages. Available URL: http://www.cc.emory.edu/Carter-Center/hope.htm.

Katz, E., Levin, M., & Hamilton, H. (1963). Tradition of research on the diffusion of innovations. *American Sociological Review*, 28(2), 237-252.

Kay, S., & Roberts, R. (1994). *Parent involvement: New challenges*. Lexington, KY: Roberts and Kay.

Kearns, D. (1989). An education recovery plan for America. In F. Schultz (Ed.), *Education 89-90*. Guilford, CT: Dushkin.

King, A. (1967). *The school at Mopass*. New York: Holt, Rinehart & Winston.

King, N. (1983). Play in the workplace. In Apple, M., & Weis, L.(Eds.), *Ideology & practice in schooling* (pp. 262-280), Philadelphia: Temple University Press.

Kohn, A. (1997). Students don't 'work'—they learn. *Education Week*. [On-line], 19 paragraphs. Available URL: http:www.EdWeek. com/htbin.

Kotlowitz, A. (1991). *There are no children here*. New York: Doubleday Anchor.

Krendl, K., & Dodd, J. (1987, October). Assessing the National Writing Project: A longitudinal study of process-based writing. (Report No. CS 210 848). (Eric Document No. ED 289 167).

Kyle, D., & Kantowicz, E. (1992). *Kids first—primero los niños*. Springfield, IL: Illinois Issues.

Lambert, W., & Taylor, D. (1984). Language in the education of ethnic minority children in Canada. In Samuda, R., Berr. J., & Laferriere, M. (Eds.), *Multiculturalism in Canada*. Toronto: Allyn & Bacon.

Lambert, W., & Tucker, R. (1972). *Bilingual education of children, the St. Lambert experiment*. Rowley, MA: Newbury House.

Lanier, J. (1983). Tensions in teaching teachers the skills of pedagogy. In Griffin, G. (Ed.), *Staff development*. Chicago: National Society for the Study of Education, University of Chicago.

Lawton, M. (1996, October 30). Study: Site management has no effect on scores. *Education Week*, 16(9), 7.

Lawton, M. (1997a, May 14). Standards advocate name to lead Achieve Group. *Education Week* [On-line]. Available URL: http://www.EdWeek.com/htbin (Archives).

Lawton, M. (1997b, September 17). Parents in N. Y. district to critique teachers. *Education Week* [On-line], 16 paragraphs. Available URL: http://www.EdWeek. com/htbin.

Lawton, M. (1997c, November 5). Chicago study credits school-based reforms. *Education Week* [On-line], 18 paragraphs. Available URL: http://www.EdWeek.com/htbin (Archives).

Lawton, M. (1997d, November 26). Ky. to showcase performance-linked curricula. *Education Week* [On-line], 19 paragraphs. Available URL: http://www.EdWeek.com/ htbin (Archives).

Lehmann-Haupt, R. (1997). Girls school seeks to overcome tech gender gap. *Wired*. [On-line], 16 paragraphs. Available URL: http://www.wired.com/news.html.

Lerman, R. (1996). Helping disconnected youth by improving linkages between high schools and careers. Paper prepared for the American Enterprise Institute Forum on America's Disconnected Youth [On-line]. Available URL: http://www.urban.org/ pubs/disconec.htm.

Levin, H. (1993). Accelerated visions. *Accelerated Schools*, 2(3), 2-3.

Levin, H. (1996). Accelerated visions. *Teacher-To-Teacher*, 5(1), 1, 13.

Levin, M. (1986). Parent teacher colloboration. In Livingstone, D. (Ed.), *Critical pedagogy and cultural power*. Toronto: Garamond.

Levine, D., & Leibert, R. (1987). Improving school improvement plans. *Elementary School Journal*, 87(4), 397-412.

Levine, D., & Levine, R. (1996). *Society and Education*. Boston: Allyn & Bacon.

Lewandowski, J. (1989). Using peer forums to motivate students. *Teaching Exceptional Children*, 21, 14-15.

Lewis, C., Schaps, E., & Winston, M. (1996). The caring classroom's academic edge. *Educational Leadership*, 16-21.

Lewis, D. (1991, Feburary 18). Society and schools: The team system. *Washington Post*.

Lieberman, A., & Miller, L. (1979). (Eds.). *Staff development*. New York: Teachers College.

Lieberman, A., & Miller, L. (1984). (Eds.). *Teachers, their world, their work*. Alexandria, VA: Association for Supervision and Curriculum Development.

Liebow, E. (1967). *Tally's corner*. Boston: Little Brown.

Lind, L. (1974). *The learning machine*. Toronto: Anansi Press.

Linnemeyer, S. & Shelton, J. (1991). Minds in the making: A community resource program. *Roeper Review*, 14(1), 35-39.

Lortie, D. (1975). *School teacher*. Chicago: University of Chicago.

Loucks, S., Cox, P. Miles, M., Huberman, M., & Eiseman, J. (1982). *Portraits of the changes, the players, and the contexts*. Andover, MA: Network.

Louis, K. (1990). Teachers, power and school change. In Clune, W., & Witte, J. (Eds.), *Choice and control in American education*, Volume II (pp. 381-390), London: Falmer Press.

Louis, K., & Kruse, S. (1995). *Professionalism and community*. Thousand Oaks, CA: Corwin.

Louis, K., Rosenblum, R., & Mulito, J. (1981). *Strategies for knowledge*. Cambridge, MA: Abt.

Mahlmann, J. (1978). *Arts education advocacy*. Washington, DC: Alliance for Arts Education.

Malen, B., Ogawa, R., & Krantz, J. (1990). What do we know about school-based management? In Clune, W., & Witte, J. (Eds.), *Choice and control in American education*, Volume II (pp. 289-352). London: Falmer Press.

Manzer, K. (2nd ed. 1990). Canadian Parents for French. In Fleming, B., & Whitla, W. (Eds.), *So you want your child to learn French* (pp. 143-146). Ottawa: Mutual Press.

Manzo, K. (1997, November 25). Scientists protest exclusion from standards writing. *Education Week* [On-line], 16 paragraphs. Available URL: http://www.EdWeek. com.ht-bin (Archives).

Manzo, K., & Sack, J. (1997, February 26). Effectiveness of Clinton reading plan questioned. *Education Week* [On-line], 43 paragraphs. Available URL: http://www. EdWeek.org/h16.

March, D., Knudsen, D., & Knudsen, G. (1987). Factors influencing the transfer of Bay area writing workshop experiences to the classroom. Paper presented to the Annual Meeting of the American Educational Research Association.

Martin, W., & MacDonnell, A. (2nd ed., 1982). *Canadian education*. Scarborough, ON: Prentice Hall.

Martinez, M. (1997, July 17). Retesting of 165 CVS freshmen being investigated. *Chicago Tribune* [On-line], 12 paragraphs. Available URL: http://www.chicago. tribune.com/print/ html.

McCarthy, J., & Still, S. (1993). Hollibrook Accelerated Elementary School. In Murphy, J., & Hallinger, P. (Eds.), *Restructuring schools*. Newberry Park, CA: Corwin Press.

McCormick, M. & Wolf, J. (1993). Intervention programs for gifted girls. *Roeper Review*, 16, 2, 85-87.

McDonald, J. (1987). Raising the teacher's voice and the ironic role of theory. In Okazawa-Rey, M., Anderson, J., & Traver, R. (Eds.), *Teaching, teachers & teacher education*. Cambridge, MA: Harvard Education Review.

McDonnell, L. (1985). Implementing low cost school improvement strategies. *Elementary School Journal*, 85 (3), 423-438.

McDonnell, L. (1994). Assessment policy as persuasion and regulation. *American Journal of Education*, 102, 394-420.

McGivney, J., & Haught, J. (1972). The politics of education: A view from the perspective of the central office staff. *Educational Administration Quarterly*, 8, 18-38.

McGrory, B. (1997, April 28). A new call to action: Political heavyweights gather to urge a spirit of volunteerism. *Boston Globe* [On line], 25 paragraphs. Available URL: http://www.boston.com/globe/htbin.

McIntyre, D., & Entwistle, S. (1983). The National Diffusion Network. In Paisley, W., & Butler, M. (Eds.), *Knowledge utilization systems in education.* Beverly Hills, CA: Sage.

McKersie, W. (1993). Philanthropy's paradox: Chicago school reform. *Educational Evaluation and Policy Analysis*, 15(22), 109-128.

McLaughlin, M., & March, D. (1979). Staff development and school change. In Lieberman, A., & Miller, L. (Eds.), *Staff development.* New York: Teachers College.

McLaughlin M., & Pfeifer, R. (1986). *Teacher evaluation: Learning for improvement and accountability—case studies.* Stanford, CA: School of Education, Stanford University.

McNeil, L. (1984). Lowering expectations: Student employment and its impact on curriculum. *Report 84-1.* Madison, WI: Center for Education Research, University of Wisconsin.

McNergney, R., Medley, D., & Caldwell, M. (1989). Making and implementing policy on teacher licensure. In F. Schultz (Ed.), *Education 89-90.* Guildford, CT: Dushkin.

McPherson, G. (1972). *Small town teacher.* Cambridge, MA: Harvard University Press.

McQuillan, P., & Muncey, D. (1995). Change takes time: a look at the growth and development of the Coaltion of Essential Schools [On-line], 30 paragraphs. Available URL: http://www.ilt.columbia.edu/ilt/papers/McQillan. html.

Meighen, R. (1986). *A sociology of educating.* London: Holt Rinehart & Winston.

Melaville, A., & Blank, M. (1993). *Together we can.* Washington, D. C.: U.S. Office of Education and U.S. Department of Health.

Metz, M. (1979). *Classroom and corridors.* Berkeley, CA: University of California Press.

Meyers, E. & McIssac, P. (Eds.). (1994). *How teachers are changing schools.* New York: IMPACT II-The Teachers Network.

Mezzacappa, D. (1997, April 23). Community service joins the syllabus in the region students volunteering/ It's a matter of course. *The Philadelphia Inquirer* [On-line], 28 paragraphs. Available URL: http://www.phillynews.com:80/inquirer/html.

Michael, B. (1990). *Volunteers in public schools.* Washington, D.C.: National Academy Press.

Michels, R. (1949). *Political parties.* Glencoe, IL: Free Press.

Miles, M. (Ed.).(1964). *Innovation and education.* New York: Teachers College.

Mirel, J. (1994). School reform unplugged: The Bensenville New American School Project, 1991-93. *American Educational Research Journal*, 31(3), 481-518.

Mitchell, S. (1966). The people shall judge. Paper presented at the Annual Meeting of the Alberta Home and School Association.

Mitchell, S. (1968). The quest of the beginnning teacher: Discovery of competence. Paper presented at the Teacher Education and Certification Conference of the Alberta Teachers Association.

Mitchell, S. (1971). *A woman's profession, a man's research*. Edmonton, Alberta: Alberta Association of Registered Nurses.

Mitchell, S. (1981). Cooperation and competition in the delivery of continuing professional education: A sociologist's view. In Baskett, H., & Taylor, W. (Eds.), *Continuing professional education* (pp. 75-77). Calgary, Alberta: University of Calgary.

Mitchell, S. (1990; 2nd ed., 1992). *Innovation and reform*. York, Ontario: Captus Press.

Mitchell, S. (1995). *Sociology for educating*. York, Ontario: Captus Press.

Mitchell, S. (1996). *Tidal waves of school reform*. Westport, CT: Praeger.

Mitchell, S. (1997). Critical questions raised in the arts. *Multicultural Education* 15(2), 4-15.

Mitchell, S. (1998). *Reforming educators: Teachers, experts and advocates*. Westport, CT: Praeger.

Moeller, G., & Charters, W. (1970). Relation of bureaucratization to sense of power among teachers. In Miles, M., & Charters, W. (Eds.), *Learning in social settings* (pp. 638-656). Boston: Allyn & Bacon.

Moffett, J. (1981). *Coming on center: English education in evolution*. Portsmouth, NH: Boynton/Cook.

Moore, D., Soltman, S., Manar, U., Steinberg,L., & Fogel, D. (1983). *Standing up for children*. Chicago: Designs for Change.

Moore, D. (1990). Voice and choice in Chicago. In Clune, W., & Witte, J. (Eds.), *Choice and control in American education*, Volume II, (pp. 153-198). London: Falmer.

Moore, W. (1970). *The Professions*. New York: Russell Sage Foundation.

Morgan, G. (1986). *Images of Organization*. Beverly Hills, CA: Sage.

Morrison, F., Pawley, C., Bonyn, R., & Unitt, J. (1986). *Aspects of French immersion at the primary and seondary levels*. Toronto: Queen's Printer.

Moses, R., Kamii, M., Swap, S., & Howard, J. (1989). The Algebra Project: Organizing in the spirit of Ella. *Harvard Education Review*, 59(4), 423-434.

Muncey, D., & McQuillan, P. (1990). *Education reform as revitalization movement.* Providence, RI: Coalition of Essential Schools, Brown University.

Murray, F. (1997, March 5). Ed schools are the key to reform. *Education Week,* [On-line], 18 paragraphs. Available URL: http://www.EdWeek.com/htbin.

Murray-Seegert, C. (1989). *Nasty girls, thugs, and humans like us.* Baltimore: Paul Brookes.

National Commission on Excellence in Education. (1983). *A nation at risk: The imperative of educational reform.* Washington, D. C.: U.S. Government Printing Office.

National Congress of Parents and Teachers. (1947). *Golden jubilee history 1897- 1947.* Chicago: National Congress of Parents and Teachers.

National Educational Goals Panel. (1997, May 2). In the summit's wake: Volunteer activity. *Daily Report Card* [On-line], 13 paragraphs. Available URL: http://www.utopia.com/mailings/reportcard/html#Index4.

National Governors' Association. (1994). *Communication with the public about education reform.* Washington, D. C.: National Governors' Association.

National Writing Project. (1995). *National Writing Project 1995 fact sheet.* Berkeley, CA: National Writing Project.

Nemser, S. (1983). Learning to teach. In Shulman, L., & Sykes, G. (Eds.), *Handbook of teaching and policy.* New York: Longman.

Network News. (1997a, Summer). News Digest. *Network News,* p. 1.

Network News. (1997b, Autumn). Janet Longmore of CIS - Canada Named CIS, Inc. Executive Director. *Network News* [On-line], 26 paragraphs. Available URL: http://www. cisnet.org/Networknews//newexec.html.

New American Schools Development Corporation. (n.d.). *NASDC facts.* Arlington, VA: New American Schools Development Corporation.

New American Schools. (1996). *Working towards excellence.* Arlington, VA: New American Schools.

New American Schools Development Corporation. (1995/1996). *Getting stronger and stronger.* Arlington, VA: New American Schools Development Corporation.

Nisbet, R. (1980). *The history of the idea of progress.* New York: Oxford University Press.

Noddings, N. (1987). Fidelity in teaching, teacher education and research in teaching. In Okazowa-Rey, M., Anderson, J., & Travers, R. (Eds.), *Teaching, teachers and teacher education.* Cambridge, MA: Harvard Education Review.

North Central Regional Educational Laboratory. (1994). School-Family partnership—a literature review. *Pathways Home Page*. [On-line], 19 paragraphs. Available URL: http://www.ncrel.org/sdrs/pidata/pioltrev.htm.

North Central Regional Educational Laboratory. (1996). The Coalition of Essential Schools: "Good schools are unique." [On-line], 10 paragraphs. Available URL: http://www.ncrel.org/ cscd/newlead/lead12/1-2d.htm.

Novak, M. (1975). *Living and learning in the free school*. Toronto: McClelland & Stewart.

O'Connell, M. (1991). *School reform Chicago style*. Chicago: The Center for Neighborhood Technology.

Office of Educational Accountability, Kentucky General Assembly. (1994). *Annual report*. Frankfort, KY: Kentucky General Assembly.

Office of Educational Research and Improvement, U. S. Department of Education. (1992). Parental satisfaction with schools and the need for standards. [On-line], 24 paragraphs. Available URL: http://www.ed.gov/pubs/ OR/ResearchRpts/parents.html.

Ogawa, R. (1994). The institutional sources of educational reform: The case of school-based management. *American Educational Research Journal*, 31(3), 519-548.

O'Hara-Escaravage, S. (n. d.). Native culture at St. Benedict's—A sincere attempt at change. Unpublished class paper, University of Calgary.

Olivero, J., & Heck, J. (1993). Staff evaluation: The Fort McMurray plan putting the pieces together for a strategic advantage. *Challenge in Educational Administration*, 30(3), 26-31.

Olson, L. (1989, April 12). 'Clinical schools': Theory meets practice on the training ground. *Education Week*. [On-line]. Available URL: http://www.EdWeek.com/htbin (Archives).

Olson, L. (1990). Teaching teachers to teach. *The Lamp*, 72(4), 6-9.

Olson, L. (1994a, November 2). Learning their lessons. *Education Week*. [On-line], 74 paragraphs. Available URL:http://www.EdWeek.com/htbin (Archives).

Olson, L. (1994b, December 7). Family ties. *Education Week*. [On-line], 54 paragraphs. Available URL: http://www.EdWeek.com/htbin (Archives).

Olson, L. (1995a, February 8). Beyond model schools. *Education Week*. [On line], 78 paragraphs. Available URL:http://www.EdWeek.com/htbin.

Olson, L. (1995b, June 21). Annenberg Institute seeks to find voice in last year. *Education Week* [On-line]. Available URL: http://www.EdWeek.com/htbin.

Olson, L. (1995c, July 12). Designs for Learning. *Education Week* [On-line]. Available URL: http://www.EdWeek.com/htbin.

Olson, L. (1996). A clean slate. In Editorial Projects in Education (Ed.), *Thoughtful teachers, thoughtful schools* (pp. 142-149). Boston: Allyn and Bacon.

Olson, L. (1997a). *The school to work revolution*. Reading, MA: Addison-Weesley.

Olson, L. (1997b, February 12). On their own, design teams must build on foundation. *Education Week* [On-line]. http://www.EdWeek.com/htbin.

Olson, L. (1997c, May 21). State progress on school-to-work reforms slow, study finds. *Education Week* [On-line]. Available URL:http://www.EdWeek.com/htbin.

Olson, L. (1998a, February 4). Will success spoil Success for All? *Education Week* [On-line], 29 paragraphs. Available URL: http://www.EdWeek.com/htbin.

Olson, L. (1998b, May 27). The importance of 'Critical Friends': Reform effort gets teachers talking. *Education Week* [On-Line], 35 paragraphs. Available URL: http//www. EdWeek.com/htbin.

O'Neal Mosley, T. (1993). Marva Collins, her way. *Technos*, 2(2), 22-25.

O'Neil, J. (1996). In Alberta on tapping the power of school-based management: A conversation with Michael Strembitsky. *Educational Leadership*, 53(4), 66-70.

O'Neill, M., & Butts, H. (1991). The Comer process: Accent on community. *Reform Report*, 2(1), 1-3.

O'Neill, M., & Valenzuela, I. (1992). Michele Clark Middle School and the Algebra Project. *Reform Report*, 2(8), 5-8, 10.

Opinion Research Centre. (1995). *Program evaluation of the mentoring program*. Dundas, Ontario: Big Brother Association of Burlington and Hamilton-Wentworth, Ontario.

Oppenheimer, T. (1997, July). The computer delusion. *Atlantic Monthly* [On-line]. Available URL: htt://www.theatlantic. com/htm.

Osborne, D., & Gaebler, T. (1992). *Reinventing government*. Reading, MA: Addison-Westley.

Pacheco, A. (1994). Spotlight on settings: University of Texas at El Paso. *Center Correspondent*, 7, 2-5.

Pauly, E. (1991). *The classroom crucible: What really works, what doesn't and why*. New York: Basic Books.

Pederson, E., Faucher, T., & Eaton, W. (1978). A new perspective on the effects of first-grade teachers on children's subsequent adult status. *Harvard Education Review*, 48, 1-31.

Perl, S., & Wilson, D. (1986). *Through teachers' eyes*. Portsmouth, NH: Heinemann.

Peterson, B., & Tenorio, R. (1994). Dynamic duo. In Wolk, R., & Rodman, B. (Eds.), *Classroom crusaders*. San Francisco: Jossey-Bass.

Peterson, P. (1985). *The politics of school reform 1870-1940*. Chicago: The University of Chicago Press.

Phillips, G. (1993). *Site-based decision-making*. Vancouver: EduServ Inc.

Pink, W., & Hyde, A. (Eds.) (1992). *Effective staff development*. Norwood, NJ: Ablex.

Plattner, A. (1994). Year of high performance. *The Alliance*, 2(1), 8.

Poe, J. (1997a, May 23). Numbers up, but still below national norm. *Chicago Tribune* [On-line], 11 paragraphs. Available URL:http://sww.chicago.tribune.com/html.

Poe, J. (1997b, June 10). Staff overhaul of school rare but not unique. *Chicago Tribune* [On-line], 10 paragraphs. Available URL: http://www.chicago.tribune.com/html.

Poe, J. (1997c, July 1). Schools start mandatory classes in an effort to improve academic. *Chicago Tribune* [On-line], 11 paragraphs. Available URL: http://www.chicago.tribune.com/html.

Poignant, R. (1969). *Education and development*. New York: Teachers College.

Pondry. L., Frost, P. , Morgan, G., & Dandridge, T. (1983). *Organization symbolism*. Greenwich, CT: JAI Press.

Ponessa, J. (1997, March 19). Professional-development schools stir debate. *Education Week* [On-line], 22 paragraphs. Available URL: http://www.EdWeek.com/htbn (Archives).

Popkewitz, T. (1983). *Change and stability in schooling*. Victoria, Australia: Deakin University Press.

Popkewitz, T. (Ed.). (1987). *The formation of school subjects*. New York: Falmer Press.

Popkewitz, T., Tabachnick, B., & Wehlage, G. (1982). *The myth of educational reform*. Madison, WI: University of Wisconsin Press.

Portner, J. (1996, May 22). Clinton calls for rewards for community service. *Education Week* [On-line]. http://www.EdWeek.com/htbin.

Poyen, Janet M. (1989). Canadian Parents for French: A National Pressure Group in Canadian Education. Master's thesis, University of Calgary.

President's Committee on the Arts and the Humanities (n. d.). *Eloquent evidence: Arts at the core of knowledge*. Washington, D.C.: President's Committee on the Arts and the

Humanities & the National Assembly of State Arts Agencies.

Presseisen, B. (1985). *Unlearned lessons*. London: Falmer Press.

Pritchard, R. (1989). The impact of American ideas on New Zealand's education policy, proactive, and thinking. Wellington, New Zealand (Eric Document: ED 338-517).

Public Agenda. (1997, October 22). Professors of education: It's how you learn, not what you learn that's most important. Available URL: http://www.publicagenda.org/about-pa/aboutpa31.htm.#sum.

Purves, A. (1992, February). Reflections on research and assessment in written composition. *Research in the teaching of English*, 26(1), 108–122.

Putka, G. (1992, September 11). 'riting and more 'riting. *Wall Street Journal*, B5.

Reinhard, B. (1997, May 28). S. F. mulls retreat from 'reconstituting' schools. *Education Week* [On-line]. Available URL: http://www.EdWeek.com/htbin (Archives).

Remer, J. (1990). *Changing schools through the arts*. New York: American Council for the Arts.

Renzulli, J. (1977). *The enrichment triad model: A guide for developing defensible programs for the gifted and talented*. Mansfield, CT: Creative Learning Press.

Reynolds, D., & and Sullivan, M. (1979). Bringing schools back in. In Burton, L. & Meighen, R., (Eds.), Schools, pupils and deviance (pp. 43-58). Driffield, England: Nafferton.

Rich, R. (Ed.). (1981). *The knowledge cycle*. Beverly Hills, CA: Sage.

Richardson, J. (1996). Inquiring minds: Teacher to teacher. *Education Week* [On line]. Available URL: http://www/EdWeek.com/htbin (Archives).

Rideout, L. (1997). *Research internship*. Chapel Island, Newfoundland: G. Shaw Collegiate.

Robertson, J. (1997). The experience of shared decision making in two Calgary high schools. Master's thesis, University of Calgary.

Rogers, E., McManus, J., Peters, J., & Kim, J. (1985). The diffusion of microcomputers in California high schools. In Chen, M., & Paisley, W. (Eds.), *Children and microcomputers*. Beverly Hills, CA: Sage.

Rogers, M. (1990). *Cold anger*. Denton, TX: University of North Texas Press.

Rooney, J. (1993). Teacher evaluation: No more "super"vision. *Educational Leadership*, 51(2), 43-44.

Rosenholtz, S. (1989). *Teachers' workplace*. New York: Longman.

Rothman, R. (1987, May 13). Writing gaining emphasis in science, math classes. *Education Week* [On-line], 54 pargraphs. Available URL: http://www.EdWeek. com/ht-bin.

Rothman, R. (1995, May 17). Redesign, don't bypass, school districts. *Education Week* [On-line]. Available URL: http://www.EdWeek. com/htbin.

Rud, A., & Oldendorf, W. (1992). *A place for teacher renewal*. New York: Teachers College.

Rudduck, J., Day, J., & Wallace, G. (1997). Students' perspectives on school improvement. In Hargreaves, A. (Ed.), *Rethinking educational change with heart and mind* (pp. 73-91). Alexandria, VA: Association for Supervision and Curriculum Development.

Ruenzel, D. (1997, December 4). The essential Ted Sizer. *Education Week*, 16(14), 32-37.

Rutter, M. (1983). School effects on pupil progress. *Child Development*, 54, 1-29.

Rutter, M., Maughan B., Mortimore, P., Ouston, J., & Smith, A. (1979). *Fifteen thousand hours*. Cambridge, MA: Harvard University Press.

Ryan, K., Newman, K., Mager, G., Applegate, J., Lasley, T., Flora, R., & Johnston, J. (1980). *Biting the apple*. New York: Longman.

Sanchez, E. (1997, May 16). School is teaching witchcraft, critics say. *Sacramento Bee* [On-line]. Available URL: http://www.sacbee.com/html.

Sanchez, R. (1997, July 3). New portrait improves profile of U. S. teachers survey shows more education, experience. *Washington Post* [On-line], 172 lines. Available URL:http://www.WashingtonPost.com/idxht.

Sapon-Shevin, M. (1994). *Playing favorites*. Albany, NY: SUNY Press.

Sarason, S. (1971; 2nd ed., 1982). *The culture of the school and the problem of change*. Boston: Allyn & Bacon.

Sarason, S. (1990). *The predictable failure of educational reform*. San Francisco: Jossey-Bass.

Sarason, S. (1993). *The case for change*. San Francisco: Jossey-Bass.

Schmitt, C., & Slonaker, L. (1996, January 14). Computers in School: Do students improve? *Mercury News* [On-line]. Available URL: http://www.sjmercury. com/news/local/schools/main114.htm.

Schorr, L. (1988). *Within our reach*. New York: Doubleday Anchor.

Schultz, E. (1996). Consumate professional. In Editorial Projects in Education (Ed.), *Thoughtful teacher, thoughful schools.* Boston: Allyn & Bacon.

Schumpeter, J. (1942). *Capitalism, socialism and democracy.* New York: Harper.

Seeley, J., Sim, R., & Loosley. E. (1956). *Crestwood Heights.* Toronto: University of Toronto Press.

Serediuk, T. (1977). Study of the implementation of the Alberta secondary social studies program using Basil Bernstein's theory of educational knowledge codes. M.A. thesis, University of Calgary.

Service Motivators in Learning and Education Service. (1992). *Smiles brochure.* Salt Lake City: Service Motivators in Learning and Education Service.

Sherrington, C. (1953). *Man on his nature.* London: Cambridge University.

Simon, R. (1982). Mysticism, management and Marx. In Gray, H. (Ed.), *The management of educational institutions.* London: Falmer Press.

Singer, J., & Butler, J. (1987). The education for All Handicapped Children Act: Schools as agents of social reform. *Harvard Education Review, 57*(3), 125-152.

Sizer, T. (1984). *Horace's compromise.* Boston: Houghton Mifflin.

Sizer, T. (1992). *Horace's school.* Boston: Houghton Mifflin.

Slavin, R. (1995). Success for All goes international. *Success Story, 5*(1), 1.

Slavin, R., Madden, N., Shaw, A., Mainzer, K., & Donnely, M. (1993). Success for All: Three case studies of comprehensive restructuring of urban elementary schools. In Murphy, J., & Hallinger, P. (Eds.), *Restructuring Schooling.* Newbury Park, CA: Corwin.

Slavin, R., Madden, N., Dolan, L., Wasik, B., Ross, S., & Smith, L. (1994). 'Whenever and wherever we choose' the replication of 'Success for All.' *Phi Delta Kappan,* 639-647.

Smith, L. & Geoffrey, W. (1968). *The complexities of an urban classroom.* New York: Holt Rinehard & Winston.

Smith, L., Klein, P., Prunty, J., & Dwyer, D. (1986). *Educational innovators.* New York: Falmer Press.

Sommerfeld, M. (1992, April 15). National commitment to parent role in schools sought. *Education Week.* [On-line], 27 paragraphs. Available URL: http://www.EdWeek. com/htbin (Archives).

Sommerfeld, M. (1993, September 8). Miss. group forms national parent network. *Education Week.* [On-line], 15 paragraphs. Available URL: http://www.EdWeek.

com/htbin (Archives).

Sommerfeld, M. (1994, April 6). Pew abandons its ambitious 10-year 'children's initiative.' *Education Week*. [On-line]. Available URL: http://www.EdWeek.com/htbin (Archives).

Sommerfeld, M. (1996a, May 1). Progress report on NASDC projects finds mixed results. *Education Week*. [On-line]. Available: URL: http://www.EdWeek.com/htbin (Archives).

Sommerfeld, M. (1996b, May 18). Gerstner signals IBM plan to increase focus on k-12 giving. *Education Week* [On-line]. Available: URL: http://www.EdWeek. com/htbin (Archives).

Spradbery, J. (1976). Conservative pupils? Pupil resistance to a curriculum innovation in mathematics. In Whitty, G., & Young, M. (Eds.), *Explorations in the politics of school knowledge*. Nafferton, England: Nafferton Books.

Sproull, L., Weiner, S., & Wolf, D. (1978). *Organizing an anarchy*. Chicago: University of Chicago.

Stanfield, R. (1994, October 1). Rebel with a cause. *National Journal*, 2278-2281.

Steele, U. (1996). Accountability for diversity—The relevance of accountability policies in public education for meeting the diverse needs of students. M.A. thesis, University of Calgary.

Steele, U., & Boyle, P. (1997). Systemic approaches to systemic discrimination. Unpublished paper.

Stern, D. (1990). Quality of students work experience and orientation towards work. *Youth and Society*, 263-282.

Stewart, D. (1987). Cutting to the core: Curriculum mishaps in Saskatchewan. In Cochrane, D. (Ed.), *So much for the mind*. Toronto: Kagan and Woo.

Stinchcombe, A. (1964). *Rebellion in a high school*. Chicago: Quadrangle.

Strike, K. (1993). Professionalism, democracy, and discursive communities: Normative reflections on restructuring. *American Educational Research Journal*, 30(2), 255-275.

Strivens, J. (1980). Contradiction and change in educational practices. In Barton, L., Meighen, R., & Walker, S. (Eds.). *Schooling and ideology and the curriculum* (pp. 93-112). Lewes, Sussex: Falmer Press.

Strom, R. & Strom, S. (1995). Intergenerational learning: Grandparents in the schools. *Educational Gerontology*, 21(4), 321-335.

Subotnik, R., & Arnold, K. (1995). Passing through the gates: Career establishment of talented women scientists. *Roeper Review*, 18(1), 55-60.

Sunstein, B. (1994). *Composing a culture*. Portsmouth, NH: Heinemann.

Sussman, L. (1977). *Tales out of school*. Philadelphia: Temple University Press.

Swindler, A. (1979). *Organizations without authority*. Cambridge, MA: Harvard University Press.

Sykes, G. (1996, March). Reform of and as professional development. *Phi Delta Kappan*, 465-467.

Tapline. (1994a, Fall). BellSouth leads literacy efforts for TAP. *Tapline*, p. 2.

Tapline. (1994b, Fall). Douglas students stage theater forums. *Tapline*, p. 11.

Taradash, G. (1994). Extending educational opportunities for middle school gifted students. *Gifted Child Quarterly*, 38,2, 89-94.

Teacher Magazine. (1992, May/June). Changing the profession. *Teacher Magazine* [On-line]. Available: URL: http://www.EdWeek.com/ htbin (Archives).

Teaching K-8. (1992). A blueprint or tomorrow. *Teaching K-8*, 34-38.

Texas Interfaith Education Fund. (1990). *The Texas IAF vision for public schools*. Austin, TX: Texas Interfaith Education Fund.

Thompson, C. (1982). *Dissemination at the National Institute of Education*. Andover, MA: Network.

Thompson, J. (1967). *Organizations in action*. New York: McGraw-Hill.

Timar, T., & Kirp, D. (1988). *Managing educational excellence*. London: Falmer Press.

Tobin, L. & Newkirk, T. (1994). *Taking stock*. Portsmouth, NH: Boynton/Cook.

Toch, T. (1991). *In the name of excellence*. New York: Oxford.

Toffler, A. (1970). *Future schock*. New York: Bantam.

Tomkins, G. (1986). *A common countenance*. Scarborough, Ontario: Prentice Hall.

Tomlinson, T., & Walberg, H. (1986). *Academic work and educational excellence*. Berkeley, CA: McCutchan.

Top, B., & Osguthorpe, R. (1987). Reverse-role tutoring: The effects of handicapped students tutoring regular class students. *Elementary School Journal*, 87(4), 413-427.

Touraine, A., Dubet, F., Wieviorka, M., & Strzelecki, J. (1980). *Solidarity, the analysis of a social movement: Poland 1980-82*. London: Cambridge University Press.

Trotter, A. (1997a, February 26). IBM shares results from field-tests of technology. *Education Week* [On-line]. Available: URL: http://www.EdWeek. com/htbin (Archives).

Trotter, A. (1997b, April 23). Parents, educators make new connection with the internet. *Education Week* [On-line], 39 paragraphs. Available URL: http://www.EdWeek.com/ htbin (Archives).

Trotter, A. (1997c, June 11). Effort to recruit mentor teachers in technology fails to connect. *Education Week*. [On-line]. Available: URL: http://www.EdWeek.com/htbin (Archives).

Turnbull, B. (1985). Using governance and support systems to advance school improvement. *Elementary School Journal*, 85 (3), 337-351.

Tyler, W. (1988). *School organization*. London: Croom Helm.

Tymko, J. (1996). *The entrepreneurial school*. Toronto: Canadian Education Association.

United States Department of Education. (1986). *What works*. Washington, D. C.: United States Department of Education.

University of Louisville (1997). *K-4/K-8 MAT your program*. Louisville: University of Louisville.

University CARLA (1996). Language immersion education. Institute of International Studies and Programs, University of Minnesota [On-line], 17 paragraphs. Available: URL: http://carla.acad.umn.edu/immersion.html.

Van Loon, L. (1996, Fall). CFP states position on united Canada. *CPF National*, 72, 1, 4.

Viadero, D. (1989, December 13). Daily news special report. *Education Week* [On-line]. Available: URL: http://www.EdWeek.com/htbin (Archives).

Viadero, D. (1991, November 6). Foreign-language instruction resurfacing in elementary schools. *Education Week* [On-line], 78 paragraphs. Available: URL: http://www. EdWeek.com/htbin (Archives).

Viadero, D. (1993, May 19). A quiet revolution is transforming teaching of writing. *Education Week* [On-line], 86 paragraphs. Available: URL: http://www. EdWeek.com/htbin (Archives).

Viadero, D. (1994a, February 2). A world of difference. *Education Week*, 13(19), 24-26.

Viadero, D. (1994b, December 7). Report casts critical eye on Reading Recovery Program. *Education Week* [On-line], 19 paragraphs. Available URL: http://www.EdWeek. com/htbin (Archives).

Viadero, D. (1995a, March 1). Diffusion network seeks to gain solid footing. *Education*

Week. [On-line], 48 paragraphs. Available URL:http://www.EdWeek.com/htbin (Archives).

Viadero, D. (1995b, July 12). Carry that weight. *Education Week* [On-line]. Available URL: http://www.EdWeek.com/htbin (Archives).

Viadero, D. (1996a). Learning to care. In Editorial Projects in Education (Eds.), *Thoughtful teachers, thoughtful schools.* (pp. 101-104). Boston: Allyn & Bacon.

Viadero, D. (1996b, March 13). Lisa Delpit says teachers must value students' cultural strengths. *Education Week* [On-line]. Available: URL: http://www.EdWeek.com/htbin (Archives).

Viadero, D. (1996c, May 8). Math texts are multiplying. *Education Week,* 15(33), 33-34.

Viadero, D. (1996d). Thinking about Thinking. In Editorial Projects in Education (Eds.), *Thoughtful teachers, thoughtful schools* (pp. 31-37). Boston: Allyn & Bacon.

Vickers, M. (1991). *Building a national system for school-to-work transition.* Cambridge, MA: Jobs for the Future.

Voege, H. (1975) The diffusion of Keynesian macroeconomics through American high school textbooks, 1936-70. In Reid, W., & Walker, D. (Eds.), *Case studies in curriculum change.* London: Routledge & Kegan Paul.

Vopat, J. (1993). Thirteen ways of looking at the parent project. *Best Practice,* 4, 10–11.

Waller, W. (1967). *The Sociology of Teaching.* New York: John Wiley.

Walters, L. (1997, February 5). Volunteer tutors: Can they teach Johnny to read? *Christian Science Monitor.* Available: URL: http://www.csmonitor.com.html.

Wang, M., Reynolds, M., & Walberg, H. (1994/1995). Serving students at the margins. *Educational Leadership,* 52(4), 12-17.

Waring, M. (1979). *Social pressures and curriculum innovation.* London: Methuen.

Washburn, G., & Martinez, M. (1997, Septmber 4). Chicago's schools add s to 3 r's: High school students will have to do service. *Chicago Tribune.* [On-line]. Available: URL: http://www.chicagotribune.com.html.

Washburn, W. (1991). Ten years of the Calgary Writing Project. *Alberta English,* 29(2), 5-6.

Washington Post. (1997, March 29). School reform, electronic forum. *Washington Post,* A16.

Wasley, P. (1991). *Teachers who lead.* New York: Teachers College.

Wasserman, M. (1970). *The school fix*. New York: Outerbridge and Diesntfrey.

Weiner, S. (1983). Participation deadlines and choice. In Baldridge, J., & Deal, T. (Eds.), *The dynamics of organizational change in education*. Berkeley, CA: McCutchan.

Weisman, J. (1991, July 31). PTA principals on corporate support fail to win over other organizations. *Education Week*. [On-line], 17 paragraphs. Available URL: http://www. EdWeek.com/htbin (Archives).

Weiss, C. (1995). The four "I's" of school reform: How interests, ideology, information, and institution affect teachers and principals. *Harvard Education Review*, 65(4), 571-592.

Weissmann, D. (1992, December). Reform heavyweights promote small schools. *Catalyst*, 4(4). 1-16.

Welch, N. (1995). *Schools, communities, and the arts*. Washington, D. C.: National Endowment for the Arts.

Werthman, C. (1963). Delinquents in school: A test for the legitimacy of authority. *Berkely Journal of Sociology*, 8, 39-60.

White, K. (1997, July 9). School technology captures public's fascination, states' dollars. *Education Week*. Available: URL: http://www.EdWeek.org/ew/com/ htbin (Archives).

Whiteside, T. (1978). *The sociology of educational innovation*. London: Methuen.

Willis, P. (1978). *Learning to labour*. Westmead, England: Saxon House.

Wilson, K. (1994). *Attempting change*. Portsmouth, NH: Heinemann.

Wise, A., Darling-Hammond, L., McLaughlin, M., & Bernstein, H. (1985). Teacher evaluation: A study of effective practices. *Elementary School Journal*, 86(1), 61-121.

Wohlstetter, P., & Mohrman, S. (1993). School-based mangement: Strategies for success. *CPRE Finance Brief*. [On-line]. Available: URL: http://www.ed.gov/pubs/CPPRE/ fb2sbm.html.

Wolcott, H. (1973). *The man in the principal's office*. New York: Holt Rhinehart & Winston.

Wolcott, H. (1977). *Teachers vs. technocrats*. Eugene, OR: Center for Educational Policy and Management, University of Oregon.

Woods, P. (1983). *Sociology and the school*. London: Routledge & Kegan Paul.

Wotherspoon, T. (1991). *Hitting the books*. Toronto: Garamond.

Wright, L., & Borland, J. (1992). A special friend: Adolescent mentors for young, economically disadvantaged, potentially gifted students. *Roeper Review*, 14, 1324-129.

Wysinger, N. (1995). Teacher profile. *Teacher-To-Teacher*, 3(2),11.

Zemelman, S., & Daniels, H.(1985). *A Writing Project*. Portsmouth, NH: Heinemann.

Zernike, K. (1997, June 10). Panel calls for overhaul of special ed. *Boston Globe*. [Online]. Available: URL: http://www.boston.com/globe/htbin.

Zigler, E., & Finn Stevenson, M. (1989). Child care in America: From problem to solution. *Educational Policy*, 3(4), 313-329.

Znaniecki, F. (1940). *The social role of the man of knowledge*. New York: Columbia University Press.

Index

About the Author

SAMUEL MITCHELL is Associate Professor, Graduate Division of Educational Research, The University of Calgary. From a background in social reform, Professor Mitchell has been increasingly involved in art and educational consulting. Among his earlier publications is *Tidal Waves of School Reform* (Praeger, 1996).

ISBN 0-275-96366-7

9 780275 963668

90000>

HARDCOVER BAR CODE